From a
Southern
Oven

Jean Anderson

Jean Anderson

From a Southern Oven

the savories, the sweets

Photography by Jason Wyche

WILEY

John Wiley & Sons, Inc.

This book is printed on acid-free paper. ∞

Copyright © 2012 by Jean Anderson. All rights reserved.
Cover image by Jason Wyche
Cover design by Jeff Faust
Interior design by Waterbury Publications
Photography copyright 2012 by Jason Wyche
Food styling by Mariana Velásquez
Prop styling by Martha Bernabe

Published by John Wiley & Sons, Inc., Hoboken, New Jersey.
Published simultaneously in Canada.

For general information on our other products and services, or technical support, please contact our Customer Care Department within the United States at 800–762–2974, outside the United States at 317–572–3993 or fax 317–572–4002.

Wiley publishes in a variety of print and electronic formats and by print-on-demand. Some material included with standard print versions of this book may not be included in e-books or in print-on-demand. If this book refers to media such as a CD or DVD that is not included in the version you purchased, you may download this material at http://booksupport.wiley.com. For more information about Wiley products, visit www.wiley.com.

Library of Congress Cataloging-in-Publication Data

Anderson, Jean
  From a southern oven: the savories, the sweets / Jean Anderson; photography by Jason Wyche
    p. cm.
  Includes index.
  ISBN 978-1-118-06775-8 (cloth) 978-1-118-30941-4 (ebk); 978-1-118-30943-8 (ebk); 978-1-118-30945-2 (ebk)
1. Baking. 2. Cooking, American--Southern style. 3. Cookbooks. I. Title.
  TX765.A55 2012
  641.5975--dc23

                                        2011046756

Printed in China

10 9 8 7 6 5 4 3 2 1

For my Southern friends and colleagues who have taught me so much over the years and continue to do so

Also by Jean Anderson

The Doubleday Cookbook * (with Elaine Hanna)

The Family Circle Cookbook (with the Food Editors of Family Circle)

Half a Can of Tomato Paste & Other Culinary Dilemmas ** (with Ruth Buchan)

The New Doubleday Cookbook (with Elaine Hanna)

The Food of Portugal ***

The New German Cookbook (with Hedy Würz)

The American Century Cookbook

The Good Morning America Cut the Calories Cookbook (co-edited with Sara Moulton)

Dinners in a Dish or a Dash

Process This! ****

Quick Loaves

A Love Affair with Southern Cooking: Recipes and Recollections *****

Falling Off the Bone

* Winner, R.T. French Tastemaker Award, Best Basic Cookbook (1975) and Best Cookbook of the Year (1975)

** Winner, Seagram/International Association of Culinary Professionals Award, Best Specialty Cookbook of the Year (1980)

*** Winner, Seagram/International Association of Culinary Professionals Award, Best Foreign Cookbook of the Year (1986)

**** Winner, James Beard Cookbook Awards, Best Cookbook, Tools & Techniques Category (2003)

***** Winner, James Beard Cookbook Awards, Best Cookbook, Americana Category (2008)

Contents

Acknowledgments

I should like to thank, first and foremost, good friends and colleagues Joanne Lamb Hayes, Kemp Minifie, and Alexis Touchet for a huge assist with recipe testing and development. They are thorough-going pros with years of experience as New York food editors and recipe developers in the test kitchens of *Gourmet*, *Family Circle*, and *Country Living*. I've worked with dozens of food pros over the years and know none more knowledgeable, more cooperative, more imaginative, or more dedicated than these three.

In addition, I'd like to thank Damon Lee Fowler, Babs Highfill, Robert Holmes, Sally Belk King, Rebecca Lang, Debbie Moose, Moreton Neal, Kathi Purvis, Maria Harrison Reuge, Bill Smith, Jr., Chip Smith, Tina Vaughan, and Jim Villas (Southerners all) for letting me pick their brains. And special thanks to my niece Kim Anderson for gathering and puréeing wild persimmons, then sharing what she'd frozen for my recipe tests.

A salute, moreover, to new friend Fran McCullough, for years a primo New York cookbook editor who now lives just up the road in Hillsborough, NC, and whose ongoing pursuit of and passion for Southern food have intensified my own. Grateful thanks also go to former New York magazine editor and colleague Lynne Whiteley Novy, computer software wizard who not only solved the riddle of tangled recipe formats but also proofed mountains of page proof spotting errors my less-than-eagle eyes had missed.

Finally, thanks to David Black, my savvy, energetic agent who found the perfect home for this book; and to my hard-working, hands-on Wiley editor, Justin Schwartz, for his wisdom, guidance, and support.

Introduction

My mother welcomed me into her kitchen as soon as I could toddle. And by the time I was four, she had taught me how to sift flour, measure sugar, and—thrill!—separate eggs.

But the biggest thrill came when I was allowed to solo for the first time. The recipe I chose was my Grandmother Johnson's Soft Ginger Cake, an old family recipe that Mother remembered from her own childhood.

On the big day, Mother was there to get me started. We set the oven at 375°F, greased the pan, measured the ingredients, and lined them up in the order that they were to be used. Something I do to this day.

Then with Mother off to join my father outside, I was on my own—fearless and eager to improvise. Why not, I thought, add nuts to the batter? Why not do cupcakes instead of a loaf? Why not shove the oven temperature way up? That way, I reasoned, the gingerbread would be ready to eat twice as fast.

Forgetting to grease the muffin tins, I slid my gingerbread cupcakes into a perilously hot oven and sailed outdoors to play. Billows of smoke sent Mother and Daddy to the rescue and me to my room. How could I have been so irresponsible? Didn't I realize I might have burned the house down? Soundly chastised, I was banned from the kitchen until I learned to follow directions. A valuable life lesson.

Fortunately, this near catastrophe didn't kill my enthusiasm for baking and before long, I was back in the kitchen—helping Mother at first, then baking cakes and cookies all by myself.

My mother introduced me to baking, but it wasn't until I entered first grade and tasted biscuits and corn breads, chess and custard pies baked that very morning in the school cafeteria kitchen that I discovered The World of Southern Baking. It was love at first bite—corny but true. Mother was a Midwesterner, ditto my father, so with one or two exceptions, everything that went into her oven was something her Illinois mother or my father's Ohio mother had baked: pot roast,

chicken fricassee, clover-leaf rolls, apple brown betty, gooseberry pie.

To her credit, however, my mother encouraged me to bake the Southern recipes that excited me—the achingly rich chess pies, the old-fashioned tea cakes, the corn breads and corn puddings, not to mention pork chops and sausage loaves. For some reason, Mother never cooked pork. Ham, yes, but only big pink packing-house hams, never the smoky mahogany-hued country hams for which the South is famous.

The older I grew, the greater my passion for Southern baking. And yes, there was an "ah-hah" moment: discovering that Southerners not only bake as many savories as sweets (maybe even more) but are also equally proud of them.

Right out of college, I'd gone to work as an assistant home demonstration agent in Iredell County, NC, a three-hour drive west of Raleigh, my hometown. Here in this land of no-nonsense country cooks, I tasted vegetable puddings, pies, and shortcakes for the first time, sauced and baked deviled eggs, sausage casseroles, rice casseroles, and no end of stuffed vegetables.

With Mother, it was ground-beef-stuffed green bell peppers, period. But these Iredell women were stuffing and baking yellow squash, and tomatoes, and onions. Even pork chops. Moreover, their stuffings (or dressings as they were more often called) might be rice-based, or cornbread-based, or sausage-based, or shrimp-based. My mother had one stuffing and it began with cubes of stale white bread.

Later as a magazine editor in New York, then food and travel writer, I grabbed the assignments that took me south to interview good home bakers as well as local chefs, invariably returning to Manhattan with steno pads full of recipes I was itching to try.

On these trips, I'd head for local bookstores, leaf through church and club fund-raiser cookbooks, hoping to spot some new Southern "something-from-the-oven." I nearly always did, bought too many cookbooks to lug home, and had them shipped to my door. When I came home to North Carolina after decades in New York, forty-eight boxes of Southern community cookbooks made the journey with me. There are hundreds in my library today and the number keeps growing.

While researching *A Love Affair with Southern Cooking* (James Beard Best Americana Cookbook, 2008), I was struck again and again by the sheer volume and variety of "unsweet" Southern puddings, pies, and shortcakes to say nothing of the endless repertoire of casseroles, gratins, and "scallops."

No, I haven't forsaken the South's luscious desserts, in fact have dished up many memorable ones in the pages that follow, a few never before published. But it was time to give the South's oven savories their due. Equal time, you might say.

Quite simply, my mission in writing this cookbook is to honor the South's great tradition of baking. All of it.

—Jean Anderson, Chapel Hill, NC
www.jeanandersoncooks.com

How to Use This Book

Before cooking, please review this section carefully. It discusses bakeware, ingredients, techniques, and other helpful basics.

IN GENERAL:

• Read each recipe at the outset—twice, if necessary—so you know exactly what ingredients and implements are needed and also understand the instructions.

• Measure all recipe ingredients before you begin and do as much advance prep as possible (peeling, coring, etc.) so there's no need to pause mid-recipe.

• Never substitute one ingredient for another unless substitutions are suggested.

• Never use one pan in place of another unless alternatives are suggested because the size and shape of a baking pan can spell success or disaster. The pan sizes given for each recipe are the ones used in testing those recipes. **Note:** I don't like dark pans for baking sweet breads, cakes and cookies, puddings, and pies because they tend to overbrown whatever is being baked in them. The same applies to pans lined with dark nonstick coatings. For these reasons, I recommend that you use light-colored pans (preferably aluminum).

• Use nonreactive pans whenever a recipe contains something acidic, for example, tomatoes, vinegar, fruit juices, beer, wine, or other spirits. This is especially important when something's cooked on top of the stove before going into the oven. Nonreactive means that a particular pan will not react with any acid ingredient cooked in it. Uncoated metal pans—especially aluminum, cast iron, copper, and tin—are highly reactive and acidic foods cooked in them will take on a "tinny" taste. Stainless steel is far less reactive and is rarely affected by acid ingredients. The best nonreactive pans, however, are porcelain-clad metal (like those made by Le Creuset) and the old-fashioned graniteware or spatterware our grandmothers used. I have a new graniteware roaster and use it often. What about pans with nonstick coatings? I personally don't use them because I worry that anything acidic coupled with burner or oven heat may "eat" into or damage the coating over time. Does that release possibly harmful chemicals? I can't say but being a "nervous Nellie," I prefer to err on the side of caution.

• Casseroles and baking dishes should also be nonreactive: ovenproof ceramic or glass, glazed earthenware, and the like.

• Make sure your oven is accurate. When I was a recipe tester at *Ladies' Home Journal* in New York, our test kitchen ovens were calibrated every two weeks—the gas ovens as well as the electric. Most home ovens run high or low—often as much as 50°F high or low—which of course can ruin a recipe. Some utility companies will calibrate your oven for you or can suggest someone who will. To know whether your oven's spot-on or way off, keep an oven thermometer in the oven and place it where the manufacturer recommends.

• "Cool" means to bring something to room temperature.

• "Chill" means to refrigerate or set in an ice bath until uniformly cold.

• Allow 20 minutes for an oven to preheat to the temperature set and 15 minutes for a broiler to preheat.

Ingredients

BACON Southerners pride themselves on their hickory-smoked bacons and for my money, none's better. Fortunately, many old-time country bacons are now available online both as slab bacon (one piece) and sliced thick or thin. Some are also nitrite-free. See Sources (page 264).

BACON DRIPPINGS Frugal cooks everywhere have always saved bacon drippings to use for frying but Southerners are particularly imaginative about using them to season all manner of vegetables as well as to mix them into crumb toppings and shorten a variety of corn breads and biscuits. I even know cooks who add bacon drippings to the fat in which they fry chicken to add a mellow, mysterious flavor. Before you freak about using bacon drippings because of the calories and cholesterol, let me just say that pork fat is significantly less saturated than butter, beef, or lamb fat. I do recommend using nitrite-free bacon, however.

BENNE SEEDS From an African word meaning "sesame," these tiny golden seeds were considered good luck by the slaves who brought them into the South during the 17th and 18th centuries. Slave families lucky enough to be given an acre of ground planted benne, black-eyed peas, okra, and sorghum, all of which arrived here via Africa. In the Georgia–South Carolina Lowcountry, sesame seeds, called benne to this day, are baked into cocktail nibbles, biscuits, and cookies. See Benne Sticks (page 35) and the more unusual Moldy Mice from the plantation country of Tidewater Virginia (page 262).

BLACK PEPPER Keep your peppermill full of black peppercorns and grind them fresh for every recipe. *Tip:* 10 energetic grinds of the peppermill = about ¼ teaspoon freshly ground black pepper, 20 grinds about ½ teaspoon.

BLACK WALNUTS In my youth, black walnut trees grew all around us in Piedmont, NC, as well as across much of the South, North, and Midwest. Indigenous to America, this member of the hickory family bears fleshy fruits that drop from the trees each fall. But it's the hard, deeply furrowed little nut inside that cooks prize. A bit sweet, a bit meaty even, I might venture, a bit musky the flavor of black walnuts is utterly unique and far more pungent than the English walnuts to which they are related. See Sources (page 264).

BUTTER Recipes in this book call for unsalted, old-fashioned stick butter. Do not substitute soft butter, margarine, or vegetable shortening of any type unless a recipe suggests substitutions. The reason for this? Each fat behaves differently when used to shorten breads, cakes, cookies, pastries, and other baked goods, a lesson I learned the hard way when I was a little girl. I substituted stick margarine for stick butter in a favorite cookie recipe with disastrous results. Instead of a dozen cookies, I ended up with a solid slab of baked cookie dough. The reason?

Margarine has greater shortening power than butter so this batch of cookies ran all over the baking sheet. **Note:** Given the complaints landing on my website from experienced home bakers, Crisco's relatively new trans fat-free shortening can't match the original for flaky pie crusts and biscuits. Feathery, fine-textured cakes either. My good Greensboro, NC, friend Bob Holmes, a dedicated hobby cook, recently sent me this e-mail:

"The Crisco saga continues. One of my cousins, a superb home cook, called me to say she just could not get her pound cakes to turn out right anymore: 'They don't rise enough and they are oily.' She's been using the old Beth Tartan recipe forever—the one with butter and Crisco. She had made one for my aunt and asked me to taste it. The texture was way too compact and the cake was actually greasy—almost as though she had used oil. So I asked if she was using Crisco? I had given her your book, *A Love Affair with Southern Cooking*, for Christmas and told her to use your recipe with all butter or to use her own with all butter. Well, she did both. Her old recipe without Crisco was perfect, she said. But she liked your cold oven pound cake way better.

"I called Crisco and talked to a really nice woman. I told her the story of my cousin and how she had been using that same pound cake recipe for well over 60 years with fine results. At first she paused, but then she told me that the now not-so-new Crisco melts more quickly in the oven than the old product and better results would result in baked goods if the shortening was kept frozen. I asked if that meant if I kept the Crisco in the freezer I'd get the fine results I once did. She said I would not, but the results would be better than they would if the Crisco was not frozen. So there you have it."

Tip: Whenever I need melted butter for a particular recipe, I slice the amount called for from a stick of butter, plop into a spouted 1-quart ovenproof glass measuring cup, and microwave uncovered on Defrost. The time varies, of course, according to the amount of butter being melted as well as the wattage of the microwave oven. If you need ¼ cup melted butter (½ stick), start with 5 minutes on Defrost, then continue nuking in 1- or 2-minute increments until the butter is liquid gold. You'll soon learn just how to do it in your particular microwave.

CATFISH According to Mark Twain, "The catfish is a good enough fish for anyone." But not my Illinois mother, who said they tasted like mud (not for nothing are they called "mudcats"). Though I grew up in Raleigh, I didn't taste catfish until I was thoroughly adult and then only because my Mississippi friend, Jean Todd Freeman, with whom I'd worked at *Ladies' Home Journal* in New York, decided it was "high time." She and her Hattiesburg sister, Cile Waite, drove me to a weathered shack beside a muddy river and ordered a platter of fried catfish. To my surprise, they were exquisitely delicate. Had they come from the lazy river directly below? Probably not. I suspect they were farm-raised catfish that had swum in environmentally correct ponds. More than 90 percent of all U.S. farm-raised catfish comes from the South—Alabama, Arkansas, Louisiana, and Mississippi. How pleased Mark Twain would be to learn that they are now our fourth most popular fish. See Sources (page 264).

CHEDDARS, JACKS, AND OTHER SEMI-HARD CHEESES It's always best, I think, to grate cheese whenever a recipe calls for it because packaged grated cheeses tend to melt less smoothly and lack the depth of flavor I'm after. For grating small amounts, a Microplane will do, and for larger ones, the food processor shredding disk. Here are some ballpark equivalents that may prove useful though amounts will vary somewhat from cheese to cheese:

2 ounces cheese = ½ cup grated
4 ounces (¼ pound) cheese = 1 cup grated
8 ounces (½ pound) = 2 cups grated
12 ounces (¾ pound) = 3 cups grated
16 pounds (1 pound) = 4 cups grated

Also see Parmigiano Reggiano (page 21) in this section.

CHICKEN Many recipes in this book called for chopped, diced, or sliced cooked chicken. Instead of boiling a hen as our grandmothers would have done, I buy a rotisserie chicken. One weighing around 3 to 3½ pounds yields 3½ to 4 cups of diced meat. My beef with today's chickens is that they're huge, particularly the breasts, which I've taken to calling "D-Cups." To bring them down to baking/braising size, I halve each half crosswise. *And here's another tip:* For a smaller bird or smaller chicken parts, "sweet-talk" the man at the rotisserie counter into selling you an uncooked bird. He may even disjoint it for you.

CITRUS JUICES My recipes all call for fresh—meaning freshly squeezed—citrus juices (lemon, lime, orange, and grapefruit). The one exception: Key lime juice. The bottled may be used if fresh Key limes are unavailable. See Sources (page 264). *Also see Key Limes (page 20) in this section.*

CLAMS Clams have never been as popular in the South as they are in New York, New Jersey, New England, and the Pacific Northwest because the sweetest, meatiest, clams come from those waters. Still, East Coast favorites—littlenecks measuring about 2 inches across and the slightly larger cherrystones (2 to 3 inches across)—are increasingly available across the South. And Southerners are beginning to substitute them on occasion for the oysters they so dearly love. The best clams to use? Freshly shucked. See Deviled Clams (page 41).

COCONUT When I was a little girl, good Southern cooks insisted upon freshly grated coconut for their cookies, cakes, and pies. Then along about World War II, fresh coconuts vanished from supermarket shelves and we all began using canned, sweetened, flaked, or grated coconut. Now that fresh coconuts are again commonplace, I urge you to try them—the difference in texture and flavor is dramatic. If you've never dealt with a fresh coconut, here's how to crack it and extract the precious meat:

1. Rap coconut all over with a hammer to loosen the meat inside.

2. Pierce two of the "eyes," drain off liquid, and reserve. This, by the way, is not coconut milk but a thin watery liquid with delicate coconut flavor. For an exceptionally moist coconut cake, some Southern bakers sprinkle it over the layers before filling and frosting.

3. Break coconut into pieces of manageable size with hammer blows.

4. Pry meat from the shell with a screwdriver.

5. Remove dark brown skin from coconut meat with a swivel-bladed vegetable peeler and discard. Wash coconut pieces under cool water and pat dry.

6. Grate coconut as coarse or fine as needed. I usually use the second coarsest side of a four-sided box grater. If finer shreds are needed, I use a coarse-textured Microplane.

CORNMEAL Whenever a recipe requires stone-ground cornmeal, I say so, but whether you use white or yellow is pretty much a matter of choice. Unlike the big brand granular yellow cornmeal most supermarkets carry, stone-ground meal is floury, nutritionally superior because it usually contains both husk and germ, and is far more flavorful. Unfortunately, it has a short shelf life, so store in an airtight container in refrigerator or freezer. Like flour, stone-ground cornmeal is usually sifted before it's measured and this, too, my recipes specify.

COUNTRY HAM AND SMITHFIELD HAM Back in 1926, the Virginia State Legislature decreed that only country ham made from peanut-fed hogs "raised in the peanut belt of Virginia or North Carolina and cured within the town limits of Smithfield in the State of Virginia" could be called Smithfield Ham. The first two requirements—the hogs' diet and residency—have been waived but genuine Smithfield hams must still be cured within the Smithfield city limits. Country hams have the same mahogany hue of Smithfield ham and equally salty/smoky flavor. Three of the South's finest country hams are the Edwards Hams of Virginia, Benton's Smoky Mountain Country Hams

of Tennessee, and Col. Newsom's Aged Kentucky Country Hams. *Tip:* If country ham is unavailable, prosciutto or serrano ham makes a good substitute (there are good domestic varieties of each). Do not, under any circumstances, substitute pink packing house ham for country ham. It lacks oomph. See Sources (page 264).

CRAB MEAT To most Southerners, crabs are blue crab, the "beautiful swimmers" of Chesapeake Bay and points south. On the Maryland and Virginia Eastern Shore, fresh crab meat is "picked," cooked, packed, and pasteurized at the source. Can sizes vary from area to area but as a rule, you can find crab meat in 8-ounce, 12-ounce, and 1-pound cans both pasteurized and fresh. Crab terminology is less straightforward as processors dream up new glorifying adjectives:

Lump Crab Snowy meat just underneath the shell that's removed in ½- to ¾-inch lumps. Prices increase as the adjectives grow more seductive—Premium Lump, Jumbo Lump, Deluxe Jumbo Lump, and so forth. The most expensive crab meat you can buy.

Backfin Snowy meat extracted from the shell only the pieces are smaller than lump crab.

Claw Meat Brownish slivers of meat extracted from the claws. Cheaper than lump or backfin crab meat. Okay to use when appearance isn't an issue.

Regular A mixture of backfin and claw meat. Moderately priced if any crab meat can be called moderately priced. Rarely available beyond the Chesapeake.

Keep fresh cooked crab meat refrigerated and use within 3 or 4 days. Pasteurized cooked crab meat must also be kept in the refrigerator. But if the sealed can remains unopened, pasteurized crab should last as long as a year but reject any that does not smell sweet and fresh or has an ammonia aroma. Caveat: According to the Seafood Marketing Authority of Maryland, pasteurized crab meat should never be frozen because its "flavor and texture will be greatly impaired." *Note:* All crab meat, even the most meticulously hand-picked lump crab, will contain bits of shell and cartilage. To remove, pick up a lump or two at a time,

gently feel, then discard any hard bits your fingers find. When finished, use the crab meat immediately—it's highly perishable. See Sources (page 264).

CRAWFISH About the size of large shrimp, crawfish tails are sweeter and less salty. Nearly all live crawfish sold in this country today come from Louisiana and the majority are farmed in muddy ponds that approximate the swampy habitat of their wild cousins. Though called "mudbugs," I've never eaten a crawfish that tasted remotely of mud. No Southerner would call them crayfish but "crawdad" is perfectly acceptable. Crawfish can be substituted for shrimp in almost any recipe. See Sources (page 264).

CREAM I grew up on raw Jersey milk from a small dairy up the road and the only cream my mother ever used was the Jersey "top milk." At nearly 40 percent butterfat, it whipped like a dream. Today most supermarkets sell heavy cream (36 to 40 percent butterfat—the ultra-pasteurized is slow to whip), whipping cream (about the same amount of butterfat but easier to whip), light cream (averaging 20 percent butterfat though some brands may be lower or higher), and half-and-half (a 50-50 blend of whole milk and cream that weighs in at 10 to 12 percent butterfat). The lower a cream's butterfat content, the more likely it is to curdle when heated. The best preventive is to blend 1 to 2 tablespoons all-purpose flour with each cup half-and-half or light cream used.

CREAM CHEESE Regular cream cheese (at least 33 percent butterfat) is the one to use in recipes unless a lighter cream cheese is suggested. In testing this book's recipes, I discovered that "light" cream cheese (Neufchâtel with about 20 percent butterfat) contains thickeners that break down when heated any length of time, giving the cheese a curdled look. Ditto reduced-fat and fat-free cream cheese.

CRUMBS, CRUMB CRUSTS, AND TOPPINGS Southerners love to scatter bread or cracker crumbs—sometimes plain but often mixed with melted butter and/or finely grated cheese—over scalloped meat, fish, fowl,

and vegetables not to mention scores of casseroles and gratins. For that reason, they may keep a stash of crumbs in the freezer. I do, myself, because I prefer them to store-bought crumbs. Using my food processor, I may buzz an entire loaf to moderately fine crumbs (a good all-purpose size), scoop into a large plastic zipper bag, label, date, and stash in the freezer. The crumbs remain fresh tasting for about 3 months.

The best bread to crumb is firm-textured or home-style white bread (Pepperidge Farm and Arnold are two familiar brands). Simply tear the slices, crusts and all, into a processor fitted with the chopping blade and alternately pulse and churn until the crumbs are as coarse or fine as you like. For the record: 1 slice bread = ½ cup crumbs. **Note:** Whenever a recipe in this book calls for a crumb topping, I specify exactly what goes into each.

Because cracker crumb toppings are less often used, I crush the crackers as needed, usually by placing them in a plastic zipper bag and pounding with a rolling pin or cutlet bat.

EGGS Unless recipes in this book specify otherwise, use LARGE eggs. You'll note that some recipes call for pasteurized eggs and that's because many old Southern recipes call for raw eggs or ones only partially cooked, which can be risky today. Though it's estimated that only one in 10,000 eggs may be infected with salmonella, using pasteurized eggs eliminates the risk of food poisoning. Fortunately, many supermarkets and high-end groceries now sell pasteurized eggs in clearly marked cartons (Davidson's is one prominent brand).

I never use pasteurized eggs in breads, cakes, or cookies that will be thoroughly baked, only in casseroles, pie fillings, meringues, and sauces where the eggs may not reach 160°F, the internal temperature the American Egg Board and U.S. Department of Agriculture deem essential to kill any microbes that might make you sick. There's a vaguely "milky" look to pasteurized egg whites and they do take a bit longer to whip to stiff peaks than raw eggs. Otherwise, I see no difference between pasteurized and unpasteurized eggs.

Note: If pasteurized eggs are unavailable, buy eggs from a small local source or farmers' market you trust.

HOW TO HARD-COOK EGGS
Bring eggs to a boil over moderate heat in a medium-size saucepan with enough cold water to cover them by about 2 inches. As soon as the water bubbles furiously, set pan off-heat, cover, and let eggs stand 15 minutes exactly. Drain eggs and plunge into ice water—this prevents that ugly dark green ring from forming between the yolks and whites. **Tip:** Eggs nearing their sell-by date peel more neatly than fresh ones, also if you crack the broad ends first, then shell under a slow stream of cold water.

ABOUT MERINGUES
According to the American Egg Board and U.S. Department of Agriculture, any recipe containing egg must reach an internal temperature of 160°F to be safe to eat. But how easy is it to get an accurate reading in an airy meringue? For that reason and because meringue-topped pies brown so quickly, I use only the whites of pasteurized eggs for my meringues or sometimes pasteurized egg whites sold in both powdered form (Just Whites) and in liquid (the Whole Foods grocery chain now stocks little cartons of liquid pasteurized whites). I personally don't like meringue powders because of their "perfumey" sweetness.

FLOUR Throughout this book, I call for sifted all-purpose flour—and sometimes sifted cake flour—meaning that you should sift flour before you measure it even if the package says "presifted." Flour compacts easily in transit and storage so if you merely spoon flour from bag to measuring cup, your 1 cup may actually be 1¼ cups. When flour is sifted, 1 cup = 1 cup and as every baker knows, precise measurements can make the difference between a feathery cake and a leaden one. **Note:** For years Southerners have used soft Southern flours in biscuits, cakes, and pie crusts. But with two favorites' recent acquisition by a big food conglomerate, I'm getting no end of complaints that White Lily and Martha White no longer behave the

way they used to. Research your area for mills that grind the soft Southern flour you seek. One near me in North Carolina is aiming for supermarkets but, the owner complains, "The big boys have bought all the shelf space." **Tip:** One way to approximate soft Southern flour is to substitute a little sifted cake flour for part of each cup of sifted all-purpose flour. Try subtracting 3 tablespoons from 1 cup of sifted all-purpose flour and adding 3 tablespoons sifted cake flour. Blend well with a whisk and I think you'll find that your cakes are finer-textured and your biscuits flakier than those made with all-purpose flour alone.

GRITS To Lowcountry South Carolinians, grits (from grist) is coarsely ground dried corn—and no, that's not a grammatical mistake. "Grits" is a singular noun. Elsewhere, grits is ground dried hominy. The grits supermarkets sell is about the texture of polenta. Demanding Southerners, however, insist upon coarser stone-ground hominy or speckled grits containing the nutritious "heart" or germ. See Sources (page 264).

HERBS With fresh herbs as near as the nearest supermarket or farmer's market, I urge you to use them as often as possible because their flavor is so far superior to dried herbs, which rapidly loose color and flavor. The only dried herbs I recommend are the dried leaves, never the ground, which tend to muddy sauces and gravies. Whenever I call for freshly chopped herbs, I mean leaves only unless the herb is so tender that smaller stems can be included (as with parsley and cilantro). Rule of thumb: 1 tablespoon freshly chopped herb = 1 teaspoon crumbled dried herb. There are exceptions, however: For unusually strong herbs like rosemary, sage, and thyme, I generally substitute ½ to ¾ teaspoon crumbled dried herb for each tablespoon of freshly chopped. **Tip:** When using dried herbs, crumble as you add—the warmth of your fingers enhances their flavor.

About Bay Leaves Once you discover the lemony evergreen flavor of fresh bay leaves, you'll abandon the dried, which not only have little flavor but also tend to shatter into bits that can cut your tongue or stick in your throat. Many supermarkets now sell slim plastic packets of fresh bay leaves. Even better, buy a little potted plant and stand it on a cool windowsill. Just make absolutely sure the plant you buy is edible—some varieties of bay are poisonous. **Note:** Always remove bay leaves from a dish before serving lest someone choke.

HICKORY NUTS Hickories belong to the New World and according to Albert F. Hill, at one time a Research Fellow in Economic Botany at Harvard, shagbark hickory nuts "are among the finest of the wild nuts of the United States and have excellent keeping qualities," a fact not lost on Native Americans. My father, also a botanist, told me long ago that hickory nuts and pecans are "cousins" and may be used interchangeably in recipes. Unlike pecans, however, hickory nuts are hard-shelled and their meat takes hours to extract. Daddy didn't mind devoting an evening to cracking the nuts that our own tall hickory rained down upon us. Thank heavens shelled-and-ready-to-use wild hickory nuts can now be ordered online. See Sources (page 264).

HOMINY What many Southerners call "big hominy" (to distinguish it from grits) is the posole of Mexican cooking. In other words, corn kernels that have been soaked with wood ashes or treated with lye until they puff and their skins slake off. You can buy hominy canned or dried, in which case you must soak it before using. To me, hominy has a slightly soapy taste but most Southerners don't mind. **Note:** To South Carolina Lowcountry cooks, hominy is cooked grits. See Sources (page 264).

HONEY The two honeys Southerners prize most are Appalachia's golden sourwood honey with a faint salty tang and the rare, delicate tupelo honey from the flowering tupelo gum trees of Florida and the Gulf Coast. **Tip:** Honey will slide out of measuring cups and spoons more easily if they've been spritzed with nonstick cooking spray. See Sources (page 264).

KEY LIMES Introduced to the Florida Keys some 175 years ago by Dr. Henry Perrine, these super-sour chartreuse- or yellow-skinned limes no bigger than golf balls are used by Key cooks in countless ways. But the one recipe Americans will forever identify with them is Key Lime Pie (you'll find the recipe in my *Love Affair with Southern Cooking*, named "best Americana cookbook" in 2008 by the James Beard Foundation). Instead of reprinting that recipe here, I've developed a Key Lime Cheesecake (page 203). Little mesh bags of Key limes periodically show up in my supermarket. But because they take forever to juice, I often use bottled Key lime juice. In baked goods it's comparable to the fresh and can be ordered online. See Sources (page 264).

LARD Every avid Southern baker, professional chef, or hobby cook uses lard for pie crusts and biscuits—snowy, creamy rendered hog fat, not vegetable shortening. The preferred brand? Lundy's refined lard, which is not hydrogenated and contains zero trans fats. Two preservatives have been added, however, to keep the lard from turning rancid: BHA and BHT. Both are controversial though the jury is still out on what actual harm they may do. BHA and BHT are widely used antioxidants that not only preserve foods, particularly those high in fat, but also cosmetics and medications. Some researchers suspect that they may be carcinogenic while others maintain just the opposite. Many Southern butchers, groceries, and supermarkets carry Lundy's lard. Ditto Hispanic groceries and if not Lundy's, surely the Armour brand. But it is hydrogenated, meaning that it contains trans fats, and has also had its shelf life extended with BHA and BHT. Pure lard, by the way, is less saturated than butter, beef suet, or lamb tallow. Moreover, it contains five times the amount of monounsaturated fat as hydrogenated vegetable shortening. So here's the thing: If you aim to bake the flakiest pie crusts and biscuits on earth, use lard. **Note:** Though I've never rendered lard, myself, other than to make a few cracklings, it can be done as a quick online search quickly proves.

MARGARINE *See Butter (page 14).*

MAYONNAISE AND SANDWICH SPREAD Most Southerners will tell you that the only mayonnaise they ever use is Duke's—creamy, ivory-hued, and oh-so-smooth and flavorful. A good home cook created the original recipe early in the 20th century—Eugenia Duke of Greenville, SC. The C. F. Sauer spice company of Richmond, VA, bought Mrs. Duke's recipe back in 1929, bottled it, and distributed it throughout the South. It's now sold in supermarkets as far north as Wisconsin and as far west as Oklahoma. Duke's also makes a good sandwich relish—mayonnaise mixed with sweet pickle relish—and it's an easy way to enrich the flavor of casseroles, deviled eggs, sauces, and the like. Of course, if Duke's is unavailable, use your own favorite mayo and sandwich relish.

MIRLITONS (ALSO CALLED CHAYOTES, CHRISTOPHENES, AND VEGETABLE PEARS) These bland pear-shaped squashes the color of celadon are said to have been an Aztec staple. And as long as I can remember, they've been a Deep South favorite, especially when scalloped or stuffed and baked. Much to my surprise, my mid-South supermarket routinely carries them.

MOLASSES Several of my recipes call for molasses that's not too dark meaning unsulfured molasses the consistency of corn syrup. Do not use blackstrap molasses. Country folk in the Appalachians grow sorghum, a type of grain, to feed their livestock. But they also press juice from the ripe seed clusters and boil it into "sweet sorghum," an amber-hued "molasses" to ladle over biscuits and corn pone. I've never substituted sorghum molasses for true molasses in any recipe, don't know if the two are interchangeable, and for that reason, don't advise it.

MUSCADINE The South's native grape—and North Carolina's State Grape—muscadines are purple-black, honey-sweet, and blessed with intense grape flavor. Unlike other grapes, they ripen singly and can be plucked from the vine one by one. Both they and their equally full-flavored cousin—the bronzy

Scuppernong—are baked into cobblers and pies, a particular favorite being one popularly known as grape hull pie (see page 182).

NUTMEG Before little bottles of grated nutmeg landed on grocery shelves, Southern cooks would grate their own and their recipes were all the better for it. Buy whole nutmegs next time and grate them as needed. Once you've tasted the lemony spiciness of freshly grated nutmeg, there's no turning back. Microplanes have replaced the funny little nutmeg graters our grandmothers used and do the job twice as fast.

OYSTERS Whether oysters come from Long Island Sound or Louisiana, Chesapeake Bay or points south, all are Eastern oysters. The water's chemical composition varies from region to region and so, too, the oysters' flavor, texture, size, and even their names—the Wellfleets of Massachusetts, Blue Points of Long Island Sound, Chincoteagues of Chesapeake Bay, Appalachicolas of the Gulf of Mexico, and so forth. Most are available in the shell (by the dozen, peck, or bushel) or shucked (by the pint or quart). Lately, however, shucked oysters seem to be more oyster juice (liquor) than oyster and for that reason, my recipes call for "drained, shucked oysters," meaning they're drained before they go into a container. I also specify medium-large oysters—"selects" (26 to 30 per pint) in seafood terminology. However, if oysters are to be chopped, there's no reason not to use the smaller, less expensive "standards" (30 to 40 per pint). **Note:** If a recipe also calls for oyster liquor and you're running short, round out the measure with bottled clam juice. Needless to add, shucked oysters are perishable and should be kept in the coldest part of the refrigerator (about 35°F is what the Maryland Seafood Marketing Authority recommends). It's also best to use them as soon as possible.

PARMIGIANO REGGIANO Throughout these pages, my recipes call for Parmigiano Reggiano, the renowned cheese of northern Italy that's still made much as it was centuries ago. Its perfect balance of flavors—sweet/salty/nutty—make it the cheese of choice for Southern casseroles, sauces, toppings, and more. It is not new to the South. Thomas Jefferson knew it as did his first cousin by marriage, Mary Randolph, who wrote the South's first cookbook, *The Virginia Housewife* (1824). Fortunately, Parmigiano Reggiano is widely available today and if you can afford it, by all means use it instead of grated domestic imitations. To save money, I buy Parmigiano Reggiano by the chunk, grate in my food processor (30 seconds is all it takes), and store in the refrigerator in a 1-pint preserving jar. For small amounts, I simply whisk a bit of Parmigiano Reggiano back and forth on a Microplane.

PEACHES The two peach varieties everyone talked about when I was little were Elbertas and Georgia Belles, both freestones, meaning the seeds could be easily popped out. Elbertas were as gold as June sunshine, the Georgia Belles white, and both gloriously sweet. One of my family's summer rituals was to drive 100 miles or so down to a pick-your-own orchard in the North Carolina Sandhills. With a bushel of Elbertas perfuming the car, we'd head home eager for the peach crisps and pies to come. Though Elbertas remain popular, many peach growers are switching to newer, more robust varieties like Redhaven (today's "industry standard"). If you don't live within easy distance of a pick-your-own orchard, you can order fresh peaches online and have them shipped to your door. See Sources (page 264).

PEANUTS Believed to be indigenous to Peru, peanuts made it to North America in a roundabout way. Early 16th-century Spanish explorers brought them from South America to Europe, then Portuguese traders introduced them to Africa and China. Groundnuts, as peanuts are known in Africa, arrived in the Colonial South possibly as early as 1670, with the founding of Charleston, SC, and its bustling slave market— America's first. Slaves, it's believed, brought with them the seeds of home—benne (sesame), peanuts, and rice—sometimes less than a handful, which they grew with great success in the New World. Today, peanuts

are a Southern staple with Georgia producing nearly half of our supply. Peanuts, of course, are not nuts but legumes that mature underground. They are highly nutritious, good sources of protein, niacin and folate (two B vitamins), vitamin E, and three important minerals (magnesium, manganese, and phosphorous). Yet peanuts contain no cholesterol, no sodium, and no trans fats, their oils being largely unsaturated. Recent research, moreover, has shown that roasted peanuts are as antioxidant-rich as blackberries and strawberries as well as a significant source of resveratrol, the anti-aging compound usually associated with red table wines. There are, of course, many different peanut varieties, but the ones I like best are the large, uniformly plump Virginia types. If you've never tasted oven-fried peanuts, you're in for a treat (see recipe, page 43). Also see Sources (page 264).

PECANS My father planted two pecan trees in our backyard and though they bore precious few nuts, there were enough to taste and, more important, to learn the value of fresh-crop nuts—the sweetness, the mellowness, and total absence of rancidity. Pecans, as I've said elsewhere, are related to hickory nuts (discussed earlier in this section), both being New World natives highly prized by Indian tribes right across the South. Today, pecan farming is big business to the delight of Southerners who bake them in breads and pies, cakes and cookies. The good news is that pecans contain significant amounts of largely unsaturated oleic acid (thought to lower LDL or "bad cholesterol") as well as phytochemicals that some researchers believe may reduce the risk of heart disease as well as colon and stomach cancer. Because canned and prepackaged pecans are rarely as sweet or fresh as I'd like, I order new-crop pecans directly from the grower. See Sources (page 264).

PERSIMMONS American persimmon trees grow wild across the South and between late September and mid-December bear intensely flavored fruits no bigger than Ping-Pong balls. Shriveled windfalls—orange with a haze of mauve—are what gleaners seek. Ditto deer,

possums, and raccoons who devour them almost as fast as they drop from the trees.

TO PURÉE PERSIMMONS
Slosh persimmons gently up and down in sink of cold water, repeat twice, then drain on several thicknesses paper toweling and pat dry. Now force persimmons through food mill set over large bowl. Discard skins and seeds. Yield: 1 quart wild persimmons = about 2 cups (1 pint) purée.

TO FREEZE PERSIMMON PURÉE
To prevent discoloring, mix ⅛ teaspoon powdered ascorbic acid (vitamin C) into each 1 quart persimmon purée. Pack in 1-pint freezer containers leaving ½ inch head space at top. Snap on lids, date, label, and set on freezing surface of 0°F freezer. Use in any recipe that calls for unsweetened persimmon purée or pulp. Storage time: 1 year. **Note:** Frozen wild persimmon purée is also available online. See Sources (page 264).

PORK In years past, hogs were as much at home on small American farms as chickens. And during the great push to tame the West, crates of piglets bumped along in covered wagons because they were sturdy and would eat almost anything. Even during my childhood, pork was the South's "red" meat of choice. But all that changed in the 1980s when the calorie-conscious began choosing chicken over pork. The pork industry's solution? Breed fat out of hogs and reposition pork as "The Other White Meat." Unfortunately it was tasteless, dry, and rarely tender even when oven-braised with liquid and vegetables. The only pork I now buy—and that used to develop recipes in this book—is the well-marbled meat of heritage breeds like Tamworth, Berkshire, Old Spot, and others. Many are available through groceries that buy from Niman Ranch. And there are online sources as well. See Sources (page 264).

PREPARED PIE CRUSTS AND PASTRY I so admire cooks who still make their own pastry and I wish I could say the same. But to be honest, like many friends and colleagues, I'm so pressed for time that I often settle

for frozen pie crusts (some of which, by the way, are first-rate), even sometimes for the new unroll-and-bake pastry sheets. Here are a few things I've learned that may be helpful.

ABOUT FROZEN PIE SHELLS

If you substitute a frozen pie shell for a from-scratch one, use the deep-dish variety. And to add a "homey" touch and minimize the risk of boil-overs, recrimp the crust making a high, fluted edge. It's as easy as pinching the dough between the thumb of one hand and index finger and thumb of the other and it takes less than a minute to recrimp in a zig-zag pattern. For added support, set unfilled pie shell—flimsy pan and all—inside a standard 9-inch pie pan and set on a heavy-duty rimmed baking sheet that was preheated along with the oven. This not only spares the oven messy spills and boil-overs but also means a crisper bottom crust.

ABOUT PREPARED PASTRY CIRCLES

Most supermarkets now sell refrigerated unroll-and-use pastry circles—they're usually near the refrigerated biscuits. I've used these when I've been pressed for time and find them perfectly acceptable. They come two to a package and are a good choice for a two-crust pie.

WHEN YOU NEED A BAKED PIE SHELL

Whether you're using a frozen pie shell or a prepared pastry circle, follow the package directions for "blind-baking" a pie shell. If you've made your own pastry, lightly prick bottom and sides of unbaked pie shell with a table fork. Line pie shell with double thickness of foil, then, so pie shell keeps its shape, pour in about 1½ cups uncooked rice or dried beans. Slide pie shell onto baking sheet on middle shelf of a preheated 450°F oven and bake 10 minutes. Remove pie shell from oven, lift out foil and rice or beans, discarding foil but saving rice or beans to weight pie shells in future. Return pie shell to baking sheet on middle oven shelf and bake 3 to 5 minutes longer until pale golden. Transfer pie shell to wire rack and cool to room temperature before filling.

RICE Many of my recipes call for "converted" or parboiled rice (Uncle Ben), but if you're making a rice pudding and creaminess is your aim, use long-grain rice (Carolina) or even short-grain rice (Arborio). Recipes specify which one to use for best results.

SALT For all-around baking, I prefer uniodized table salt. I personally find kosher or coarse salt too grainy for breads, cakes, cookies, puddings, and pies though perfectly fine for savories.

SALTWATER FISH According to Maryland's Seafood Marketing Authority, more than 200 different kinds of fish swim in Chesapeake Bay, "the world's greatest inland sea with more than 4,000 miles of shoreline." Some varieties—striped bass (often called rockfish or simply "rock") and white perch—are permanent residents of the bay, but dozens of others—croaker, flounder, herring, sea trout, shad, and spot—swim in from the Atlantic to feed. The Southern Atlantic teems with bluefish, too, with drum, redfish (a variety of drum), red snapper, and the highly prized, white-fleshed pompano. Many of these same fish also swim the warmer waters of the Gulf of Mexico and pompano caught here is considered the choicest fish of all. I'm lucky to have a first-rate fishmonger, who drives his refrigerated truck to the Carolina coast every Thursday, buys the local catch, then sells it on Fridays and Saturday mornings. Most supermarket fish, even that of high-end groceries, has been frozen, then thawed. It's perfectly acceptable if handled properly from trawler to table but can never match fresh-caught fish for flavor and texture.

SCALLOPS Though tiny bay scallops live in Southern inlets and backwaters, they've never been as popular among Southerners as the big sea scallops even though these are rarely taken south of New Jersey and supplies of those from Maine to Labrador are depleted. Many of the sea scallops now sold in this country are farm-raised in Asia (mainly Japan) and frozen. These, moreover, may have been bleached and "plumped" with a phosphate solution that not only increases their weight by as much as 30 percent but also

imparts a slightly soapy taste. The choicest scallops are "divers"—handpicked by divers instead of being scraped from the sea floor by commercial trawling rakes. Look for scallops marked "chemical-free" or "dry-packed." As for size, sea scallops (the meat, not the shell) average 1½ to 2 inches across.

SCUPPERNONG *See Muscadine (page 20).*

SHORTENING (VEGETABLE SHORTENING) *See Butter (page 14).*

SHRIMP The most widely available shrimp come from warm waters and though sometimes masquerading as "Gulf shrimp" or "pink shrimp" are actually brown shrimp or the more common white shrimp. Both are bright pink when cooked. It's hard not to be wooed by the adjectives flung about to describe shrimp—"colossal," "extra-jumbo," "jumbo," and so forth—but these are not standardized or even officially recognized terms.

The way to buy shrimp is by "count," i.e. the number of shrimp (head-on, in-the-shell) per pound. Common market sizes: 16/20 (16 to 20 shrimp per pound, sometimes labeled "extra-jumbo"), 20/25 (20 to 25 shrimp per pound), 26/30, 31/35, 36/42, and so on with shrimp getting smaller as the numbers increase. Counts preceded by "UN" or "U" are heavyweights. For example, U-10 comes to about 10 shrimp per pound. It goes without saying that the bigger the shrimp, the bigger the price.

Most shrimp coming to market today have been frozen, then thawed, and are so perishable they should be used as soon after purchase as possible. Needless to add, they should be stored in the coldest part of the refrigerator. It's now possible to buy frozen, cooked, shelled and deveined shrimp, the majority farm-raised in Thailand. Scrutinize package labels. Before using frozen shrimp, thaw in refrigerator, drain well, and pat dry on paper toweling. For obvious reasons, I prefer local shrimp and the fresher the better.

SOUR CREAM In some parts of the country, I'm told, sour cream is no longer available in 8-ounce cartons. No problem. Simply pack sour cream into a 1-cup measure—the kind you use for measuring flour—and level off the top with the broad side of a small spatula. *Note:* Unless I suggest "light" or low-fat sour cream for a particular recipe, do not use it. Many are thickened with gums or gelling agents that break down when heated, meaning a curdled casserole, cheesecake, or sauce.

SUGAR Unless otherwise specified, the sugar used in my recipes is granulated sugar but whenever two different sugars are used within a single recipe—granulated and confectioner's for example—each one is specified. A number of my recipes call for raw sugar (also known as turbinado), a pale brown granulated sugar that tastes more of caramel than molasses. Light and dark brown sugar are nothing more than granulated sugar darkened with molasses. Of the two, I prefer the more delicate light brown sugar.

VANILLA AND OTHER EXTRACTS Always use pure vanilla extract, never imitation, which to me tastes nothing like true vanilla and is disagreeably perfumey. The same applies to all extracts used in this book—almond, orange, lemon, rum, and so forth. So use pure extracts, only. The faux can ruin a good cake or cookie, pudding or pie. See Sources (page 264).

Measuring Tips

There are two basic types of measuring cups, one for liquids, the second for dry or soft, thick ingredients. Here are the correct ways to use them.

Spouted Measuring Cups

Technique: Set measuring cup on a flat surface and fill to desired amount (¼ cup, ½ cup, 1 cup, etc.), then bend down and confirm the amount at eye level.

For liquids: Broths, fruit and vegetable juices, milk and cream, oils and vinegars, soft drinks, wines, whiskeys and other spirits, water, honey, molasses, and syrups.

"Dry" Measures
(Nested cups in ¼, ⅓, ½, and 1-cup sizes):

For the following ingredients, spoon ingredient into measuring cup of desired size, packing as you go, and level off the top with the broad side of a small spatula.

- *Brown sugar* (light or dark)
- *Chutneys and pickle relishes*
- *Fruit and vegetable purées, applesauce, mashed Irish or sweet potatoes*
- *Jams, jellies, marmalades, and preserves*
- *Ketchup, chili sauce, tomato paste, and bottled pasta sauces*
- *Lard, soft butter or margarine, and vegetable shortening*
- *Mayonnaise and mustard*

- *Peanut butter, Nutella, tahini, and other nut and seed pastes*
- *Sour cream and yogurt*

For the ingredients that follow, simply spoon into the measuring cup and level off with the edge of a small spatula:

- *Bread and cracker crumbs*
- *Cereals* (uncooked) Bran, flakes, oatmeal (rolled oats), and other grains
- *Cheeses* (grated or shredded)
- *Cornmeal* (stone-ground or granular)
- *Dried fruits* (raisins, currants, chopped dates, and Craisins, etc.)
- *Dried peas, beans, and lentils*
- *Flour* All-purpose, cake, whole wheat, rice, and rye, etc.
- *Fresh fruits* Chopped, diced, or sliced apples, bananas, peaches, and pears, etc.
- *Herbs* Freshly chopped parsley, cilantro, and basil, etc. Also finely chopped fresh ginger.
- *Macaroni* (uncooked) and other small pasta
- *Nuts* Halves, pieces, and chopped
- *Rice* (uncooked) Converted, long-grain, short-grain, brown, basmati, quick-cooking (Minute Rice), wild rice, rice mixtures, and rice-pasta mixtures
- *Sugar* Granulated, raw, and confectioner's (10X)
- *Vegetables* Chopped, diced, or sliced bell peppers, celery, carrots, and onions, etc.

part 1

The
Savories

Baking.

The very word conjures visions of tall, tiered cakes swirled about with icing, of cookie jars filled to the brim, of fruit pies and custard pies and chess pies not to mention tea breads, crisps, and cobblers galore. In other words, Sweets with a capital S.

But, oh, so much more goes into Southern ovens. While researching *A Love Affair with Southern Cooking* (2007), I was startled to discover how many savories Southerners have been baking since Colonial days: appetizers, an impressive repertoire of main dishes (meat, fish, fowl, cheese, eggs, pasta, rice), vegetables (maybe creamed or scalloped, maybe gratinéed, or perhaps stuffed) plus yeast breads and corn breads, biscuits and muffins. The list is long.

In the beginning, baking was done on open hearths, then in brick ovens, then in cast-iron behemoths stoked with wood, then scaled-down versions fueled with coal, wood and/or kerosene. Gas ovens arrived in Southern kitchens toward the turn of the 20th century but didn't outnumber wood stoves till the 1930s. About the same time electric ovens began claiming place of pride in big-city Southern kitchens but not in small towns or rural areas still off the electric grid. My mother didn't get an electric stove till the start of WWII—in thoroughly electrified Raleigh, NC.

Even more welcome than electric stoves were thermostatically controlled oven temperatures that minimized the risk of overbrowning (read "burning") as well as undercooking. Need a moderate oven? Set the thermostat at 350°F. Need a hot oven? Turn the dial to 400°, 450°,

or more. Gone were the days of the iffy "elbow tests" grandmother used—the faster she pulled her elbow from the oven, the hotter it was. But only experienced bakers knew how hot "hot" was.

I guess you could say I've been researching the South's oven savories ever since I was a little girl, but for this chapter, I added an intensive year of study. Some of the recipes I've assembled here date back to Colonial America, others are unabashedly modern. New or old, however, all have been tested for accuracy—once, twice, and in the case of a few maddeningly vague historic recipes, three times. My aim, as always, is to create recipes that work for today's cooks in today's kitchens using today's ingredients.

The recipe titles that follow give some notion of the scope and appeal of the savories Southerners bake: Pecan-Cheddar Pennies • Benne Sticks • Little Shrimp Half-Moons • Mushroom Tassies • Jekyll Island Crab Pie • Oysters Johnny Reb • Baked Shrimp Salad • Shrimp and Artichoke Hearts au Gratin • Fish Corned the Eastern Shore Way • Chicken Jambalaya Casserole • Colonial Chicken Pudding • Atlanta Brisket • Moravian Baked Pork Chops • Pimiento Mac 'n' Cheese • Asparagus Pie • Lady Cabbage • Baked Breaded Cauliflower • Creamed Celery with Pecans • Eggplant Gratin • Vidalia Shortcake • Tomato Pudding • Gulf Coast Green Rice • Eggs Creole • Bacon Biscuits • Peanut Butter Bread • Casserole Corn Bread • Philpy • Peach Muffins • Sweet Potato Focaccia.

And these, mind you, are only the beginning.

chapter one

Appetizers,

nibbles & snacks

Breathes there a Southern hostess who doesn't adore cheese daisies? If so, I've not met her. Even my Illinois mother took to cheese daisies and made them using a Southern neighbor's recipe. This is a new spin on that recipe that substitutes freshly grated Parmigiano Reggiano (unheard of in my mother's day) for Cheddar and ramps up the cayenne. *Note:* I've tried shooting this dough through my cookie gun with so-so success. If the weather's humid, better to shape the dough into balls and flatten as the recipe directs.

Peppery Cheese Rounds

Makes About 6½ Dozen

2½ to 2¾ cups sifted unbleached all-purpose flour

½ to 1 teaspoon ground hot red pepper (cayenne), depending on how hot you like things

¼ teaspoon freshly grated nutmeg

¼ teaspoon salt

1 cup (2 sticks) refrigerator-cold unsalted butter, cut into slim pats

8 ounces freshly grated Parmigiano Reggiano

1. Preheat oven to 350°F.

2. Whisk 2½ cups flour, cayenne, nutmeg, and salt together in large shallow bowl. Add butter, then with pastry blender, cut into dry ingredients until texture of coarse meal.

3. Add cheese and work in with fingers until uniformly crumbly. Squeeze bit of mixture and if holds together, dough is ready. If not, work in a little additional flour.

4. Shape dough into ¾-inch balls, space about 2 inches apart on ungreased baking sheets, then with floured, smooth-surfaced meat pounder or bottom of sturdy glass, flatten into rounds ¼ inch thick. Or if you're a cookie gun maestro, shoot into daisies (see Note above).

5. Bake, one sheet at a time, on middle oven shelf 10 to 12 minutes until color of parchment.

6. Transfer cheese rounds at once to wire racks and cool to room temperature. Store in airtight containers.

No Southern tea table—or cocktail party, for that matter—is complete without cheese straws (or daisies) made with a Cheddar that's well aged and good and sharp. And no stinting on cayenne, either. What I've done here is give this Old South staple a new spin by working freshly ground pecans into the dough. Instead of shooting the dough through a cookie gun, I roll it into logs, chill or freeze, then slice and bake as needed. How easy is that? *Tip:* The fastest way to grind pecans is in a food processor. Just pulse and churn until the texture of kosher salt—no longer or you'll have paste. For ½ cup ground pecans, you'll need about ½ cup nuts. Grind the pecans before you begin the recipe, measure, and set aside.

Pecan-Cheddar Pennies

Makes About 5 Dozen

½ cup (1 stick) unsalted butter, cut into pats, plus 3 tablespoons, at room temperature

6 ounces sharp Cheddar cheese, coarsely grated

1 teaspoon salt

1 teaspoon sweet Hungarian paprika, or if you prefer, pimenton (smoky Spanish paprika)

½ teaspoon freshly grated nutmeg

¼ to ½ teaspoon ground hot red pepper (cayenne), depending on how hot you like things

½ cup finely ground pecans (see Tip above)

1½ cups unsifted all-purpose flour

1. Cream butter, cheese, salt, paprika, nutmeg, and cayenne in food processor by alternately pulsing and churning until smooth. Pulse in pecans, then flour but only until dough comes together—no longer or cheese pennies will be tough.

2. Divide dough in half and shape into two logs about 7½ inches long and 1½ inches in diameter. Wrap each snugly in foil and refrigerate overnight or, if you prefer, freeze.

3. When ready to proceed, preheat oven to 350°F. With sharpest knife, slice dough into rounds about ¼ inch thick and space 1½ inches apart on ungreased baking sheets.

4. Slide onto middle oven shelf and bake 7 to 10 minutes until pennies feel firm—they should not brown.

5. Transfer at once to wire racks, cool to room temperature, and serve. Or layer in airtight containers between sheets of foil or wax paper, store on a cool, dry shelf, and serve within 2 weeks.

Note: Frozen, these cocktail nibbles will keep fresh for about 4 months.

"Benne," as I've said elsewhere, is what sesame seeds are called in the Lowcountry, particularly in and around Charleston, SC. They were brought to this country by the Africans imported as slave labor, and they were among the African foods that soon made it from slave cabin to "big house." Good Lowcountry cooks today bake benne into biscuits, cookies, and cocktail snacks as a riffle though *Charleston Receipts* quickly proves. This Junior League classic, first published in 1950, is for me the quintessential local cookbook because of its distinct sense of time and place. Now, dozens of printings later, *Charleston Receipts* is still going strong. This particular recipe, however, is my own. *Note:* To toast benne, spread in an ungreased pie pan and set on the middle shelf of a preheated 275°F oven for 8 to 10 minutes until pale amber, stirring seeds once or twice to redistribute. Cool benne before using.

Benne Sticks

Makes About 12 Dozen

1¼ cups sifted all-purpose flour

¼ cup lightly toasted benne seeds (see Note above)

2 tablespoons freshly grated Parmigiano Reggiano

½ teaspoon salt

⅛ to ¼ teaspoon ground hot red pepper (cayenne), depending on how hot you like things

3 tablespoons cold unsalted butter, cut into pats

3 tablespoons cold lard (not vegetable shortening), diced

¼ cup ice water (about)

1. Combine flour, benne, cheese, salt, and cayenne in large shallow bowl. Scatter butter and lard on top, then with pastry blender, cut in until texture of lentils. Forking flour mixture briskly, add ice water until soft dough forms. Shape into ball, flatten, wrap in plastic food wrap, and refrigerate 30 minutes.

2. When ready to proceed, preheat oven to 400°F. Remove dough from refrigerator, divide in half, and roll one piece at a time on lightly floured surface into 9-inch square as thin as pie crust.

3. Using metal-edge ruler to guide you, cut dough into strips about ⅜ inch wide with pastry wheel (cutter). Now cut each strip into 3-inch lengths.

4. Arrange strips about 1 inch apart on ungreased baking sheets. Bake, one sheet at a time, on middle oven shelf about 8 to 10 minutes until very lightly browned.

5. Transfer at once to wire racks and cool to room temperature. Serve with cocktails or put out on an open-house buffet.

Note: Layered in airtight tins between sheets of wax paper, these benne sticks remain crisp and fresh for about 2 weeks.

Southern hobby bakers, like those elsewhere, welcome frozen pie shells and pastries because of the time they save. Moreover, many of them—frozen puff pastry, to name one—are first-rate and an effective way to glamorize old favorites. That's why I use it instead of plain pastry for these crunchy little shrimp appetizers. *Note:* Frozen puff pastry will thaw more evenly in the refrigerator than at room temperature, but this takes about 6 hours.

Little Shrimp Half-Moons

Makes 2½ Dozen Appetizers

6 ounces cooked, shelled, and deveined large shrimp, halved crosswise

1 large scallion, trimmed and cut in 1-inch chunks (include some green tops)

2 tablespoons mayonnaise or mayonnaise-relish sandwich spread

1 tablespoon fresh lemon juice

1½ teaspoons anchovy paste

½ teaspoon hot red pepper sauce, or to taste

¼ teaspoon freshly ground black pepper

3 sheets frozen puff pastry (1½ packages, 17.3 ounces each), thawed according to package directions

1. Whiz all but final ingredient (pastry) in food processor until smooth. Scoop into bowl, cover, and refrigerate at least 1 hour.

2. When ready to proceed, preheat oven to 400°F. Spread thawed pastry sheets on lightly floured smooth surface, then with lightly floured rolling pin, roll one at a time into rectangle 12 inches long and 9½ inches wide.

3. Cut into rounds with lightly floured 3-inch round cutter. Drop slightly rounded teaspoon shrimp mixture into middle of each round and brush pastry edges with cold water. Fold pastry over filling, forming little half-moons, and crimp edges firmly with fork to seal.

4. Arrange half of pastries, not touching, on each of two ungreased baking sheets. Slide one baking sheet onto middle oven shelf and bake pastries 12 to 15 minutes until puffed and browned. Repeat with second sheet of pastries.

5. Arrange shrimp half-moons on large heated platter and serve warm with cocktails.

One of the beauties of this winning Southern appetizer is that the toast cups can be made 2 to 3 months in advance and frozen. *Note:* Firm-textured bread, also known as "home-style," is sturdy enough to shape into cups–even the very thin slices, which you need here. *Tip:* Pulse bread trimmings into moderately fine crumbs in a food processor, empty crumbs into a plastic zipper bag, and freeze. Then whenever a recipe calls for a bread crumb topping, you're ahead of the game.

Crab Cups

Makes About 4 Dozen

TOAST CUPS

2 loaves (1 pound each) very thinly sliced firm-textured white bread (see Note and Tip above)

1 cup (2 sticks) unsalted butter, melted

CRAB FILLING

2 tablespoons unsalted butter

2 large scallions, finely chopped (include some green tops)

2 tablespoons all-purpose flour

¾ cup milk

2 tablespoons medium-dry sherry, Madeira, or Port

2 ounces Gruyère cheese, moderately coarsely shredded

8 ounces backfin crab meat, coarsely flaked and bits of shell and cartilage removed

1 tablespoon moderately coarsely chopped fresh parsley

1½ teaspoons fresh lemon juice

½ teaspoon finely grated lemon zest

½ teaspoon Dijon mustard

¼ teaspoon salt, or to taste

⅛ teaspoon hot red pepper sauce, or to taste

¼ cup moderately fine soft white bread crumbs tossed with 1 teaspoon melted unsalted butter (Topping)

1. Preheat oven to 450°F.

2. *Toast Cups:* Arrange 48 bread slices into 24 stacks of two and cut into rounds with 2¾-inch biscuit cutter. Brush both sides of each round with melted butter, then press into ungreased mini muffin pans forming 48 little cups.

3. Slide onto middle oven shelf and bake 5 to 8 minutes until golden brown. Cool toast cups in pans to room temperature. Reduce oven temperature to 375°F.

4. Meanwhile prepare ***Crab Filling:*** Melt butter in medium-size nonreactive saucepan over moderate heat, add scallions, and cook, stirring now and then 2 to 3 minutes until limp and golden. Blend in flour and cook and stir 1 minute. Add milk and cook, stirring constantly, 3 to 5 minutes until thickened and no raw floury taste lingers.

5. Remove from heat, add sherry and cheese, and stir until cheese melts. Fold in crab and all remaining ingredients except Topping. Spoon filling into toast cups, dividing total amount evenly; you'll need about ½ tablespoon per toast cup, then scatter a scant ¼ teaspoon Topping over each.

6. Slide onto middle oven shelf and bake uncovered about 10 minutes until bubbly and tipped with brown.

7. Arrange toast cups on warm large platter and pass with drinks.

By definition, tassies are bite-size pastries and in the South that nearly always means mini pecan tarts though sometimes mini lemon chess. But must "tassie" be used exclusively for sweets? By definition, "tassie" is the Scottish diminutive of *tasse*, French for "cup" or "goblet." So I don't think I'm committing heresy by calling these bite-size mushroom appetizers tassies. They are Southern, they rival Pecan Tassies for popularity, and I think they're equally delicious. Moreover, they're easier to make because the crust is nothing more than white sandwich bread cut into rounds, fitted into mini muffin pan cups, and toasted. *Note:* Most supermarkets sell 8-ounce packages of presliced mushrooms and I often use them to trim prep time, but only if the mushrooms look good and fresh—no darkening, no withering, no signs of going soft. *Tip:* In some parts of the country, I'm told, sour cream is no longer available in 8-ounce containers. No problem. Simply substitute 1 cup firmly packed sour cream.

Mushroom Tassies

Makes 2 Dozen

24 (3½-inch) rounds cut from firm-textured white sandwich bread (you'll need 24 slices, about 2 loaves, 1 pound each)

2 tablespoons unsalted butter

8 ounces white or cremini mushrooms, stemmed, wiped clean, and moderately coarsely chopped (see Note above)

4 large scallions, trimmed and moderately coarsely chopped (include some green tops)

2 tablespoons finely chopped Italian parsley

2 teaspoons finely chopped fresh thyme or ½ teaspoon dried leaf thyme, crumbled

2 tablespoons all-purpose flour

1 carton (8 ounces) sour cream (see Tip above)

½ teaspoon finely grated lemon zest

½ teaspoon salt, or to taste

¼ teaspoon ground hot red pepper (cayenne), or to taste

2 tablespoons freshly grated Parmigiano Reggiano

1. Preheat oven to 375°F. Lightly spritz 24 mini muffin pan cups with nonstick cooking spray and set aside.

2. Gently flatten rounds of bread with fingers and fit into muffin pan cups forming little tart shells. Slide onto middle oven shelf and bake about 10 minutes until nicely toasted. Remove from oven and cool to room temperature in pans.

3. Meanwhile, melt butter in medium-size heavy skillet over moderate heat, add mushrooms, scallions, parsley, and thyme, and cook, stirring now and then, about 7 minutes until soft and juices evaporate.

4. Blend in flour and cook and stir 2 minutes to eliminate raw floury taste. Smooth in sour cream, lemon zest, salt, and cayenne and cook and stir 1 to 2 minutes more—easy does it. You don't want cream to curdle. Taste for salt and cayenne and adjust.

5. Spoon mushroom mixture into tart shells, dividing amount evenly, then top each tassie with a light sprinkling of cheese. Slide onto middle oven shelf and bake about 10 minutes until bubbly and touched with brown.

6. Arrange on colorful platter, serve warm with cocktails, and get ready for compliments.

If a fruit or vegetable is cup-shaped or hollow, a Southerner will stuff it. And if nature gave the fruit or vegetable no cup or hollow, a Southerner will make one. Thumb through any community fund-raiser published south of the Mason-Dixon and you'll find everything from baked stuffed onions and mirlitons to baked stuffed cherry tomatoes and sugar snaps. I've caught the "fever" and worked up a recipe for crab-stuffed mushrooms. Few cocktail appetizers are more elegant or delicious. *Note:* In this Age of Salmonella, I either use a pasteurized egg (which many supermarkets now carry) in this recipe or one from a local source I trust because the crab stuffing may brown before the egg in it reaches the 160°F the U.S. Department of Agriculture deems safe.

Baked Crab-Stuffed Mushrooms

Makes 3 Dozen Hors d'Oeuvre

3   tablespoons unsalted butter

4   large scallions, trimmed and finely chopped (include some green tops)

1   small celery rib, trimmed and finely chopped

1   cup firmly packed mayonnaise

1   large pasteurized egg, well beaten (see Note above)

1   tablespoon minced fresh parsley (Italian or curly)

1   tablespoon fresh lemon juice

½   teaspoon salt

1   teaspoon hot red pepper sauce

1   cup moderately fine soft white bread crumbs (2 slices firm-textured bread)

1   pound backfin crab meat, bits of shell and cartilage removed

3   dozen mushrooms of uniform size (2 to 2¼ inches across), stemmed and wiped clean (reserve stems for soup or stew another day)

    Paprika (preferably sweet Hungarian paprika)

1. Preheat oven to 375°F. Lightly butter a large rimmed baking sheet and set aside.

2. Melt butter in small heavy skillet over moderate heat, add scallions and celery, and cook, stirring occasionally, 5 to 7 minutes until golden. Scoop into mixing bowl, add next six ingredients (mayonnaise through hot red pepper sauce) and mix well. Add bread crumbs and toss lightly, then fold in crab.

3. Fill each mushroom cap with about 1 tablespoon crab mixture, mounding it up slightly. Arrange mushrooms in single layer on baking sheet and sprinkle lightly with paprika.

4. Slide onto middle oven shelf and bake uncovered 15 to 20 minutes until mushroom filling browns lightly.

5. Transfer mushrooms to warm large platter and pass with cocktails.

Deviled crab is familiar to most of us. But deviled clams? Anyone living within the sound of the surf—in this case Chesapeake Bay—knows how to devil most of the shellfish that watermen net. In these parts, deviled clams run a close second to deviled crab. *Note:* I like to bake deviled clams in scallop shells, but if you have none, use a shallow 1-quart casserole or au gratin pan lightly spritzed with nonstick cooking spray.

Deviled Clams

Makes 6 First-Course Servings

24 cherrystone clams, freshly shucked and well drained

1 cup coarse soda cracker crumbs mixed with ¾ teaspoon dry mustard

2 tablespoons melted unsalted butter

3 tablespoons finely grated yellow onion

¾ teaspoon salt, or to taste

½ teaspoon freshly ground black pepper

½ teaspoon hot red pepper sauce

¾ cup moderately fine soft white bread crumbs tossed with 1 tablespoon melted unsalted butter (Topping)

1. Preheat oven to 400°F. Spritz 6 pristine large scallop shells with nonstick cooking spray, arrange not touching on rimmed baking sheet, and set aside (see Note above).

2. Combine all ingredients except Topping and divide among scallop shells. Scatter Topping evenly over all.

3. Slide onto middle oven shelf and bake uncovered about 15 minutes until bubbly and brown.

4. Serve at once at the start of an elegant meal.

Certain recipes pop up out of God knows where, catch the public fancy, and in no time are the new "gotta-haves." Case in point: Texas Torte. All the rage among stylish Southern hostesses back in the '70s, it was easy to make, easy to serve, and substantial enough to stave off "the tipsies" at cocktail parties. Did it originate in Texas? Maybe. But the Deep South surely claims it.

Texas Torte

Makes About 4 Dozen Hors d'Oeuvre

2 large eggs

2 tablespoons all-purpose flour

1 teaspoon dried leaf oregano, crumbled (preferably Mexican oregano)

½ teaspoon salt

¼ teaspoon dried leaf thyme, crumbled

⅛ to ¼ teaspoon ground hot red pepper (cayenne), depending on how hot you like things

1 can (5 ounces) evaporated milk

1 can (4 ounces) diced green chilis, with their liquid

8 ounces sharp Cheddar cheese, moderately coarsely shredded

8 ounces Monterey Jack, moderately coarsely shredded

1. Preheat oven to 350°F. Coat 13 × 9 × 2-inch ovenproof glass baking dish with nonstick baking spray and set aside.

2. Whisk eggs with flour, oregano, salt, thyme, and cayenne until frothy in large bowl, then whisk in milk. Fold in chilis and both cheeses, stirring until combined.

3. Pour into baking dish, slide onto middle oven shelf, and bake uncovered 30 to 35 minutes just until lightly golden and set.

4. Cool 5 minutes in pan, then cut into bite-size pieces; I find that 6 cuts the length of the baking dish and 8 crosswise are exactly right.

5. Arrange on warm large platter and serve with drinks.

Another food introduced to the South by African slaves, peanuts are still widely grown in Virginia, the Carolinas, and Georgia. If you've never tasted oven-fresh peanuts, you're in for a treat. "Green" or raw peanuts—shelled, blanched, and oven-ready—can be ordered online. The best ones to use? One of the plump, deeply flavorful, widely grown Virginia varieties, sometimes called "Virginia Runners." See Sources (page 264). *Note:* For more about peanuts, see page 21.

Oven-Fried Peanuts

Makes 2 Pounds

2 pounds shelled, blanched, raw peanuts (see headnote)

5 tablespoons refrigerator-cold unsalted butter, cut into small dice

Salt to taste

1. Preheat oven to 300°F.

2. Spread peanuts on two large rimmed baking sheets, dividing amount equally, then dot with butter, distributing evenly.

3. "Oven-fry," one pan at a time, on middle oven shelf about 1 hour, stirring several times, or until richly and uniformly golden.

4. Remove from oven, sprinkle with salt, and toss well. Taste and adjust salt as needed.

5. Serve at room temperature with cocktails or as an anytime snack. Stored in airtight canisters, oven-fried peanuts remain fresh-tasting for 3 to 4 weeks.

chapter two

Main Dishes

(meat, fish, fowl & more)

True "cue" is a pit-roasted hog basted with the cue master's secret sauce—usually a mix of vinegar, hot pepper sauce, oil, sugar, and sometimes tomato, as well. There must be a deeply smoky flavor (preferably hickory) and meat so tender it drops from the bone, all of which takes hours and hours. Still, Southerners call chicken baked this way "barbecued" and its flavor definitely measures up.

Oven-Barbecued Chicken

Makes 6 Servings

4 pounds meaty chicken parts (breasts, drumsticks, thighs, etc.), breasts halved crosswise, if large

4 large garlic cloves, smashed and skins removed

1½ cups water

SAUCE

1 cup tomato juice

¼ cup (½ stick) unsalted butter, cut in pats

¼ cup cider vinegar

1 tablespoon honey or raw sugar

1 tablespoon Worcestershire sauce

1 teaspoon salt, or to taste

½ teaspoon hot red pepper sauce, or to taste

¼ teaspoon freshly ground black pepper

¼ teaspoon dry mustard

1. Preheat oven to 375°F.

2. Arrange chicken skin side down in single layer in large shallow nonreactive baking pan. Drop in garlic and add water. Slide onto middle oven shelf and bake uncovered 45 minutes, turning pieces once or twice.

3. Meanwhile, combine all sauce ingredients in small heavy nonreactive pan. Set over low heat and bring slowly to a boil. Turn heat to lowest point, slide a diffuser underneath pan, and keep sauce warm. **Note:** If you can't keep heat low enough, set pan off-heat.

4. When chicken has cooked 45 minutes, make sure all pieces are skin side up. Pour reserved sauce evenly over all and bake uncovered 40 to 45 minutes longer, basting frequently with sauce. To test chicken for doneness, insert instant-read thermometer in meatiest part of breast or thigh not touching bone; it should read 165°F. **Note:** If sauce in pan thickens too much before chicken is done, mix in ½ to 1 cup boiling water.

5. To serve, arrange chicken on heated large platter. Strain sauce, discarding solids, and pass separately. The traditional accompaniment? Coleslaw and hushpuppies or corn bread.

One of the classic ways Southerners recycle leftover chicken or turkey is to cream it and ladle over rice, but I like to combine the chicken, rice, and cream sauce in a casserole along with thinly sliced mushrooms. Now that my supermarket sells baby bellas (cremini or baby portabella mushrooms), I use them instead of the more familiar white mushrooms; they have more flavor. And for welcome crunch, I top my casserole with coarsely chopped pecans—no need to toast them in advance.

Casserole of Chicken (*or turkey*), Rice, and Mushrooms

Makes 6 Servings

3 tablespoons unsalted butter or vegetable oil

8 ounces baby bella or white supermarket mushrooms, trimmed, wiped clean, and thinly sliced

¼ cup dry white wine or vermouth

1 large yellow onion, coarsely chopped

¼ cup unsifted all-purpose flour

½ teaspoon salt, or to taste

½ teaspoon freshly ground black pepper, or to taste

¼ teaspoon dried leaf thyme, crumbled

¼ teaspoon rubbed sage

2 cups chicken broth

1 cup half-and-half

1½ cups converted rice, cooked according to package directions

3 cups diced cooked chicken or turkey

½ cup coarsely chopped pecans

1. Preheat oven to 375°F. Lightly butter 2½-quart casserole and set aside.

2. Melt 1 tablespoon butter in large heavy skillet over moderate heat, add mushrooms, and cook, stirring often, 8 to 10 minutes until juices evaporate. With slotted spoon, transfer mushrooms to small bowl, add wine, toss lightly, and set aside.

3. Add remaining butter to skillet and stir-fry onion 6 to 8 minutes until lightly browned. Blend in flour, salt, pepper, thyme, and sage, and when smooth, add broth gradually, stirring briskly to incorporate flour. Mix in half-and-half and cook, stirring constantly, 3 to 5 minutes until mixture boils and thickens. Taste for salt and pepper and adjust as needed.

4. Return mushrooms to skillet along with any wine in bowl, then mix in cooked rice and diced chicken. Transfer to casserole, spreading to edge, and top with pecans.

5. Slide onto middle oven shelf and bake uncovered about 25 minutes until bubbling and lightly browned.

6. Serve hot with baby green peas, butter beans, or if you prefer, asparagus or broccoli.

"Stuffing" to most people is "dressing" down South, where it's often served in lieu of potatoes, used to stuff fish and fowl, shaped into patties and fried, and added to all manner of casseroles. Though the recipe that follows is a long-ago favorite, you might also try this way of recycling the Thanksgiving bird. If you have about 5 cups of leftover turkey dressing, skip Steps 1 and 2 below. Spread leftover dressing in casserole and bake as directed in Step 3. If you've 1½ cups leftover turkey gravy, mix with 4 cups diced cooked turkey, spread over partially baked dressing, sprinkle with chopped parsley, and proceed as directed in Steps 6 and 7.

Chicken (*or turkey*) and Dressing Casserole

Makes 6 to 8 Servings

4 cups ½-inch bread cubes (8 to 10 slices firm-textured white bread)

¾ teaspoon rubbed sage

¼ teaspoon salt, or to taste

¼ teaspoon freshly ground black pepper, or to taste

¼ cup (½ stick) unsalted butter

1 large yellow onion, coarsely chopped

2 large celery ribs, thinly sliced

2 large eggs

2 cups chicken broth

2 tablespoons all-purpose flour

4 cups diced leftover or rotisserie chicken or Thanksgiving turkey

2 tablespoons coarsely chopped fresh parsley

1. Preheat oven to 375°F. Spritz shallow 2-quart casserole or baking pan with nonstick cooking spray and set aside.

2. Toss bread cubes with sage, salt, and pepper in large mixing bowl. Melt 2 tablespoons butter in large skillet over moderate heat, add onion and celery, and cook 5 to 7 minutes, stirring occasionally, until tender. Add to bread mixture. Lightly beat one egg with ½ cup broth in small bowl, add to bread mixture, and toss well.

3. Pat bread mixture in even layer over bottom of casserole, slide onto middle oven shelf, and bake uncovered 20 minutes until beginning to brown.

4. Meanwhile, whisk remaining broth and flour in medium-size saucepan until smooth. Add remaining butter and cook over moderate heat, stirring often, until consistency of light cream.

5. Lightly whisk second egg in small bowl, blend in about ½ cup hot thickened sauce, then stir back into pan. Bring just to a simmer, stirring constantly. Taste for salt and pepper, adjusting as needed, then fold in chicken. Spoon chicken mixture over dressing in casserole and sprinkle with parsley.

6. Slide onto middle oven shelf and bake uncovered about 20 minutes longer until bubbly and beginning to brown.

7. Serve hot with a simply seasoned green vegetable—asparagus, snap beans, and broccoli are all good choices.

Back when I was a junior food editor at *Ladies' Home Journal* in New York, I created a party dish using three of my favorite Southern foods: chicken, rice, and pecans. Everyone loved it, I'm pleased to say. I've tweaked the recipe over the years and still find it perfect for company although it's difficult to find small broiler-fryers these days let alone a butcher who will disjoint them and bone each piece. *Note:* My solution is to use boneless chicken breasts and bone-in thighs, which are easy to bone. Just make sure that you have a sharp knife. Insert it in the center of each thigh—the underside. Once you've found the bone, draw knife the length of it, peel back flesh, and remove bone. *Tip:* To toast pecans, spread in a pie pan and set on middle shelf of a 350°F oven for 8 to 10 minutes. Watch carefully.

Orange Chicken Nested in Pecan Pilaf

Makes 6 to 8 Servings

CHICKEN

½ cup extra-virgin olive oil (about)

1 pound medium mushrooms, stemmed, wiped clean, and thinly sliced (reserve stems for soup or stew another day)

3 medium yellow onions, coarsely chopped

1 large garlic clove, finely minced

1 large whole bay leaf (preferably fresh)

2 teaspoons dried leaf marjoram, crumbled

1 teaspoon dried leaf thyme, crumbled

2 teaspoons salt, or to taste

½ teaspoon freshly ground black pepper, or to taste

¾ cup fresh orange juice

½ cup dry white wine

½ teaspoon finely grated orange zest

1½ cups unsifted all-purpose flour

6 small boneless chicken breasts (not chicken scallops)

6 chicken thighs, boned (see Note above)

PILAF

2½ cups converted rice, cooked according to package directions

1 cup coarsely chopped, lightly toasted pecans (see Tip above)

¾ teaspoon salt

¼ teaspoon freshly ground black pepper

1. *For Chicken:* Preheat oven to 300°F. Spritz 13 × 9 × 2-inch baking dish or large shallow casserole with nonstick cooking spray and set aside.

2. Heat 3 tablespoons olive oil in large heavy skillet over moderately high heat 1 minute, add mushrooms and onions, and sauté, stirring often, 8 to 10 minutes until mushrooms give up their juices and these evaporate.

3. Add garlic, bay leaf, and half each of the marjoram, thyme, salt, and pepper. Cook and stir 1 minute, then mix in orange juice, wine, and orange zest. Bring to a boil, reduce heat so mixture bubbles gently, then simmer uncovered 5 to 7 minutes until reduced by about one-fourth. Discard bay leaf, set mushroom mixture off-heat, and reserve.

4. Combine flour and remaining marjoram, thyme, salt, and pepper by shaking in large plastic zipper bag. Dredge chicken breasts and thighs, several pieces at a time, by shaking in flour mixture.

5. Heat 3 tablespoons remaining olive oil in second large heavy skillet

continued on page 52

continued from page 50

1½ to 2 minutes over moderately high heat until ripples appear on skillet bottom. Brown chicken in batches in oil, adding more oil if needed and allowing 3 to 5 minutes per side per batch. As chicken browns, lift to paper toweling to drain.

6. *For Pilaf:* Leaving rice in pan in which it cooked, add all remaining ingredients and toss well.

7. *To assemble:* Bed pilaf in bottom of baking dish and spoon half the mushroom mixture over it. Toss well, then spread to corners. Lay browned chicken skin side up on top of pilaf, pushing in slightly, and ladle remaining mushroom mixture evenly over all.

8. Cover snugly with aluminum foil, slide onto middle oven shelf, and bake 1 to 1½ hours until an instant-read thermometer, inserted in meaty piece of chicken not touching bone, registers 165°F.

9. Serve hot as the centerpiece of a dinner party.

Note: Doubled, this recipe is just the thing for a large buffet.

Not so long ago my young Georgia friend Rebecca Lang e-mailed to ask if I knew anything about an old Southern recipe called Chicken Boudine. To be honest, I'd never heard of it. A week or two later, Rebecca e-mailed back to say that she'd tracked down the elusive recipe and that it—surprise!—originated in Athens, GA, the very town where she lives. She further discovered that Chicken Boudine had been created by a 1920s/'30s Athens caterer, a certain Mrs. Cobb who'd cooked for several Georgia governors as well as for countless stylish parties. In Rebecca's welcome new cookbook *Quick-Fix Southern*, you'll find her speedy spin on Mrs. Cobb's long-winded Chicken Boudine. The version that follows is my own fairly quick riff. According to Rebecca, sherry's the "magic" ingredient (pretty daring back during Prohibition) and is what gives this popular party casserole its *je ne sais quoi*. *Note:* For 4 cups bite-size pieces cooked chicken, you'll need a rotisserie broiler weighing 3 to 3½ pounds. If you have Thanksgiving leftovers going begging, by all means use turkey in place of chicken. *Tip:* In some parts of the country, I'm told, sour cream is no longer available in 8-ounce containers. No problem. Simply substitute 1 cup firmly packed sour cream.

Chicken (*or turkey*) Boudine

Makes 6 to 8 Servings

4 cups bite-size pieces boned and skinned cooked chicken or turkey (see Note above)

2½ cups (6 ounces) medium-wide egg noodles, cooked and drained by package directions

1 jar (4 ounces) diced pimientos, well drained

¼ cup (½ stick) unsalted butter

6 medium scallions, trimmed and thinly sliced (include some tops)

1 package (8 ounces) sliced white or baby bella (cremini) mushrooms (halve large slices)

2 tablespoons all-purpose flour

1½ cups chicken broth

½ cup medium-dry sherry

1½ cups moderately coarsely shredded sharp Cheddar cheese (about 6 ounces)

1 carton (8 ounces) sour cream, at room temperature

1 teaspoon salt, or to taste

½ teaspoon freshly ground black pepper, or to taste

1. Preheat oven to 350°F. Spritz 13 × 9 × 2-inch baking dish with nonstick cooking spray and set aside.

2. Place chicken, noodles, and pimientos in large bowl and set aside.

3. Melt butter in large heavy skillet over moderately high heat, add scallions and cook, stirring occasionally, 3 to 4 minutes until golden. Add mushrooms and sauté, stirring now and then, about 5 minutes until limp and tender.

4. Blend in flour and cook and stir 1 minute, then add broth and sherry and cook, stirring constantly, 3 to 4 minutes until thickened. Remove from heat, add 1 cup shredded cheese, stir until melted, then mix in sour cream, salt, and pepper.

5. Add to chicken mixture and toss lightly to combine. Scoop into baking dish, spreading to edge, and sprinkle remaining ½ cup shredded cheese evenly on top.

6. Slide onto middle oven shelf and bake uncovered 25 to 30 minutes or until bubbling and tipped with brown.

7. Serve at once accompanied by a green vegetable of your choice, simply dressed—green beans, perhaps, garden peas, or asparagus spears.

Back when we were an English colony, this Virginia recipe would have begun with a young barnyard fowl—killed, plucked, eviscerated, and readied for the pot. I have some notion of what that involved because during World War II we kept chickens for eggs and for eating. Even though I was a little girl at the time, one of my jobs was to keep the flock fed and watered. Another job, which I hated, was to catch a bird, dispatch it, and deliver it to my mother to be cooked. How easy it is for us today with supermarkets carrying prepackaged, ready-to-eat whole birds, disjointed birds, even chicken parts and "scaloppini." Harder to come by are young broilers weighing 3 to 3½ pounds. *Tip:* Head to the deli counter and "sweet-talk" the person running the rotisserie into selling you an uncooked broiler. He (or she) may even disjoint it for you. Mine does.

Colonial Chicken Pudding

Makes 6 Servings

1   young broiler weighing 3 to 3½ pounds, cut up for frying and each half breast halved crosswise (see Tip above)

2   medium yellow onions, peeled and each stuck with 2 whole cloves

2   medium celery ribs, thickly sliced (include leafy tops)

2   large sprigs fresh Italian parsley

2   large sprigs fresh thyme (preferably lemon thyme) or 1 teaspoon dried leaf thyme, crumbled

2   large whole bay leaves (preferably fresh)

1   slice of lemon about ½ inch thick

10 peppercorns

½   teaspoon salt, or to taste

1   can (14 ounces) chicken broth plus enough (about 3 cups) cold water to cover chicken

5   tablespoons unsalted butter

3   tablespoons all-purpose flour

1   cup heavy cream, at room temperature

8   large eggs, lightly beaten

1. Place chicken in large, heavy, broad-bottomed nonreactive Dutch oven, add next nine ingredients (onions through broth mixture), and bring to a boil over moderate heat. Reduce heat so liquid bubbles gently, cover, and cook 25 to 30 minutes until chicken is tender. Toward end of cooking preheat oven to 350°F.

2. With tongs or large slotted spoon, lift chicken pieces to several thicknesses paper toweling to drain. Strain stock (cooking liquid), discarding solids. Reserve 2½ cups strained stock for sauce and freeze the rest to use another day.

3. Arrange chicken pieces in ungreased 2½-quart casserole and set aside.

4. Melt butter in medium-size heavy saucepan over moderate heat, blend in flour, and cook and stir 1 minute. Add 2½ cups reserved chicken stock and cook 3 to 5 minutes, stirring constantly, until lightly thickened and smooth. Mix in heavy cream. Blend about 1 cup hot sauce into beaten eggs, stir mixture back into pan, then cook and stir 2 minutes. Do not boil or sauce may curdle.

5. Pour sauce evenly over chicken. Set casserole in large shallow roasting pan on pulled-out shelf in lower third of oven, and add enough boiling water to pan to come 1½ inches up sides of casserole.

6. Gently slide shelf back into oven and bake chicken pudding uncovered about 40 minutes until lightly browned and set like custard; a cake tester, inserted in middle of sauce, should come out clean.

7. Serve at table and accompany with steamed broccoli florets, asparagus spears, or green beans.

My adaptation of an old Alabama recipe that appeared half a century ago in a little spiral-bound cookbook published by the North Carolina Federation of Home Demonstration Clubs. A headnote introduces the recipe as "a favorite of the mother of Mr. J. W. Roberts of Barbour County, Alabama," who fought in the War Between the States, returned to the Old Roberts Plantation, and "lived to a ripe old age." *Note:* Long ago, tough over-the-hill hens were simmered till tender, their meat stripped from the carcasses and used countless ways. Because few of us have little, if any, leftover cooked chicken on hand, I suggest using the meat of a rotisserie bird. My modern Confederate pie also substitutes frozen corn for fresh, a significant time-saver.

Confederate Corn and Chicken Pie

Makes 6 to 8 Servings

PASTRY

- 1 cup unsifted all-purpose flour
- ¼ teaspoon salt
- ¼ cup firmly packed lard (not vegetable shortening) or 2 tablespoons each lard and unsalted butter
- 2 to 3 tablespoons ice water
- 1½ teaspoons cider vinegar

FILLING

- 2 tablespoons unsalted butter
- 1 medium yellow onion, coarsely chopped
- 3 cups chicken broth blended with ⅓ cup unsifted all-purpose flour
- 2 teaspoons sugar
- ½ teaspoon dried leaf thyme, crumbled
- 1 bag (16 ounces) solidly frozen whole-kernel corn
- 1 teaspoon salt, or to taste
- ½ teaspoon freshly ground black pepper, or to taste
- 4 cups bite-size pieces cooked chicken (see Note above)

1. Preheat oven to 375°F. Lightly oil or butter 2½-quart round casserole or spritz with nonstick cooking spray and set aside.

2. *For Pastry:* Combine flour and salt in large mixing bowl, then with pastry blender, cut in lard until texture of lentils. Combine 2 tablespoons ice water with vinegar and while forking flour mixture briskly, sprinkle over all. Continue forking until soft pastry forms. If mixture seems dry, fork in another ½ to 1 tablespoon ice water.

3. Roll pastry between sheets of floured wax paper into round 1 inch larger than top of casserole. Remove top sheet of wax paper and cut pastry into 12 strips of equal width. Set peeled-off wax paper back in place, ease pastry circle onto plate, and set in freezer while you prepare filling.

4. *For Filling:* Melt butter in large heavy saucepan over moderate heat. Add onion and cook 5 to 7 minutes, stirring frequently, until beginning to brown.

5. Add broth mixture, sugar, and thyme and cook, stirring constantly, about 5 minutes until mixture boils and thickens. Mix in corn, salt, and pepper and simmer 3 minutes more.

6. Layer half of chicken in casserole, spread with half of corn mixture, then repeat layers.

7. Remove pastry from freezer and peel off top sheet of wax paper. Working on bottom sheet, weave pastry strips into a lattice, then gently ease from wax paper to casserole. Pinch strip ends and any leftover pastry together around edge of casserole, then crimp for a decorative finish.

8. Place casserole on rimmed baking sheet, slide onto middle oven shelf, and bake uncovered 40 to 45 minutes until crust browns and filling bubbles.

9. Serve with wedged or sliced red-ripe tomatoes.

Despite its name, this popular Southern party casserole did not originate at that bigger than Rhode Island southeast Texas spread fictionalized, it's said, in *Giant*, 1956's box-office smash starring Elizabeth Taylor, Rock Hudson, and James Dean. Nor, as far as I know, was King Ranch Chicken ever a specialty at King Ranch. So why is it named for this National Historic Landmark where the King/Kleberg family grew rich on Santa Gertrudis cattle, quarter horses, thoroughbreds, and oil? My friend Karen Haram, for years food editor of the *San Antonio Express-News*, thinks it may be because the recipe, itself, is so rich. There are countless versions of King Ranch Chicken, some of them unnecessarily long-winded. My streamlined variation takes advantage of rotisserie chicken, presliced mushrooms, and bottled salsa. *Note:* For deeper flavor, choose a Mexican salsa (see Sources, page 264). *Tip:* To soften corn tortillas, here's the microwave method Rick Bayless used on his PBS show, *One Plate at a Time*: Sprinkle a kitchen towel with cold water, stack tortillas in towel, microwave 4 minutes on medium, and let stand 2 minutes.

King Ranch Chicken

Makes 6 Servings

3 tablespoons unsalted butter

1 small yellow onion, finely chopped

2 large garlic cloves, finely chopped

1 package (8 ounces) sliced white or baby bella (cremini) mushrooms (halve large slices)

¼ teaspoon ground hot red pepper (cayenne)

¼ teaspoon ground cumin

2 tablespoons all-purpose flour

¾ cup chicken broth

½ cup milk blended with 2 tablespoons sour cream

½ teaspoon salt, or to taste

¼ teaspoon freshly ground black pepper, or to taste

8 corn tortillas, softened (see Tip above)

3½ cups diced cooked chicken

1 jar (16 ounces) tomato salsa, as mild or hot as you like (see Note above)

1½ cups coarsely grated mild Cheddar cheese (about 6 ounces)

1. Preheat oven to 350°F. Spritz 12 × 7½ × 2-inch baking dish with nonstick cooking spray and set aside.

2. Melt butter in large heavy skillet over moderate heat, add onion and garlic, and cook, stirring occasionally, 2 to 3 minutes until limp and golden. Add mushrooms, cayenne, and cumin and cook, stirring now and then, 6 to 8 minutes until mushrooms release their juices and most of these evaporate.

3. Blend in flour and cook and stir 1 minute. Add broth, milk mixture, salt, and black pepper and cook, stirring constantly, about 3 minutes until thickened.

4. Cover bottom of baking dish with 4 tortillas, then layer remaining ingredients in dish this way, each time spreading to cover layer below: half diced chicken, one-third mushroom mixture, half salsa, half cheese, then half remaining mushroom mixture, the remaining tortillas, chicken, salsa, cheese, and finish with remaining mushroom mixture.

5. Slide onto middle oven shelf and bake uncovered 30 to 35 minutes until bubbling and tipped with brown.

6. Serve at once with a tartly dressed green salad. Or maybe a spinach and bacon salad.

This is my spin on a recipe given to me decades ago by Jean Todd Freeman, fellow *Ladies' Home Journal* editor. A brilliant writer, Jean grew up in Hattiesburg, MS, and even before graduating from Mount Holyoke was selling short stories to *McCall's, Redbook,* and *Ladies' Home Journal. Journal* husband and wife editors-in-chief, Bruce and Beatrice Blackmar Gould, had the smarts to hire Jean right out of college. By the time I joined the magazine, she was a senior editor in the Philadelphia "literary office" while I was an entry-level food editor in New York where all the homemaking departments were located. Having heard of Jean's brilliance from Day One, having also heard that she was the Goulds' pet who could do no wrong, I frankly expected to hate her. Instead, we became lifelong friends. Neighbors, too, after the Philadelphia staff moved to New York. Soon I was a regular at Jean's frequent dinner parties where this chicken and artichoke casserole invariably drew raves as did her other standby—Shrimp and Artichoke Hearts au Gratin (page 107).

Chicken and Artichoke Casserole with Mushrooms and Madeira

Makes 6 Servings

1 cup unsifted all-purpose flour

½ tablespoon sweet paprika

1 teaspoon dried leaf thyme, crumbled

1 teaspoon salt

½ teaspoon freshly ground black pepper

3 to 3½ pounds chicken parts (a mix of light and dark meat), oversize breasts halved crosswise

¼ cup extra-virgin olive oil

2 packages (8 ounces each) sliced white or baby bella (cremini) mushrooms (halve large slices)

1 cup chicken broth

¼ cup medium-dry Madeira, Port, or sherry

3 jars (4 ounces each) marinated artichoke hearts, well drained

1. Preheat oven to 375°F. Lightly spritz shallow 4-quart casserole with nonstick cooking spray and set aside.

2. Combine flour, paprika, thyme, salt, and pepper by shaking in large plastic zipper bag. Dredge chicken, several pieces at a time, by shaking in flour mixture. Tap off excess flour. Save 3 tablespoons dredging flour to thicken sauce.

3. Heat oil in large heavy skillet over moderately high heat 1½ to 2 minutes until ripples appear on pan bottom. Brown chicken in batches in oil, skin side up at first, allowing 3 to 4 minutes per side. Drain on paper toweling.

4. Pour drippings from skillet, then spoon 2 tablespoons back in. Reduce heat to moderate, add mushrooms, and sauté 8 to 10 minutes, stirring occasionally, until juices evaporate.

5. Sprinkle reserved dredging flour over mushrooms and stir well. Add broth and cook, stirring constantly, 2 to 3 minutes until thickened. Add wine and simmer 2 minutes more.

6. Arrange chicken skin side up in casserole, tuck artichokes in and around, and pour hot mushroom mixture evenly over all. Cover casserole with lid or foil.

7. Slide onto middle oven shelf and bake 40 minutes. Remove lid and bake 20 minutes more until instant-read thermometer, inserted in meaty chicken part not touching bone, reads 165°F.

8. Serve at table accompanied by fluffy boiled rice and a crisp green salad.

Here's another Southern casserole of leftovers, this time chicken and ham. To Cajuns and Creoles, this isn't a true jambalaya. Never mind. It's easy, it's delicious, a one-dish dinner that's perfect for a casual supper with family or friends.

Chicken Jambalaya Casserole

Makes 6 Servings

2 tablespoons bacon drippings or vegetable oil

3 mild or hot link sausages (8 to 9 ounces in all), sliced about ¼ inch thick

1 large yellow onion, coarsely chopped

1 large green bell pepper, cored, seeded, and coarsely chopped

2 large garlic cloves, finely chopped

½ teaspoon dried leaf thyme, crumbled

2 large whole bay leaves (preferably fresh)

1½ cups diced cooked chicken, about equal parts light and dark meat

1 cup diced cooked ham, preferably country ham

1 cup uncooked long-grain rice

⅓ cup coarsely chopped fresh Italian parsley

2 cups chicken broth

1 can (14.5 ounces) diced tomatoes, with their liquid

1 teaspoon salt, or to taste

½ teaspoon freshly ground black pepper, or to taste

1. Preheat oven to 350°F. Spritz 2½-quart casserole with nonstick cooking spray and set aside.

2. Heat drippings in heavy 12-inch skillet over moderately high heat 1 to 1½ minutes until ripples appear on pan bottom. Add sausages and brown, stirring occasionally, 3 to 5 minutes. With slotted spoon, lift to bowl and reserve.

3. Reduce heat to moderate, add onion, bell pepper, garlic, thyme, and bay leaves to drippings and cook, stirring occasionally, 8 to 10 minutes until limp and lightly browned. Return sausages and accumulated juices to skillet, add all remaining ingredients, and bring to a boil. Transfer to casserole, making sure all rice is covered with liquid, and cover with snug lid or foil tightly smoothed over casserole.

4. Slide onto middle oven shelf and bake about 45 minutes until rice is tender, flavors marry, and almost all liquid is absorbed; remove and discard bay leaves.

5. Dish up at table and serve—no accompaniments needed, though a crisp tossed salad wouldn't be amiss.

Southerners, it seems to me, are particularly clever about recycling leftovers. Take this recipe: It calls for 2½ cups cooked chicken or turkey as well as 1½ cups cooked rice. The crumbs, too, can be buzzed up out of stale bread. *Note:* Our grandmothers would have used canned mushrooms for the sauce but fresh mushrooms, now a supermarket staple, will mean a sauce of deeper flavor, especially if you choose creminis (baby bellas), portabellas, shiitakes, morels, or chanterelles. For this recipe, presliced mushrooms work just fine as long as they are moist and fresh.

Chicken (*or turkey*) Loaf with Mushroom Sauce

Makes 6 Servings

LOAF

- 2½ cups finely chopped or coarsely ground cooked chicken or turkey, about equal parts light and dark meat
- 1½ cups cooked long-grain rice
- 1½ cups moderately coarse stale bread crumbs (3 slices firm-textured white bread)
- ½ cup moderately coarsely chopped yellow onion
- ½ cup finely diced celery
- ¼ cup canned diced pimientos, well drained
- ¼ cup moderately finely chopped fresh parsley (Italian or curly)
- 1 teaspoon poultry seasoning
- 1 teaspoon salt
- ½ teaspoon freshly ground black pepper
- 1 cup evaporated milk beaten with 3 large eggs

SAUCE

- ¼ cup (½ stick) unsalted butter
- 1 package (8 ounces) sliced white or baby bella (cremini) mushrooms, large slices halved (see Note above)
- 4 large scallions, trimmed and thinly sliced (include some green tops)
- ½ teaspoon dried leaf thyme, crumbled
- 4 tablespoons all-purpose flour
- 2½ cups milk, at room temperature
- 1 teaspoon salt, or to taste
- ¼ teaspoon freshly ground black pepper, or to taste.

1. For Loaf: Preheat oven to 350°F. Spritz 9 × 9 × 2-inch baking pan with nonstick cooking spray and set aside.

2. Place all loaf ingredients in large bowl, mix well with hands, then scoop into pan. Spread mixture to corners and pat firmly so loaf is firm when baked.

3. Slide onto middle oven shelf and bake uncovered 45 to 50 minutes until nicely browned and instant-read thermometer, inserted in middle of loaf, reads 165°F. Transfer pan to wire rack and cool loaf in pan 15 to 20 minutes while you prepare Sauce.

4. *For Sauce:* Melt butter in heavy 12-inch skillet over moderately high heat, add mushrooms, scallions, and thyme, and cook, stirring now and then, until mushroom juices evaporate, about 5 minutes.

5. Reduce heat to moderate, smooth in flour, and cook and stir 1 minute. Stirring hard, add milk in slow steady stream and simmer, stirring constantly, until sauce thickens and no longer tastes of raw flour, about 5 minutes. Season with salt and pepper.

6. To serve, cut loaf into 6 squares of equal size and ladle mushroom sauce over each portion.

I can't believe I'd never heard of this recipe until I was halfway through writing this cookbook and then only because my good friend Fran McCullough, a primo New York cookbook editor now retired and living in the historic town of Hillsborough just north of Chapel Hill, e-mailed one morning full of enthusiasm: "Have you ever heard of Atlanta Brisket?" She'd eaten it for the first time the night before at some local "food do" and was blown away by its flavor and succulence. A quick online search turned up this shocker. Eli N. Evans, my across-the-hall Gramercy Park co-op neighbor for nearly 20 years, is an aficionado of Atlanta Brisket. Who knew? President Emeritus of The Charles H. Revson Foundation of New York and like me a born-and-bred Tar Heel, Eli is the author of three acclaimed books: *The Provincials: A Personal History of Jews in the South*, *Judah P. Benjamin: The Jewish Confederate*, and *The Lonely Days Were Sundays: Reflections of a Jewish Southerner*. The irony here is that I'd hand recipe "tests" across the hall to Eli and his family, never dreaming that he knew a thing about cooking.

Atlanta Brisket

Makes 10 to 12 Servings

5 pounds fresh beef brisket, trimmed of excess fat

2 bottles (16.5 ounces each) Coca-Cola (not Diet Coke)

1 teaspoon kosher salt

1 teaspoon freshly ground black pepper

3 tablespoons vegetable oil

GRAVY

2 cups Coca-Cola marinade, reserved from above

1 envelope dry onion soup mix (from a 2-ounce package)

1 can (8 ounces) salt-free tomato sauce

½ cup tomato ketchup

3 large yellow onions, halved lengthwise and each half sliced about ⅜ inch thick

3 large whole bay leaves (preferably fresh)

1. Place brisket in large nonreactive roaster with snug-fitting lid (I used one measuring 15½ inches long, 12 inches wide, and 4 inches deep). Pour Coca-Cola evenly over brisket, cover, and refrigerate 24 hours, turning brisket once or twice in Coca-Cola marinade.

2. When ready to proceed, preheat oven to 325°F. Lift brisket from roaster and pat dry. Line large fine sieve with coffee filter and set over medium-size bowl. Pour in Coca-Cola marinade and let drip through.

3. Rub brisket well on both sides with salt and pepper. Heat oil in very large (15-inch) heavy skillet about 1 minute over high heat until ripples appear on pan bottom. Add brisket and brown 3 to 4 minutes on each side. Return brisket to roaster, now rinsed and dried.

4. *For Gravy:* Combine 2 cups filtered Coca-Cola marinade, soup mix, tomato sauce, and ketchup and pour over brisket. Scatter sliced onions on top and drop in bay leaves. **Note:** If you use fresh bay leaves, crinkle them a bit as you drop them into the roaster to release their flavor.

5. Cover roaster, slide into lower third of oven, and braise brisket 4 hours. Check roaster at half time and if liquid seems skimpy—not likely—add a little more filtered Coca-Cola marinade, or beef broth, or water.

6. Remove roaster from oven and set on trivet on counter. Remove lid and cool brisket at least 30 minutes to allow juices to settle and meat to firm up. **Note:** Some cooks bring the brisket to room temperature before serving. Discard bay leaves and remaining Coca-Cola marinade.

7. To serve, lift brisket to cutting board and slice about ¼ inch thick—across the grain and slightly on the bias. Overlap brisket slices on large platter and smother with pan gravy and onions. The best accompaniment? For me nothing beats a tart and creamy coleslaw.

Whenever I travel about the South, I head for the nearest bookstore and have a look at the local cookbooks, those spiral-bound paperbacks published by churches and clubs to raise funds for good works. I have hundreds of these now, dozens from every Southern state. One recipe that keeps cropping up in these local fund-raisers—apparently old, but new to me—is this unusual but oh, so easy pork chop casserole. *Note:* As with the Moravian Baked Pork Chops (page 68) and Baked Pecan-Stuffed Pork Chops (page 69), use good heritage pork here instead of prepackaged supermarket chops.

Spiced Pork Chops Baked with Rice and Sour Cherries

Makes 6 Servings

6   pork loin chops, each about 1¼ inches thick (about 4¼ pounds in all; see Note above)

1   teaspoon salt

½   teaspoon freshly ground black pepper

3   tablespoons bacon drippings, unsalted butter, or vegetable oil

1   cup uncooked converted rice

1   can (14 ounces) chicken broth plus enough water to total 2 cups

2   cans (14.5 ounces each) pitted tart red cherries, well drained

2   tablespoons sugar blended with 1½ teaspoons finely grated lemon zest and ¼ teaspoon ground cinnamon (spiced sugar)

1. Preheat oven to 350°F. Pat pork chops dry with paper toweling, then rub both sides of each chop with salt and pepper and set aside.

2. Heat drippings in large heavy skillet over moderately high heat 1½ to 2 minutes until ripples appear on pan bottom. Add chops and brown about 2 minutes on each side.

3. Meanwhile, spread rice over bottom of ungreased shallow 4-quart casserole (15 × 10½ × 2 inches is a good size). Combine broth mixture and cherries, spoon over rice layer taking care not to dislodge it, then sprinkle with half the spiced sugar. Nestle browned pork chops side by side in cherries, sprinkle remaining spiced sugar on top, and cover casserole.

4. Slide onto middle oven shelf and bake about 1¼ hours until chops are tender.

5. Serve hot with a simply steamed and seasoned green vegetable—broccoli, perhaps, or Brussels sprouts, or green beans.

These country-style pork chops baked in gravy were popular years ago among the Moravians of Forsyth County, NC, and in some families, still are. For deeply flavorful, juicily tender pork, buy chops from heritage breeds like Berkshire, Tamworth, Old Spot, etc., which many Southern farmers now raise on a small scale and sell at farmers' markets. You'll also find heritage pork at high-end groceries. *Note:* For better flavor, brown the pork chops in bacon drippings. For rich gravy, use chicken broth and evaporated milk; for medium-rich, broth and water.

Moravian Baked Pork Chops

Makes 6 Servings

6 pork loin chops cut 1 to 1¼ inches thick (about 4¼ pounds in all)

1 cup unsifted all-purpose flour mixed with 1¼ teaspoons salt, ½ teaspoon freshly ground black pepper, and ¼ teaspoon rubbed sage (seasoned flour)

¼ cup bacon drippings or vegetable oil or 2 tablespoons each bacon drippings and oil (see Note above)

1 can (12 ounces) evaporated milk (reduced fat, if you like) or 1½ cups water (see Note above)

1 cup chicken broth

1. Preheat oven to 325°F.

2. Dredge each pork chop well on both sides in seasoned flour, shaking off excess and reserving 3 tablespoons to thicken gravy. Heat drippings in large heavy skillet over moderately high heat until ripples appear on pan bottom, 1 to 1½ minutes. Brown chops well, about 5 minutes per side. Transfer to large shallow roasting pan (14 × 9 × 3 inches is about right), arranging one layer deep.

3. Add milk to skillet drippings; stir to loosen browned bits. Whisk reserved 3 tablespoons seasoned flour into the broth and add to milk in skillet. Cook, stirring constantly, until thickened and smooth—about 3 minutes. Pour evenly over pork chops and cover pan with foil.

4. Slide onto middle oven shelf and bake about 1 hour until chops are tender.

5. Remove chops to serving platter and keep warm. Skim fat from milk gravy in pan. Transfer gravy and any remaining drippings from roasting pan to blender and whiz until smooth.

6. Pour ½ cup water into roasting pan, stir to loosen browned bits, and transfer to measuring cup or small bowl. With blender running, gradually add as much reserved pan liquid as needed for good gravy consistency, blending until smooth between each addition. Transfer gravy to small saucepan, set over moderate heat, and bring just to a boil.

7. Serve with boiled rice or potatoes and ladle gravy over all.

Why were Grandma's pork chops so juicy and flavorful when ours are anything but? Because the pork Nana bought came from well-marbled heritage breeds like Berkshire, Duroc, Gloucester Old Spot, and Tamworth and the fat they contained guaranteed flavor and succulence. In the '80s things changed dramatically. Chicken sales soared in diet-conscious America and pork sales plummeted. To regain market share, pork producers began breeding much of the fat out of their hogs. Result? Pork chops so dry and tasteless no amount of TLC seemed to help. Today, thank God, boutique farmers scattered about the South are once again raising heritage hogs and selling their well-marbled meat at farmers' markets.

Baked Pecan-Stuffed Pork Chops

Makes 4 Servings

3　tablespoons bacon drippings or vegetable oil

1　medium yellow onion, coarsely chopped

1　medium celery rib, trimmed and coarsely chopped (include a few leaves)

½　teaspoon rubbed sage

½　teaspoon dried leaf thyme, crumbled

1½　cups moderately fine soft white bread crumbs

½　cup coarsely chopped pecans

2　tablespoons coarsely chopped fresh parsley (curly or Italian)

1　teaspoon salt, or to taste

½　teaspoon freshly ground black pepper, or to taste

4　double (2-rib) pork rib chops cut 1½ inches thick (about 3 pounds)

GRAVY

3　tablespoons pork chop drippings (or round out measure with bacon drippings or vegetable oil)

3　tablespoons all-purpose flour

1　cup chicken broth

¾　cup milk, at room temperature

　Salt and freshly ground black pepper to taste

1. Preheat oven to 350°F. Line medium-size shallow baking pan with foil, placing dull side up; set aside.

2. Heat drippings in large heavy skillet over moderately high heat 1 to 1½ minutes until ripples appear on pan bottom. Add onion, celery, sage, and thyme and sauté, stirring occasionally, 3 to 5 minutes until limp and golden. Remove from heat, add crumbs, pecans, parsley, ½ teaspoon salt, and pepper and toss well to mix. Cool to room temperature.

3. With sharp paring knife, cut down between ribs of each double chop to form a pocket large enough to stuff. Rub outside of chops with remaining salt. Stand pork chops on rib ends on wax-paper-covered counter and spoon stuffing into pockets, mounding it up but not packing it down.

4. Stand pork chops on rib ends, side by side but not touching, in foil-lined pan, slide onto middle oven shelf, and bake uncovered 55 minutes to 1 hour until instant-read thermometer, inserted in middle of chop touching neither stuffing nor bone, registers 155° to 165°F if you prefer well-done pork. Remove chops from oven and let stand in pan while you prepare gravy.

5. *For Gravy:* Blend pork drippings and flour in small heavy saucepan and cook and stir over moderate heat 3 minutes. Whisking hard, add broth and milk and cook, continuing to whisk, about 5 minutes until thickened, smooth, and no raw floury taste remains. Season to taste with salt and pepper.

6. Arrange pork chops on large heated platter, spoon a little gravy on top, and pass the rest.

Ham and eggs is a combo we all know, but ham and cauliflower? Equally delicious, and in fact, ham's a natural with the whole huge cabbage family and that includes cauliflower, which Mark Twain once called "a cabbage with a college education." *Note:* Use cooked ready-to-eat country ham here—a good cured and smoked ham like the Smithfield or Edwards hams of Virginia. If unavailable, substitute thickly sliced prosciutto or a domestic serrano (see Sources, page 264), better than mass-produced pink packing house hams, most of which have been injected with water or brine. *Note:* I processor-chop the ham—quick and easy though the ham must be cut into 1-inch chunks before it goes into the machine. For ⅔ cup coarsely ground or chopped ham, you'll need about 6 ounces if the ham has a thick outer covering of fat, which should be removed. If not, 4 ounces will do. *Tip:* Newsom's of Kentucky sells ground cooked country ham (see Sources, page 264).

Country Ham and Cauliflower Casserole

Makes 6 Servings

1   large cauliflower (about 3 pounds), trimmed and divided into florets about 1½ inches across

3   large egg yolks

1   cup heavy cream blended with 2 tablespoons all-purpose flour

½   cup firmly packed sour cream

½   teaspoon freshly grated nutmeg

½   teaspoon freshly ground black pepper

¼   teaspoon salt

⅔   cup coarsely ground, trimmed, cooked country ham (see Note and Tip above)

¾   cup fine dry bread crumbs tossed with 2 tablespoons each freshly grated Parmigiano Reggiano and melted unsalted butter (Topping)

1. Preheat oven to 375°F. Spritz a 13 × 9 × 2-inch baking dish with nonstick cooking spray and set aside.

2. Parboil cauliflower florets 5 to 8 minutes in just enough lightly salted boiling water to cover until crisp-tender. Drain well and arrange in single layer in baking dish.

3. Beat egg yolks well with heavy cream mixture, sour cream, nutmeg, pepper, and salt. Add ham, mix until evenly distributed, and spoon over cauliflower, again making sure ham is well distributed. Scatter Topping evenly over all.

4. Slide onto middle oven shelf and bake uncovered until bubbling and tipped with brown, 20 to 25 minutes

5. Serve at once as the centerpiece of a light lunch or supper or, if you prefer, as an accompaniment to roast chicken, turkey, or pork.

It bears repeating, I think, that Southerners will stuff almost anything that's hollow—bell peppers, avocados, you name it. And if a favorite fruit or vegetable has no hollow—artichokes, onions, tomatoes, yellow squash, and so forth—they'll scoop out the "innards," turn them into a stuffing, spoon into the hollows they've created, and bake. *Note:* Should bell peppers be parboiled before they're stuffed? I prefer to stuff them raw because the peppers are less likely to collapse as they bake. Moreover, I like peppers with a bit of crunch. However, if you like softer peppers, lay scooped-out peppers on their sides in a large, heavy nonreactive Dutch oven, add enough lightly salted boiling water to cover them by about an inch, cover, and parboil over moderate heat just until crisp-tender, 6 to 8 minutes. Drain peppers well, stand cut side down on several thicknesses of paper toweling, and let "drip-dry."

Baked Ham, Rice, and Sausage Stuffed Peppers

Makes 6 Servings

6 large green or red bell peppers (see Note above)

12 ounces bulk sausage meat, as mild or hot as you like

1 medium yellow onion, coarsely chopped

8 ounces moderately finely ground leftover baked or boiled ham

1 can (14.5 ounces) diced tomatoes, well drained

1½ cups cooked long-grain rice

¼ teaspoon salt, or to taste

¼ teaspoon freshly ground black pepper, or to taste

½ cup moderately fine soft white bread crumbs tossed with 2 tablespoons freshly grated Parmigiano Reggiano and 1 tablespoon melted bacon drippings or butter (Topping)

1. Preheat oven to 375°F.

2. Slice about ½ inch off top of each bell pepper and set tops aside. Scoop seeds and veins from each pepper and discard. Stand peppers upside down on paper toweling. Remove and discard pepper stems, then coarsely chop pepper tops and reserve.

3. Cook sausage in large, heavy nonreactive skillet over moderately high heat 4 to 5 minutes, breaking up large clumps, until lightly browned. With slotted spoon, lift sausage to small bowl and reserve.

4. Reduce heat to moderate, then add onion and chopped bell pepper tops to skillet drippings and cook, stirring occasionally and scraping up brown bits, 8 to 10 minutes until limp and lightly browned. Mix browned sausage and accumulated juices into skillet mixture along with all but final ingredient (Topping).

5. Stuff peppers one by one, dividing sausage mixture evenly. Sprinkle Topping over each stuffed pepper, again dividing total amount evenly.

6. Stand stuffed peppers shoulder to shoulder in shallow baking pan just big enough to hold them—peppers should touch and support one another. Then pour water into pan around peppers to depth of ¾ inch.

7. Slide stuffed peppers onto middle oven shelf and bake uncovered about 40 minutes until crisp-tender and lightly browned.

8. To serve, using two large spoons, lift peppers to heated large round platter or to individual plates. If peppers you've stuffed are red, serve with a green vegetable—snap beans, perhaps, or broccoli, even butter beans. If peppers are green, accompany with baby carrots, golden beets, or yellow squash. Whatever the vegetable, steam and dress simply.

Until recently, summer squash (yellow, cymlings or pattypans, even mirlitons) were more popular than winter squash down South. Not so today, knowing as we do that orange-fleshed winter squash (acorn, butternut, and so forth) are powerhouses of beta carotene (vitamin A). Given the Southerner's love for stuffing things, is it any surprise that acorn squash win the popularity contest? They're the right size—two will serve four. Moreover, they have natural hollows just begging to be stuffed. *Note:* Because country sausage is heavily spiced, this recipe calls for no salt or pepper. Still, you might taste the finished stuffing before spooning into the squash and add a little salt and pepper, if needed.

Twice-Baked Acorn Squash with Country Sausage Stuffing

Makes 4 Servings

2 medium acorn squash (about 2 pounds)

1 tablespoon unsalted butter, melted

STUFFING

8 ounces bulk country sausage meat (as mild or hot as you like)

1 large yellow onion, coarsely chopped

½ teaspoon dried leaf sage, crumbled

¼ teaspoon dried leaf thyme, crumbled

2 cups moderately coarse soft white bread crumbs (4 slices firm-textured white bread)

4 teaspoons freshly grated Parmigiano Reggiano

1. Preheat oven to 375°F.

2. Arrange whole squash, not touching, in ungreased small baking pan, slide onto middle oven shelf, and bake 1 to 1¼ hours until soft-firm.

3. *Meanwhile, prepare Stuffing:* Brown sausage in large heavy skillet over moderately low heat, 15 to 20 minutes, breaking up clumps. With slotted spoon, lift to paper toweling to drain.

4. Pour drippings from skillet and reserve. Spoon 3 tablespoons drippings back into skillet, add onion, sage, and thyme, and cook, stirring often, about 10 minutes until lightly browned. Return sausage to skillet along with 1 tablespoon reserved drippings and continue breaking up clumps until fairly fine. Add bread crumbs, toss to combine, and set aside.

5. When squash are done, remove from oven but leave oven on. Halve each squash lengthwise when cool enough to handle, scoop out "strings" and seeds, and discard. Brush squash hollows with melted butter, spoon in stuffing, and top with cheese.

6. Arrange squash, not touching, in ungreased pan just large enough to hold them, slide onto middle oven shelf, and bake uncovered about 30 minutes until touched with brown.

7. Serve as a main course, and to round out the meal? Buttered broccoli or Brussels sprouts. Or, if you prefer, a tartly dressed salad of mixed greens.

I won't pretend that Tetrazzini is a Southern recipe but Southerners have made it their own by substituting ham for turkey. The original recipe—a casserole of creamed turkey, mushrooms, pasta, and cheese—was created in honor of Luisa Tetrazzini, the early 20th-century Italian soprano whom James Beard described as a woman of "astounding girth and thrilling voice." Beard believed that Turkey Tetrazzini was created at San Francisco's luxurious Palace Hotel where the diva often stayed. Others claim that the recipe originated in New York at the old Knickerbocker, a once posh Times Square hotel where Tetrazzini lived while appearing at the Metropolitan Opera a few blocks away. *Note:* To trim prep time, I use presliced mushrooms—1½ eight-ounce packages—but only if the mushrooms look fresh.

Ham Tetrazzini

Makes 6 Servings

3 cups diced boiled or baked ham

¼ cup (½ stick) unsalted butter

1¾ pounds small white mushrooms, stemmed, wiped clean, and thinly sliced (see Note above)

6 large scallions, trimmed and thinly sliced (white part only)

3 tablespoons all-purpose flour

1¾ cups chicken broth

1 cup light or heavy cream

3 tablespoons medium-dry sherry

¾ cup freshly grated Parmigiano Reggiano

¾ teaspoon salt, or to taste

¼ teaspoon freshly ground black pepper, or to taste

8 ounces spaghettini (extra-thin spaghetti), broken in half, cooked and drained according to package directions

1 jar (4 ounces) diced pimientos, well drained

1. Preheat oven to 375°F. Spritz shallow 2½-quart casserole with nonstick cooking spray and set aside. Place ham in large bowl and set aside also.

2. Melt 2 tablespoons butter in large heavy skillet over moderately high heat, add mushrooms and scallions, and cook 6 to 8 minutes until limp; add to ham.

3. Melt remaining butter in small heavy saucepan over moderate heat, blend in flour, add broth, and cook, stirring constantly, 3 to 5 minutes until thickened and smooth.

4. Mix in cream, sherry, ¼ cup cheese, salt, and pepper, and cook and stir 2 minutes; add to ham mixture along with hot, drained spaghettini and pimientos. Toss well, scoop into casserole, and spread to edge. Sprinkle remaining cheese on top.

5. Slide onto middle oven shelf and bake uncovered 25 to 30 minutes until bubbling and tipped with brown. Serve oven-hot with a green vegetable or salad of your choice.

VARIATIONS

Turkey (or Chicken) Tetrazzini: Prepare as directed, substituting 3 cups diced cooked turkey or chicken (dark and light meat) for ham. Also, if you like, add 1 cup well drained, thawed frozen baby green peas. Makes 6 Servings.

Tuna Tetrazzini: Prepare as directed, substituting two 12-ounce cans water-pack solid white albacore tuna for ham; drain each can well and flake tuna. Also add 1 cup well drained, thawed frozen baby green peas and ¼ cup coarsely chopped parsley. Makes 6 Servings.

Note: I sometimes omit the sherry and add ¼ cup well-drained tiny capers, 1 to 2 tablespoons fresh lemon or lime juice, and 1 tablespoon snipped fresh dill, always tasting as I improvise.

Mayhaws, if you don't know them—and I didn't until I was well into my 30s—are the tart red fruits of a wild hawthorne that flourishes in swampy areas of the Deep South. My Mississippi friend, Jean Todd Freeman, fiction editor of *Ladies' Home Journal* when I was a mid-level food editor, was the one who introduced me to mayhaw jelly. We lived around the corner from one another in the West Village and whenever Jean entertained, there was always a bowl of rosy jelly on the dinner table. "It's mayhaw," she explained, then added that women would gather the windfalls and boil them into jelly. I doubt that many bother these days, but no matter. You can buy mayhaw jelly online (see Sources, page 264). Almost as good—crabapple jelly, wild plum jelly, even apple jelly if it's tart and rosy enough. The key to a glaze that's bright and glistening is using a jelly that's equally so. I find this meatloaf a delicious way to recycle leftover rice not to mention baked or boiled ham. Shaped and baked in a shallow pan, this meatloaf can be sliced right in the pan. *Tip:* To "grind" ham, dice and pulse in a food processor till hamburger-like.

Mustard-and-Mayhaw-Glazed Ham and Rice Loaf

Makes 6 to 8 servings

1½ pounds ground baked or boiled ham (see Tip above)

1½ cups firmly packed, unseasoned cooked rice (see headnote)

1½ cups soft white bread crumbs (3 slices firm-textured white bread)

1 can (12 ounces) evaporated milk (use low-fat, if you like)

3 large eggs

6 large scallions, trimmed and moderately finely chopped (include some green tops)

⅓ cup coarsely chopped fresh Italian parsley

1 teaspoon dried leaf marjoram, crumbled

1 teaspoon dry mustard

½ teaspoon freshly ground black pepper

¼ teaspoon ground cinnamon

¼ teaspoon ground ginger

½ cup mayhaw jelly (see headnote) blended until smooth with ⅓ cup prepared yellow mustard (Glaze)

1. Preheat oven to 350°F. Line 13 × 9 × 2-inch baking pan with foil, placing dull side up, then lightly spritz with nonstick cooking spray and set aside.

2. Place all but final ingredient (Glaze) in large bowl and mix thoroughly with hands. Scoop into pan and shape into loaf about 10 inches long, 5 inches wide, and 3 inches high.

3. Slide onto middle oven shelf and bake uncovered 50 minutes. Remove loaf from oven and spread evenly with Glaze.

4. Return to oven and bake uncovered 15 to 10 minutes longer until loaf glistens and instant-read thermometer thrust into middle reads 165°F.

5. Transfer loaf to wire rack and cool 20 minutes so juices have time to settle and meat to firm up.

6. To serve, slice loaf right in pan, spacing cuts about ½ inch apart and angling slightly on the bias. Best accompaniments? Something from the cabbage family—broccoli, perhaps, Brussels sprouts, or cauliflower simply cooked and seasoned.

Southerners are lucky because our supermarkets sell locally made country-style pork sausage meat. In my own state (North Carolina) Neese's (see Sources, page 264) has been delivering its preservative-free fresh sausage meats daily since 1917. Originally available only near the source (the Greensboro area), Neese's is now a supermarket staple in South Carolina and Virginia as well as across the Tar Heel State. Neatly wrapped 1-pound packages of bulk sausage come in three styles: regular (made from a 100-year-old family recipe), extra sage (used for this recipe), and hot. Southern friends, now in New York, beg for care packages of the sausages of home, and I've obliged them a few times even though fresh sausage is highly perishable. So far, so good (God bless "blue ice," insulated containers, and express overnight delivery). *Note:* Because fresh sausage meat contains considerable fat, as indeed it should, I call for lean (about 10 percent fat) ground pork. But if your sausage seems to lack fat, choose ground pork flecked with plenty of it. Rarely one to use mixes, I call for an onion soup mix here because its intense flavor isn't overpowered by the seasonings of fresh country sausage—not so freshly chopped onions, even the richly browned. It's a shortcut cooks in a hurry will welcome. But, make a note, both the soup mix and sausage are so salty the meatloaf, itself, needs none. *Additional Time-Savers:* Processor-crumb the bread (for 2 cups you'll need 4 slices firm-textured white bread) and add to mixing bowl, then empty envelope of soup mix on top of crumbs. Now processor-chop about ¾ cup washed and wrung-dry parsley leaves, and add to bowl along with all remaining ingredients.

Sausage Loaf

Makes 6 to 8 Servings

2 cups moderately coarse soft white bread crumbs (see Additional Time-Savers above)

1 envelope dry onion soup mix (from a 2-ounce package; see Note above)

½ cup moderately finely chopped fresh parsley

1 teaspoon dried leaf sage, crumbled

½ teaspoon dried leaf thyme, crumbled

½ teaspoon freshly ground black pepper

1½ pounds lean ground pork (see Note above)

1 pound fresh country-style bulk sausage meat (regular or with extra sage; see headnote)

1 can (10 ounces) diced tomatoes with green chilis, with their liquid (as mild or hot as you like)

2 large eggs

1. Preheat oven to 350°F. Spritz 9 × 5 × 3-inch loaf pan with nonstick cooking spray and set aside.

2. Simply place all ingredients in large mixing bowl and mix thoroughly with hands.

3. Pack sausage mixture into pan, mounding in center and making little trough around edge to catch drippings.

4. Slide pan onto middle oven shelf and bake uncovered 1 hour and 20 to 25 minutes until loaf is richly browned, firm, and has pulled from sides of pan.

5. Cool loaf in upright pan on wire rack 20 to 30 minutes.

6. Turn out, if you like, on heated small platter. Or do as I do: Slice loaf right in the pan, spacing cuts at ⅜-inch intervals, then plate, spooning a few drippings over each slice (there won't be many). Best accompaniments: mashed potatoes or sweet potatoes plus boiled collards or turnip greens. **Note:** Leftovers make dandy sandwiches—dream up your own "Dagwood."

I have no clue how this centuries-old Southern recipe—a crumb-crusted beef, ham, and pork loaf—came by its name but I do know that it's special enough for a small dinner party. Back in plantation days, each meat had to be ground by hand. Not so today with supermarkets routinely selling ground beef and even, on occasion, ground pork. On the other hand, ground ham is rarely available so you'll have to beg your butcher to grind it for you or chop it, yourself, in a food processor. Like many early meat recipes, this one is heavily spiced with cinnamon (a valuable preservative back when there were no refrigerators) and freshly grated nutmeg. One early recipe calls for a whole tablespoon of ground cinnamon and two freshly grated nutmegs—way too much for today's tastes so I've reduced both significantly.

Blind Hare

Makes 8 Servings

1 pound ground pork shoulder (if unavailable, substitute ground chicken or turkey)

1 pound ground smoked ham (see headnote)

1 pound ground beef chuck

2 cups moderately fine soft white bread crumbs (4 slices firm-textured white bread)

3 large eggs, lightly beaten

1 teaspoon salt

½ teaspoon freshly ground black pepper

½ teaspoon freshly grated nutmeg

¼ teaspoon ground cinnamon

1 cup moderately coarse soft white bread crumbs tossed with 2 tablespoons melted butter (Crust)

GRAVY

3 tablespoons pan drippings or drippings plus melted butter to total 3 tablespoons

¼ cup unsifted all-purpose flour

Pinch freshly grated nutmeg

1½ cups beef broth

1 cup half-and-half, at room temperature

Salt and freshly ground black pepper to taste

1. Preheat oven to 350°F. Line large rimmed baking sheet with foil, dull side up, and set aside.

2. Using your hands, mix all meatloaf ingredients—except Crust—well in large bowl. Scoop mixture onto prepared baking sheet and shape into loaf about 8 inches long, 5 inches wide, and 3 inches high, patting meat firmly as you shape. Now pat on Crust, pressing crumbs into loaf, scooping up and reapplying any that fall onto foil.

3. Slide loaf onto middle oven shelf and bake uncovered about 50 minutes to 1 hour until nicely browned and an instant-read meat thermometer, inserted in middle of loaf, registers 165°F. **Note:** If loaf is browning too fast, tent with foil. Remove loaf from oven and let rest 20 minutes.

4. *Meanwhile, prepare Gravy:* Blend drippings, flour, and nutmeg in small heavy saucepan and cook and stir over moderate heat 3 minutes. Whisk in broth and half-and-half, then cook, whisking constantly, about 5 minutes until thickened, smooth, and no raw floury taste remains. Season to taste with salt and pepper.

5. To serve, ease loaf onto heated large platter, and cut on the bias into slices ½ to ¾ inch thick. Top each portion with a little gravy and pass the rest. Best accompaniments? Rice or mashed potatoes to catch every drop of gravy plus carrots and maybe garden peas.

Long before the Tex-Mex craze swept across this country, Southerners were baking tamale pies for brunches, lunches, and light suppers. Cooks in a hurry use a corn bread mix for the topping, but I find them unpleasantly sweet and prefer to make my own buttermilk corn bread. To save time, I measure the ingredients while the meat filling simmers. Couldn't be easier.

Tamale Pie

Makes 6 Servings

2 tablespoons corn or vegetable oil

2 medium-large yellow onions, coarsely chopped

1 medium red bell pepper, cored, seeded, and coarsely chopped

1 medium green bell pepper, cored, seeded, and coarsely chopped

2 large garlic cloves, finely chopped

2 teaspoons chili powder

1 teaspoon dried leaf oregano, crumbled (preferably Mexican oregano)

1 pound ground lean beef chuck

3 tablespoons all-purpose flour

1 jar (16 ounces) chunky salsa (as mild or hot as you like)

2 tablespoons tomato paste

1 package (9 ounces) solidly frozen whole-kernel corn

1 teaspoon salt, or to taste

½ teaspoon freshly ground black pepper, or to taste

2 tablespoons coarsely chopped fresh cilantro or parsley

TOPPING

1 cup unsifted all-purpose flour

¾ cup unsifted yellow cornmeal (not stone-ground)

2 teaspoons baking powder

1 teaspoon baking soda

1 teaspoon salt

1 teaspoon chili powder

1 teaspoon dried leaf oregano, crumbled (preferably Mexican oregano)

¼ teaspoon freshly ground black pepper

1 cup buttermilk

¼ cup corn oil or vegetable oil

1 extra-large egg

1. Preheat oven to 400°F.

2. Heat oil in heavy deep nonreactive 12-inch ovenproof skillet 1½ to 2 minutes over moderate heat until ripples appear on pan bottom. Add onions, red and green bell peppers, and garlic and stir-fry 5 to 8 minutes until limp. Add chili powder, oregano, and beef, breaking up clumps.

3. Cover and cook 10 minutes. Blend in flour, then add salsa and tomato paste, stirring well to incorporate. Add corn and simmer uncovered 5 to 10 minutes, stirring often, until meat is no longer pink. Mix in salt, pepper, and cilantro and set off-heat.

4. *For Topping:* Combine all dry ingredients (flour through black pepper) in large bowl and make well in center. Combine buttermilk, oil, and egg, pour into well, and mix briskly just until dough holds together. Spread over meat filling, leaving 1- to 1½-inch margins all round.

5. Slide onto middle oven shelf and bake uncovered 15 to 20 minutes until bubbly and brown.

6. Serve at once as the main course accompanied by a tart cabbage slaw or, if you prefer, a salad of greens—Caesar or Green Goddess dressing would be my choice.

There's an ongoing fad down South that scares me and that's the one that calls for mixing up eggy casseroles of bread and cheese and God knows what else, then refrigerating overnight and baking the next day. OK, perhaps, when our eggs were farm-fresh and wholesome, but with frequent recalls of salmonella-contaminated eggs, my advice is to bake these casseroles straightaway. It's OK to prep everything ahead of time, just don't combine the ingredients until you're ready to slide the casserole into the oven. Call me a Nervous Nellie but I didn't spend years in bacteriology labs at Cornell without learning a thing or two. Better safe than sorry.

Sausage and Egg Breakfast

Makes 6 Servings

1 pound bulk sausage meat (as sage-y or peppery as you like)

6 large eggs

1 cup half-and-half

1 cup milk

2 tablespoons Dijon mustard

½ teaspoon dried leaf thyme, crumbled

½ teaspoon salt

¼ teaspoon freshly ground black pepper

6 lightly toasted slices firm-textured white bread, halved lengthwise, then crosswise

8 ounces sharp Cheddar cheese, moderately coarsely shredded

1. Preheat oven to 325°F. Spritz 13 × 9 × 2-inch ovenproof glass baking dish with nonstick baking spray and set aside.

2. Crumble sausage into large heavy skillet, set over moderately high heat, and cook 6 to 8 minutes, breaking up large clumps, until uniformly brown. With slotted spoon, scoop sausage to paper toweling to drain; discard drippings.

3. With hand electric mixer at moderate speed, beat eggs, half-and-half, milk, mustard, thyme, salt, and pepper to combine and set aside.

4. Layer half the toast in baking dish, then half the sausage and half the cheese. Pour in half the egg mixture. Repeat layers.

5. Cover baking dish with foil, slide onto middle oven shelf, and bake 45 to 50 minutes until set like custard and slightly puffed.

6. Serve at once as the centerpiece of a hearty breakfast or brunch or even an informal luncheon or supper. To accompany? Nothing better than sliced red-ripe tomatoes lightly glossed with olive oil.

Southerners love good country sausage—make that bulk sausage—and many supermarkets carry a variety of superior local brands with varying degrees of heat (pepper) as well as several choices of seasoning. "Extra sage-y" is my own favorite and the one I use here. What's good about this casserole is that it can be partially—and safely—made ahead, refrigerated overnight, and finished the next morning in time for a lazy Sunday breakfast. Some breakfast casseroles contain eggs as well as sausage and rice or grits. Others substitute a pound of crumbled, crisply fried bacon or sausage. This simpler recipe is the one I serve houseguests and so far, no complaints. *Note:* Because sausage is so highly seasoned, this recipe isn't likely to need salt or pepper. But taste just before serving and adjust seasoning as needed.

Sunday Breakfast Rice and Sausage Casserole

Makes 6 Servings

1 pound extra sage-y bulk sausage meat

1 large yellow onion, coarsely chopped

1 large celery rib, coarsely chopped

½ teaspoon dried leaf thyme, crumbled

1 cup uncooked converted rice

2 cups chicken or beef broth

1. Preheat oven to 350°F (but only if making the casserole the morning you'll serve it). Spritz 2½-quart casserole with nonstick cooking spray and set aside.

2. Crumble sausage into large heavy skillet, set over moderately high heat, and cook, breaking up large clumps, 5 to 7 minutes until no longer pink and most of drippings have cooked out. With slotted spoon, transfer sausage to casserole.

3. Drain drippings from skillet, then spoon 3 tablespoons back in. If insufficient, round out measure with bacon drippings or unsalted butter. Add onion, celery, and thyme and sauté, stirring now and then, about 5 minutes until limp and lightly browned. Add to sausage in casserole and toss well. **Note:** Casserole can be covered and refrigerated overnight at this point.

4. Mix rice into casserole, add broth, and stir well. Cover, slide onto middle oven shelf, and bake about 1½ hours until rice is fluffy and tender. Taste for salt and pepper and adjust.

5. Stir rice and sausage lightly, then serve. Accompany, if you like, with fried or scrambled eggs, and biscuits fresh from the oven. That's the Southern way. So is it any wonder that many Southerners consider Sunday breakfast the best meal of all?

Little known outside the South—make that Deep South—mirlitons (also called chayotes, christophenes, and vegetable pears) are deeply furrowed, pale green or ivory, pear-shaped members of the squash family. White of flesh, they contain one large slim seed, and when removed, leave halves perfect for stuffing (see Shrimp-Stuffed Mirlitons, page 110). But Southern cooks also turn mirlitons into casseroles like this one, even a sweet Mirliton Pie (page 197). Like other "vegetables of the vines" (i.e. the whole huge "gourd" family), mirlitons are a New World squash. Believed to have been an Aztec staple, they are so popular in Louisiana that New Orleans celebrates them each fall with a boisterous Mirliton Festival in its river's edge Bywater District. Now available across much of the upper South, mirlitons are still "exotics" few people know how to cook. *Note:* Raw mirlitons ooze a sticky liquid when cut—it's harmless and rinses off easily. Still, it's advisable to wear gloves when working with mirlitons lest your hans itch or burn.

Mirliton and Sausage Casserole

Makes 4 Servings

3 large mirlitons (about 2 pounds; see Note above)

1 pound bulk sausage meat (as mild or hot as you like)

1 tablespoon vegetable oil (if sausage very lean)

1 large yellow onion, coarsely chopped

1 large garlic clove, finely chopped

½ teaspoon salt, or to taste

¼ teaspoon freshly ground black pepper, or to taste

1 cup soft white bread crumbs tossed with 1½ tablespoons melted unsalted butter (Topping)

1. Preheat oven to 350°F. Spritz shallow 1½-quart casserole or au gratin pan with nonstick cooking spray and set aside.

2. Halve mirlitons lengthwise, scoop out and discard seeds, then peel each half and halve lengthwise. Finally, cut each piece crosswise into slices about ½ inch thick.

3. Place mirlitons in large nonreactive saucepan, add just enough water to cover, and bring to a boil over moderately high heat. Adjust heat so water bubbles gently, cover, and cook 15 to 20 minutes until mirlitons are tender; drain well and set aside.

4. Crumble sausage into large heavy skillet, add vegetable oil if sausage seems lean, and cook over moderately high heat, breaking up large clumps, until no longer pink—3 to 4 minutes. With slotted spoon, scoop sausage to bowl and set aside.

5. Reduce heat to moderate, add onion and garlic to drippings, and cook, stirring occasionally, about 5 minutes until nicely browned. Add drained mirlitons to skillet along with sausage and accumulated juices.

6. Cook and stir 2 to 3 minutes, then season to taste with salt and pepper.

7. Scoop into casserole, spreading to edge, and scatter Topping evenly over all.

8. Slide onto middle oven shelf and bake uncovered about 25 minutes until bubbling and nicely browned.

9. Serve as the main course of an informal lunch or supper and accompany with a green vegetable—snap beans, for example, or broccoli. Something with crunch and color.

Each summer when I was little, my family would load up the old Ford and head north to our cottage on Chesapeake Bay. My brother and I loved it there because we could catch crabs in the shallows right out front and all we needed was a piece of string, a safety pin, and a piece of bacon. In no time we'd have a bucketful, which Mother would boil on an antiquated wood stove, then serve with melted butter, bibs, and little wooden mallets. I've eaten plenty of crabs over the years, but none as good as blue crabs. Not the Peekytoes of Maine, not the West Coast Dungeness, not Alaska King or snow crab, not even the beloved Sapateiras of Portugal. None, in my opinion, can match the sweetness, tenderness, and delicacy of the Chesapeake's "beautiful swimmers." I once judged a blue crab/Dungeness competition in Baltimore with East and West Coast chefs strutting their stuff and judges from New York, Baltimore, San Francisco, and Seattle. To my delight—but not surprise—blue crabs grabbed the gold. Our most revered blue crab dishes, however, aren't likely to have been created by trendy chefs. Southerners prefer handed-down family recipes—everything from Crab Meat Norfolk to Deviled Crab to that most luscious of Chesapeake classics, Crab Imperial. Some cooks gussy it up with onions, green bell pepper, prepared mustard, even. For me, less is more. Why overpower the exquisite taste of blue crabs? *Note:* When picking over lump crab, be careful not to tear the meat apart.

Eastern Shore Crab Imperial

Makes 4 Servings

⅔ cup mayonnaise (use "light," if you like)

1 tablespoon moderately finely chopped fresh parsley

½ teaspoon dry mustard

½ teaspoon salt

½ teaspoon hot red pepper sauce

1 pound fresh lump crab meat, bits of shell and cartilage removed (see Note above)

1 cup fairly fine soft white bread crumbs mixed with 1½ tablespoons melted unsalted butter (Topping)

1. Preheat oven to 375°F. Lightly butter shallow 1½-quart casserole and set aside.

2. Combine mayonnaise, parsley, mustard, salt, and hot red pepper sauce in large bowl. Fold in crab, taking care not to break up lumps. Turn into casserole, spreading to edge, and scatter Topping evenly over all.

3. Slide onto middle oven shelf and bake uncovered 15 to 20 minutes until bubbling and tipped with brown.

4. Serve at once as the main course of an elegant dinner. To accompany? Something green—asparagus spears, steamed and drizzled with melted butter, would be perfect.

You might call this a cost-conscious Imperial because it not only calls for backfin crab meat (less expensive than lump) but also stretches the crab with cubed bread. It's plenty rich nonetheless and elegant enough for a small dinner party. *Note:* If backfin crab is unavailable, substitute lump crab.

Annapolis Imperial Crab

Makes 4 Servings

¼ cup (½ stick) unsalted butter

2 tablespoons finely grated yellow onion

1 tablespoon all-purpose flour

½ cup half-and-half

½ cup mayonnaise or mayonnaise-relish sandwich spread

1 tablespoon fresh lemon juice, or to taste

1 teaspoon Worcestershire sauce

½ teaspoon hot red pepper sauce, or to taste

¼ teaspoon salt, or to taste

1 pound backfin crab meat, bits of shell and cartilage removed (see Note above)

2 slices firm-textured white bread, crusts removed and bread cut in ½-inch cubes

½ teaspoon sweet paprika (about)

1. Preheat oven to 400°F. Lightly spritz shallow 4- to 5-cup casserole with nonstick cooking spray and set aside.

2. Melt 3 tablespoons butter in small heavy nonreactive saucepan over moderate heat, add onion, and cook and stir 1 to 2 minutes until golden. Blend in flour and cook and stir 1 minute. Add half-and-half and cook, stirring constantly, about 3 minutes until mixture bubbles and thickens. Remove from heat and blend in mayonnaise, lemon juice, Worcestershire, hot red pepper sauce, and salt; set aside.

3. Melt remaining 1 tablespoon butter in large heavy nonreactive skillet over moderately low heat and brown slowly 7 to 8 minutes, stirring now and then, until color of topaz. Add crab and turn in butter to coat. Mix in bread cubes and reserved sauce, stirring only enough to combine. Turn into casserole and blush with paprika.

4. Slide onto middle oven shelf and bake uncovered 15 to 20 minutes until bubbling and tipped with brown.

5. Serve at once accompanied by a simply steamed and seasoned green vegetable like broccoli, asparagus, or green beans.

Does every cook have a favorite recipe for deviled crab, perhaps a cherished family one handed down the generations? If you eat your way around Tidewater Virginia or the Eastern Shore of Maryland and Virginia sampling deviled crab as I have, you'll discover that some deviled crab is devilishly hot, some tepid, and some surprisingly bland. This particular recipe, picked up years ago on the Eastern Shore, strikes a delicious balance. Unlike much deviled crab, it contains no mayonnaise. Also unique? A smidgeon of bacon drippings, which not only mellows the seasonings but also adds a touch of mystery. *Note:* Because of the saltiness of the crab, bacon drippings, and mustard, this recipe needs little salt.

Chesapeake Deviled Crab

Makes 6 Servings

3   tablespoons unsalted butter

1   small red or green bell pepper, cored, seeded, and moderately finely chopped

1   medium yellow onion, moderately finely chopped

⅓   cup finely diced celery

1   pound fresh lump crab meat, bits of shell and cartilage removed

1   cup moderately fine soft white bread crumbs (2 slices firm-textured white bread)

1   large egg, hard-cooked, peeled and moderately finely chopped (see How to Hard-Cook Eggs, page 18)

2   tablespoons melted bacon drippings or unsalted butter

2   tablespoons Dijon mustard

1   tablespoon moderately finely chopped fresh curly parsley

½   teaspoon hot red pepper sauce

¼   teaspoon salt (see Note above)

1   cup fairly fine soft white bread crumbs mixed with 1 tablespoon melted unsalted butter (Topping)

1. Preheat oven to 375°F. Lightly butter 1½- to 2-quart shallow casserole and set aside.

2. Melt butter in small heavy skillet over moderate heat, add bell pepper, onion, and celery and sauté, stirring often, 5 to 8 minutes until limp but not brown. Transfer to large mixing bowl.

3. Add remaining ingredients except Topping and toss well to combine. Scoop mixture into casserole, spreading to edge, then scatter Topping evenly over all.

4. Slide onto middle oven shelf and bake uncovered about 20 minutes until bubbling and lightly browned.

5. Serve hot with a cool green salad simply dressed with oil and vinegar.

Unlike meat loaves that cook in bread-loaf pans, this one works better in a shallow, square ovenproof glass baking dish—the kind we use for brownies and other bar cookies. Do not use a metal pan—your crab loaf will taste "tinny". Once baked, the loaf is cut into large squares—do it at table, if you like, or plate in the kitchen. *Note:* I like my crab loaf "straight up" but a simple sour cream–caper sauce wouldn't be amiss. Just combine ¾ cup sour cream ("light," if you like) and about ¼ cup well-drained tiny bottled capers. What could be easier?

Lowcountry Crab Loaf

Makes 4 to 6 Servings

3 tablespoons unsalted butter

¼ cup finely chopped scallions, shallots, or yellow onion

¼ cup finely chopped green bell pepper

1 tablespoon all-purpose flour

1½ teaspoons Old Bay seasoning

¾ cup half-and-half or evaporated milk, at room temperature

1 large egg, well beaten

2 tablespoons mayonnaise or mayonnaise-relish sandwich spread

2 teaspoons fresh lemon juice

2 teaspoons Dijon mustard

1 pound lump crab meat, bits of shell and cartilage removed

4 slices firm-textured white bread, crusts removed and bread cut in ½-inch cubes

1. Preheat oven to 350°F. Spritz an ovenproof glass 8 × 8 × 2-inch baking dish with nonstick cooking spray and set aside.

2. Melt 2 tablespoons butter in small heavy saucepan over moderate heat, add scallions and bell pepper, and sauté 3 to 4 minutes until golden. Smooth in flour and Old Bay and cook and stir 1 minute. Add half-and-half and cook, stirring constantly, until thickened and smooth, about 3 minutes.

3. Whisk about ¼ cup hot sauce into beaten egg, stir back into pan, and set off-heat. Blend in mayonnaise, lemon juice, and mustard, then transfer to large mixing bowl. Fold in crab and half of bread cubes. Melt remaining 1 tablespoon butter and toss with remaining bread cubes; set aside.

4. Scoop crab mixture into baking dish, spreading to corners, and top with buttered bread cubes.

5. Slide onto middle oven shelf and bake uncovered 30 to 35 minutes until bubbling and touched with brown.

6. Cut into squares, set out a bowl of sour cream–caper sauce, if you like (see headnote), and a plate of thinly sliced red-ripe tomatoes. Nothing more needed for the main course.

Southerners have long known that one of the best ways to stretch a pound of pricey lump crab is to mix in finely chopped hard-cooked eggs—in this case four large ones. This particular recipe comes from one of Georgia's Golden Isles where blue crabs swim in offshore waters but are rarely cheap. St. Simon's cooks bake and serve deviled crabs in well-scrubbed blue crab shells but scallop shells work equally well, so too an au gratin pan or shallow casserole.

St. Simon's Deviled Crab

Makes 6 Servings

4 large eggs, hard-cooked, peeled, and finely chopped (see How to Hard-Cook Eggs, page 18)

¼ cup (½ stick) unsalted butter, at room temperature

3 tablespoons finely grated yellow onion

3 tablespoons minced fresh parsley

2 tablespoons fresh lemon juice

1 tablespoon cider vinegar

1 tablespoon dry mustard

1½ teaspoons Worcestershire sauce

¾ teaspoon salt, or to taste

½ teaspoon freshly ground black pepper, or to taste

1 pound lump crab meat, bits of shell and cartilage removed

⅓ cup heavy cream

⅔ cup fine soft white bread crumbs tossed with 1 tablespoon melted unsalted butter (Topping)

1. Preheat oven to 400°F. Spritz 6 pristine large crab or scallop shells or one 1½-quart au gratin pan or shallow casserole with nonstick cooking spray and set aside.

2. Combine first 10 ingredients (hard-cooked eggs through black pepper) in large bowl, then fold in crab meat and cream, taking care not to break up lumps of crab.

3. Divide crab mixture among crab shells or spoon into au gratin pan, spreading to edge. Scatter with Topping, distributing evenly.

4. Arrange filled crab shells, not touching, on rimmed baking sheet, slide onto middle oven shelf, and bake uncovered 15 to 20 minutes until bubbling and tipped with brown. **Note:** Baking sheet not needed for au gratin pan and baking time is just the same.

5. Serve hot as the main course of an elegant luncheon or dinner and accompany with a tossed salad of mixed greens, and if you like, fresh-baked biscuits or yeast rolls.

When is a casserole a pie? When it's a long-ago Southern recipe—usually fish or fowl—baked in a shallow dish under a blanket of bread or cracker crumbs. This crab casserole, sampled while zig-zagging along Georgia's coast and offshore islands, is just such a "pie." If memory serves, the turreted, Victorian Jekyll Island Club is where I ate it ages ago and also where I found the thin spiral-bound community fund-raiser that contained a similar recipe. I simply cannot resist buying these little local cookbooks, particularly long-out-of print ones, which brim with snippets of lore as well as generations-old recipes found nowhere else. The crab pie that follows was inspired by those of Jekyll Island.

Jekyll Island Crab Pie

Makes 6 Servings

3 large eggs

2 tablespoons melted unsalted butter

2 tablespoons finely minced scallions

2 tablespoons moderately finely chopped red bell pepper

1 tablespoon Worcestershire sauce

1 teaspoon dry mustard

½ teaspoon salt

½ teaspoon hot red pepper sauce

1 cup heavy cream blended with 2 tablespoons all-purpose flour

¾ cup milk

1 pound lump crab meat, bits of shell and cartilage removed

⅔ cup moderately fine soda cracker crumbs tossed with 1 tablespoon melted unsalted butter (Topping)

1. Preheat oven to 350°F. Lightly spritz 1½-quart au gratin pan or shallow baking dish with nonstick cooking spray and set aside.

2. Whisk first 10 ingredients (eggs through milk) together in large mixing bowl to combine, then gently mix in crab. Pour into au gratin pan, gently spreading to distribute crab evenly, and scatter Topping over all.

3. Slide onto middle oven shelf and bake uncovered 35 to 40 minutes until lightly browned and set like custard.

4. Remove from oven and let stand 10 minutes, then serve as the main course of an elegant dinner or luncheon accompanied by a colorful vegetable like asparagus or snow peas.

When I was a little girl, we would return to our Chesapeake Bay summer cottage in the early "R" months of fall to enjoy fresh Chincoteagues. I loved hopping in the boat with Daddy and chugging up Anti-Poison Creek to a dockside pound that sold the Chesapeake's best fish and shellfish, among them the glorious Chincoteagues. To non-Southerners, Chincoteague will forever be associated with the half-wild pinto pony immortalized in Marguerite Henry's late '40s book, *Misty of Chincoteague*, and the subsequent 1961 movie largely shot on the island. Its premier was held there with Misty, herself, leading the parade down Main Street. But Chincoteague also means oysters—the finest on earth—Virginians, say. Being allergic to them, I've never tasted Chincoteagues, but have watched the rest of my family scarf them down by the dozen. This recipe, given to my mother ages ago by an old-timer who lived near our cottage, is the classic way to scallop Chincoteagues (of course any good oysters will do). *Note:* After draining, you should have 4 cups oysters. Save liquor drained from oysters and if there's less than the amount called for below, round out the measure with bottled clam juice.

Oysters Scalloped the Chesapeake Way

Makes 4 to 6 Servings

3	tablespoons unsalted butter or bacon drippings
1	medium yellow onion, coarsely chopped
2	tablespoons all-purpose flour
¼	teaspoon freshly grated nutmeg
1	quart (4 cups) drained, shucked medium-large oysters (preferably Chincoteagues), coarsely chopped (see Note above)
¾	cup oyster liquor, strained, or ¾ cup bottled clam juice (see Note above)
¼	cup heavy cream
2	tablespoons fresh lemon juice
½	teaspoon salt
¼	teaspoon freshly ground black pepper
1	cup moderately coarsely crushed soda crackers
½	cup moderately fine dry bread crumbs mixed with 1 tablespoon melted unsalted butter (Topping)

1. Preheat oven to 375°F. Spritz 1½-quart shallow baking dish or au gratin pan with nonstick cooking spray and set aside.

2. Melt butter in small heavy nonreactive skillet over moderate heat, add onion, and stir-fry about 5 minutes until limp and golden. Blend in flour and nutmeg, turn heat to lowest point, and allow to mellow while you prepare oysters.

3. Heat oysters and oyster liquor in medium-size heavy nonreactive saucepan over moderately low heat 3 to 5 minutes. just until oyster skirts ruffle. Do not boil or the oysters will be tough.

4. Reduce heat to low, stir in onion mixture along with cream, lemon juice, salt, and pepper, and cook, stirring gently, 1 minute. Set off-heat and mix in crushed crackers.

5. Scoop into baking dish, spreading to edge, then scatter Topping evenly over all.

6. Slide onto middle oven shelf and bake uncovered 25 to 30 minutes until bubbling and tipped with brown.

7. Serve at once as the main course accompanied by a green vegetable like asparagus or broccoli.

Oysters grow plump and sweet in the bays and sounds of the southern Atlantic where good cooks prepare them every which way. I wouldn't have thought to devil oysters, but this dish is popular up and down the North Carolina coast. Hostesses here may serve deviled oysters as an entrée, or they may bake them in scallop shells and serve at the start of an elegant dinner. *Note:* If you want to bake the deviled oysters in scallop shells, you'll need eight pristine ones measuring 5 to 5½ inches across. You'll also need to anchor each stuffed shell in kosher salt on rimmed baking sheets to keep them from wobbling. *Tip:* Oysters vary hugely in size and in the amount you get per pint. I used Virginia (Chesapeake Bay) oysters—about 22 medium-large oysters per pint. So in the oyster recipes that follow, aim for those of equal size.

Deviled Oysters

Makes 8 First-Course Servings, 4 Main-Course

2	tablespoons unsalted butter
2	tablespoons all-purpose flour
½	teaspoon salt
½	teaspoon freshly ground black pepper
1	cup heavy cream
2	large whole bay leaves (preferably fresh)
2	large egg yolks, beaten with ¼ teaspoon freshly grated nutmeg
2	tablespoons coarsely chopped fresh parsley
1	tablespoon Worcestershire sauce
1	tablespoon tomato ketchup
1	tablespoon Dijon mustard
1	quart (4 cups) drained, shucked medium-large oysters, coarsely chopped and patted dry on several paper towels (see Note and Tip above)
1	cup moderately fine soft white bread crumbs tossed with 1 tablespoon melted unsalted butter (Topping)

1. Preheat oven to 400°F. Spritz 1½-quart au gratin pan or shallow casserole or 8 large (5- to 5½-inch) scallop shells with nonstick cooking spray and set aside.

2. Melt butter in small heavy saucepan over moderate heat, blend in flour, salt, and pepper and cook and stir 1 minute. Add cream and bay leaves, bruising slightly as you drop into pan, then cook and stir 3 to 5 minutes until thickened and smooth; discard bay leaves.

3. Blend about ⅓ cup sauce into egg yolks, stir back into pan, and cook and stir 1 minute more; do not boil or sauce may curdle. Off-heat, mix in parsley, Worcestershire, ketchup, and mustard. Combine with oysters, scoop into au gratin pan, spreading to edge, and scatter with Topping.

4. Slide onto middle oven shelf and bake uncovered until bubbling and brown—20 to 25 minutes for au gratin or casserole, 18 to 20 minutes for stuffed scallop shells.

5. Serve hot. Good main-course accompaniments: steamed asparagus or green beans, or maybe a crisp cucumber and red onion salad.

Johnny Rebs were the "boys in gray," Confederate soldiers in a war some Southerners still call "The War Between the States" or "War for Southern Independence" or most euphemistically of all, "The Late Unpleasantness." No one seems to know when or where this rich oyster casserole originated, but my good friend Damon Lee Fowler of Savannah, culinary historian of all things Southern, believes the recipe may have been created in a Deep South restaurant back in the late '30s or early '40s when *Gone with the Wind* mania was epidemic. He also believes it to be "a riff on Mary Randolph's old Scalloped Oysters recipe, with crackers instead of bread crumbs. It's a Deep South standard." Randolph's *The Virginia Housewife*, published in 1824, was America's first Southern cookbook. Web-surfing, another good friend, Bob Holmes of Greensboro, NC, discovered that Oysters Johnny Reb had been a signature dish at the late, lamented Old Southern Tea Room in Vicksburg, MS. I ate there years ago while on assignment for *Food & Wine* but don't recall seeing Oysters Johnny Reb on the menu though the recipe appears in the Old Southern Tea Room recipe booklet published in 1960. What follows is a fusion of several variations found in local fund-raiser cookbooks. *Note:* Six dozen medium-large oysters are needed for this recipe—and that's 1½ quarts (6 cups), when well drained.

Oysters Johnny Reb

Makes 6 to 8 Servings

3 cups moderately coarse soda cracker crumbs

9 large scallions, trimmed and finely chopped (include some green tops)

½ cup finely minced fresh Italian parsley

6 tablespoons melted unsalted butter

3 tablespoons fresh lemon juice

1 tablespoon Worcestershire sauce

2 teaspoons hot red pepper sauce, or to taste

¾ teaspoon salt, or to taste

¾ teaspoon freshly ground black pepper, or to taste

1½ quarts (6 cups) drained, shucked medium-large oysters, patted dry on paper toweling (see Note above)

¾ cup heavy cream

1 teaspoon sweet paprika

1. Preheat oven to 350°F. Lightly spritz shallow 2-quart casserole with nonstick cooking spray and set aside.

2. Combine first nine ingredients (crumbs through black pepper) in medium-size bowl. Sprinkle half the crumb mixture over bottom of casserole, cover with oysters, and pour cream evenly over all.

3. Slide onto middle oven shelf and bake uncovered 20 minutes. Remove casserole from oven and raise oven temperature to 400°F. Top casserole with remaining crumb mixture and sprinkle with paprika.

4. Return casserole to middle oven shelf and bake uncovered about 20 minutes until bubbling and lightly browned. Transfer casserole to wire rack and cool 15 minutes to allow juices to settle.

5. Serve Oysters Johnny Reb as the main course of an elegant small luncheon or dinner. To accompany? What better than a tartly dressed salad of crisp greens? Or roasted asparagus?

To Northerners, nothing tops oysters-on-the-half-shell except maybe perfect oyster stew. But Southerners also dote on Oyster Pie and a bite of this one, a recipe I picked up eons ago while I was on assignment in Georgia's Golden Isles, shows why. *Note:* Because oysters ooze considerable liquid as they cook, drain off as much of their liquor as possible. Reserve ½ cup oyster liquor for this recipe and freeze the rest for soup another day. But if the oysters you buy have little liquor, round out the ½ cup needed with bottled clam juice. *Tip:* Old-hand Southern cooks know that if their pie crusts are to be tender and flaky, they must use lard. Never mind that few supermarkets carry it. You'll find it in abundance at the nearest Latino grocery. Just make sure the lard you buy is snowy and sweet and fresh. Rancid lard will ruin your pastry.

Golden Isles Oyster Pie

Makes 6 Servings

PASTRY

2 cups sifted all-purpose flour

¼ teaspoon salt

½ cup firmly packed, well-chilled lard (not vegetable shortening; see Tip above)

⅓ cup ice cold water (about)

1 tablespoon fresh lemon juice

¼ teaspoon finely grated lemon zest

1 large egg white, beaten until frothy

OYSTER FILLING

1 quart (4 cups) drained, shucked medium-large oysters

½ cup oyster liquor, strained (see Note above)

3 tablespoons unsalted butter

¼ cup unsifted all-purpose flour

½ teaspoon salt, or to taste

¼ teaspoon freshly ground black pepper, or to taste

¼ teaspoon ground hot red pepper (cayenne), or to taste

¼ teaspoon freshly grated nutmeg

¼ teaspoon finely grated lemon zest

1½ cups heavy cream, at room temperature

1. *For Pastry:* Set heavy-duty rimmed baking sheet on middle oven shelf and preheat oven to 425°F.

2. Combine flour and salt in large mixing bowl. With pastry blender, cut lard into flour until texture of lentils. Combine water, lemon juice, and zest, then forking flour mixture briskly, sprinkle liquid evenly over all; continue forking until soft dough forms. If mixture seems dry, fork in another 1 to 2 tablespoons cold water.

3. Divide dough into two pieces, one slightly larger than other, and shape into two balls. Wrap smaller ball in plastic food wrap and refrigerate. Roll larger ball into 14-inch circle on lightly floured pastry cloth. Ease pastry circle into 1½-quart deep-dish pie plate or pan measuring 9 to 9 ½ inches across the top. Press pastry over bottom and up sides of pan, then brush bottom and sides—but not overhang—with beaten egg white and set aside to air-dry.

4. *For Oyster Filling:* Warm oysters and oyster liquor over moderately low heat in heavy nonreactive 12-inch, skillet 10 to 12 minutes, stirring occasionally, until oyster skirts ruffle. Drain oysters well, discarding liquid. Pat oysters dry on several thicknesses paper toweling and set aside.

5. Melt butter in medium-size heavy nonreactive saucepan over moderate heat, blend in flour, salt, black and cayenne peppers, nutmeg, and lemon zest and cook and stir 1 minute until smooth. Add cream and cook, stirring constantly, 5 to 7 minutes until very thick and smooth. Remove from heat, press plastic wrap flat on surface of sauce, and set aside.

6. For top crust, roll remaining pastry as before but this time into 12-inch circle.

7. Remove plastic wrap from sauce and discard, fold oysters into sauce, then spoon into pie shell, spreading to edge.

8. Ease top crust into place. Trim top and bottom crusts all around to overhang pan 1 inch, then roll up onto pan rim and crimp into high fluted edge. Cut several decorative steam vents in top crust.

9. Slide pie onto preheated baking sheet on middle oven shelf and bake 10 minutes. Reduce oven temperature to 375°F and bake 25 to 30 minutes longer until filling is bubbly and crust nicely browned. Transfer pie to wire rack and cool 15 minutes so juices settle.

10. Serve pie at table, cutting into generous wedges and making sure everyone gets plenty of oysters. To accompany? Nothing's better than a tartly dressed salad of mixed greens except maybe thickly sliced red-ripe tomatoes right off the vine.

Do we Southerners deep-fry everything? Not as much as we used to, which got me to thinking. If breaded chicken scallops oven-fry so well, why not breaded sea scallops? After a few tries, I came up with this easy recipe. Key here is choosing sea scallops of about the same size so they'll cook evenly and be done at the same time. Also key: buying the freshest sea scallops you can find. Don't settle for frozen. They'll ooze quantities of liquid and the breading will be mush.

Crispy Oven-Fried Scallops

Makes 4 Servings

1 cup (2 sticks) melted unsalted butter mixed with 1 tablespoon fresh lemon juice and ½ teaspoon finely grated lemon zest (I also sometimes add ½ teaspoon finely minced fresh lemon thyme)

1½ cups moderately fine soft white bread crumbs mixed with 2 tablespoons each freshly grated Parmigiano Reggiano and moderately finely chopped fresh Italian parsley (Breading)

1 medium garlic clove, smashed and skin removed

1¼ pounds fresh sea scallops, each about 2 inches across, drained and patted dry on paper toweling

¼ teaspoon salt

¼ teaspoon freshly ground black pepper

1. Preheat oven to 375°F. Place melted butter in small bowl and Breading in pie pan. Drop garlic into butter and allow to stand 10 minutes; remove garlic and discard.

2. Sprinkle scallops with salt and pepper, dip into melted butter, then Breading, patting it on thickly.

3. Arrange scallops in shallow baking pan large enough to accommodate them in one layer and drizzle remaining butter on top, taking care not to dislodge Breading.

4. Slide onto middle oven shelf and bake uncovered, basting several times with pan drippings, 15 to 20 minutes until lightly browned.

5. Serve hot with a green vegetable—broccoli florets, perhaps, or asparagus—or if you prefer, with a tartly dressed salad of mixed greens.

Although I was born and brought up in Raleigh, my Illinois mother cooked "Midwestern," so school lunch was my introduction to Southern cooking. There were no vending machines back then coughing up colas and chips, crackers and cookies, only good country cooks making soups and stews and meatloaves of one kind or another. My particular favorite was the salmon loaf served every few weeks, made, my flavor memories tell me, with canned salmon, soda cracker crumbs, chopped onion, dill pickle, and parsley. To that magic formula, I've added tiny capers and a squeeze of fresh lemon juice. *Note:* Because of the saltiness of the capers, crackers, and salmon this recipe needs no additional salt.

Salmon Loaf

Makes 6 to 8 Servings

2 cans (14.75 ounces each) pink Alaska salmon, drained, flaked, bits of dark skin removed, and liquid reserved

2 cups moderately coarse soda cracker crumbs (you'll need about 60 two-inch-square crackers)

Reserved salmon liquid plus enough evaporated milk to total 2 cups

3 large eggs, lightly beaten

6 large scallions, trimmed and finely chopped (white part only)

1 medium celery rib, finely chopped (include a few leaves)

⅓ cup moderately finely chopped well-drained dill pickle

⅓ cup moderately finely chopped fresh parsley

¼ cup well drained small capers

2 tablespoons fresh lemon juice

½ teaspoon dill weed

½ teaspoon freshly ground black pepper

SAUCE

1½ cups firmly packed sour cream

¼ cup firmly packed mayonnaise

¼ cup well drained small capers

3 tablespoons finely snipped fresh dill

1 to 2 tablespoons milk if needed to thin sauce

1. Preheat oven to 325°F. Spritz 9 × 5 × 3-inch loaf pan with nonstick cooking spray and set aside.

2. Using hands, combine all loaf ingredients thoroughly in large mixing bowl. Pack salmon mixture into pan, mounding in center and making little trough around edge to catch drippings.

3. Slide pan onto middle oven shelf and bake uncovered 1 hour and 15 to 20 minutes until loaf is richly browned, firm, and has pulled from sides of pan.

4. Cool loaf in upright pan on wire rack to room temperature.

5. *Meanwhile, prepare Sauce:* Combine all ingredients.

6. Turn cooled salmon loaf out on small platter, if you like. Or do as I do: Slice loaf right in the pan, spacing cuts at ⅜-inch intervals.

7. To serve, overlap slices on small platter, spoon a little sauce down the middle, and pass the rest.

Like salmon, shad are ocean fish that swim upriver to spawn in fresh water, sometimes hundreds of miles upriver. They are prized up and down the Atlantic but nowhere more than in the South, where they are stuffed with their own roe—sometimes in tandem with backfin crab meat—bundled in foil, and baked just until the fish almost flakes at the touch of a fork. Reserve this recipe for a special dinner party when shad are in season. That means March or April along the mid-Atlantic or, as they say in Tidewater Virginia, "when the shadbush blooms." *Note:* Have your fishmonger prepare your shad for stuffing and that means boning the fish so you can open it like a book as well as cleaning and dressing it. If he balks, ask for two skin-on boneless shad fillets. If you have a shad fisherman in your family who'll do this messy job for you, praise be!

Baked Stuffed Shad

Makes 6 Servings

1   3½-pound shad, cleaned, dressed, and boned (see Note above)

1   teaspoon fine sea salt (about)

½   teaspoon freshly ground black pepper (about)

1   pair fresh shad roe (about 8 ounces in all), membranes removed, and roe mashed until smooth

8   ounces backfin or lump crab meat, bits of shell and cartilage removed

2   tablespoons unsalted butter, cut into small dice

1   medium yellow onion, peeled, halved lengthwise, then each half thinly sliced

6   slices richly smoked bacon

1. Preheat oven to 400°F. Criss-cross two long sheets heavy-duty foil in large shallow baking pan, placing dull side up and letting each end overhang pan slightly more than half the length of the shad.

2. Center shad on foil, open like book, and sprinkle inside and out with salt and pepper. Spread roe over bottom half of shad, top with crab, dot with butter, then sprinkle lightly with salt and pepper. Fold top half of shad over bottom enclosing stuffing. (**Note:** If using two shad fillets, place first fillet skin side down and proceed with stuffing as directed above, then top with second fillet, placing skin side up.)

3. Cover shad with onion slices, then lay bacon slices crosswise on top and tuck ends underneath fish. Fold foil ends in and bundle shad in a snug package.

4. Slide pan onto middle oven shelf and bake shad about 30 minutes until flesh almost flakes. Open foil package and ease shad from it onto large ovenproof platter trying not to disturb onions or bacon and reserving cooking juices. Preheat broiler.

5. Slide platter of fish into broiler, placing about 5 inches from heat, and broil 2 to 3 minutes to crisp and brown the bacon.

6. To serve, spoon some cooking juices evenly over shad and accompany with spring's best asparagus and tiny redskin potatoes, boiled in their skins. **Note:** Shad is extremely bony, so warn dinner guests to proceed with caution as a few bones may be lurking in the flesh.

Forever a favorite along the Maryland-Virginia Eastern shore, this four-ingredient recipe couldn't be easier to make. But you must be choosey about the fish you use. Old-timers will tell you that fatty fish corn best—channel bass, mackerel, shad, even not-as-fatty bluefish. And the fresher the better. *Note:* Cooking times will vary according to the thickness of the fillets. Those cut from the head end of the fish will be thicker and require a little longer cooking than thinner fillets from the tail end.

Fish Corned the Eastern Shore Way

Makes 6 Servings

6 ready-to-cook, skin-on mackerel fillets (2 to 2½ pounds; see Note above)

⅓ cup firmly packed light brown sugar

1½ teaspoons salt

½ to 1 teaspoon freshly ground black pepper (depending on how hot you like things)

1. Line rimmed large baking sheet with aluminum foil (dull side up), then spritz lightly with nonstick cooking spray.

2. Arrange fish fillets skin side down and not touching on foil. Combine sugar, salt, and, pepper, and sprinkle evenly over fish. Cover pan and refrigerate fish at least 3 hours.

3. When ready to proceed, set pan of fish on counter, remove cover, and preheat oven to 400°F.

4. Slide fish onto middle oven shelf and bake uncovered 10 to 15 minutes until sugar mixture bubbles and fish almost flakes when touched with fork.

5. Serve fish on heated plates and accompany with fresh-baked corn bread and a good sweet-sour coleslaw.

For decades, perhaps centuries, Crisfield on Maryland's Eastern Shore has been "crab central," the place where the Chesapeake's "beautiful swimmers" (blue crabs) are picked and packed for sale up and down the East Coast. Though condos are beginning to edge the shore and yachts tie up in Somers Cove, Crisfield remains a salty "waterman's" town with no shortage of restaurants serving the catch of the day. My own favorite, this spicy shrimp and crab combo. *Note:* If fresh shrimp are unavailable, buy frozen, cooked, shelled, and deveined shrimp from a market you trust. Some high-end groceries sell frozen shrimp that's already thawed. Otherwise, thaw shrimp in the refrigerator before using and drain well.

Crisfield Shrimp and Crab Bake

Makes 6 Servings

1 pound lump crab meat, bits of shell and cartilage removed

1 pound cooked, shelled, and deveined medium-size shrimp (see Note above)

3 tablespoons unsalted butter

2 large scallions, trimmed and coarsely chopped (include some green tops)

2 tablespoons all-purpose flour

1 cup half-and-half

3 tablespoons medium-dry sherry such as Amontillado or a Verdelho Madeira

2 teaspoons Dijon mustard

1 teaspoon hot red pepper sauce

½ teaspoon salt, or to taste

¼ teaspoon freshly ground black pepper, or to taste

2 tablespoons coarsely chopped fresh parsley

1 cup moderately fine soft white bread crumbs mixed with ½ cup freshly grated Parmigiano Reggiano and 1½ tablespoons melted unsalted butter (Topping)

1. Preheat oven to 350°F. Spritz shallow 2-quart casserole or au gratin pan with nonstick cooking spray and set aside.

2. Place crab and shrimp in large bowl and set aside. Melt butter in small heavy saucepan over moderate heat, add scallions, and cook, stirring occasionally, 3 to 4 minutes until golden. Blend in flour and cook and stir 1 minute.

3. Stirring constantly, add half-and-half and cook about 3 minutes until thickened and smooth. Blend in sherry, mustard, hot red pepper sauce, salt, black pepper, and parsley, add to crab and shrimp, and toss lightly to combine. Scoop all into casserole, spreading to edge, and scatter Topping evenly over all.

4. Slide casserole onto middle oven shelf and bake uncovered 20 to 25 minutes until bubbling and touched with brown.

5. Serve hot with coleslaw or a tossed salad of crisp greens.

Often called "Little Charleston," Georgetown lies some 60 miles north of its "big sister" along the Ocean Highway (US 17)—about halfway to Myrtle Beach. Though it was founded after Charleston (1670) and Beaufort (1711) farther south near Savannah, some historians believe that Lucas Vásquez de Ayllón sailed into Winyah Bay with African slaves as early as 1526 and established a Spanish colony on Waccamaw Neck near present-day Georgetown. But what would have been Europe's first North American settlement succumbed to fever and slave rebellion. The surviving Spaniards sailed away abandoning their slaves, who had the good sense to befriend local Indians. Centuries later, Georgetown's aristocracy grew rich on rice; indeed by 1840 they were producing more than half of America's supply of "Carolina gold." To see a South long "gone with the wind," you've only to visit Georgetown's majestic rice plantations during the annual spring tour—Arundel, Hampton, Hopsewee, and Mansfield (now a posh B & B). You can also tour the Lowcountry's abandoned rice "fields" by boat, cruising dark waters beneath Spanish-moss-hung live oaks. This ecological gumbo was not only ideal for growing rice but also teemed—and still does—with some of the sweetest shrimp on earth. So is it any wonder that early Georgetown cooks liked to combine the local rice and shrimp? Few shrimp and rice dishes are easier—or better—than this old favorite. But make a note, it's "crustless" and more casserole than pie. *Note:* I've taken a few modern shortcuts here—like using canned tomatoes instead of homegrown and using frozen shelled and deveined raw shrimp when fresh-caught are unavailable. I do insist, however, on Atlantic or Gulf Coast shrimp.

Georgetown Rice and Shrimp Pie with Bacon

Makes 4 Servings

3 tablespoons bacon drippings or vegetable oil

1 large yellow onion, coarsely chopped

1½ pounds shelled and deveined raw medium-size shrimp (see Note above)

1 can (14.5 ounces) diced tomatoes, with their liquid plus enough water to total 2 cups

1 teaspoon sweet paprika

1 teaspoon Worcestershire sauce

½ teaspoon salt, or to taste

¼ to ½ teaspoon ground hot red pepper (cayenne), depending on how hot you like things

¾ cup long-grain rice, cooked according to package directions until fluffy-dry

4 slices lean richly smoky bacon

1. Preheat oven to 400°F. Spritz 2-quart shallow casserole with nonstick cooking spray and set aside.

2. Melt bacon drippings in large heavy skillet over moderately high heat, add onion, and sauté, stirring occasionally, 8 to 10 minutes until nicely browned.

3. Add shrimp and stir-fry 2 to 3 minutes just until pink. Add tomatoes, paprika, Worcestershire, salt, and cayenne, and bring to a simmer. Remove from heat and fold in rice.

4. Scoop all into casserole and spread to edge. Lay bacon slices on top, not touching one another.

5. Slide onto middle oven shelf and bake uncovered 30 to 35 minutes until bacon crisps and browns.

6. Serve at once with a green salad or vegetable of your choice. I personally favor pole beans, broccoli, or asparagus.

My good friend and colleague Elaine Hanna moved years ago from Upper Saddle River, NJ, to Savannah and wasted no time discovering the glory and versatility of shrimp pulled from local waters. The two of us met longer ago than either of us would care to admit in the New York test kitchens of *Ladies' Home Journal* and became fast friends. So when Doubleday asked me to write a big, basic, all-inclusive cookbook, I agreed on one condition: that Elaine, one of the most imaginative and trustworthy food professionals I've ever known, coauthor. This easy casserole, one of Elaine's recent creations, is her dinner party staple. And now mine as well.

Savannah Party Shrimp and Rice

Makes 4 to 6 Servings

5 tablespoons extra-virgin olive oil

1 medium-large yellow onion, coarsely chopped

2 large garlic cloves, finely chopped

1 package (8 ounces) sliced white or baby bella (cremini) mushrooms (halve large slices)

1½ pounds shelled and deveined raw medium-size shrimp

1¼ cups uncooked converted rice

1¼ teaspoons salt

⅛ teaspoon ground hot red pepper (cayenne)

⅛ teaspoon sweet paprika

⅛ teaspoon ground saffron

3 tablespoons tomato paste

2⅔ cups chicken or vegetable broth

1½ cups frozen baby green peas, thawed and drained

2 tablespoons coarsely chopped fresh Italian parsley

1. Preheat oven to 350°F. Spritz shallow 2-quart casserole with nonstick cooking spray and set aside.

2. Heat oil in large heavy skillet over moderate heat 1½ to 2 minutes until ripples appear on pan bottom. Add onion and garlic and sauté, stirring often, about 5 minutes until golden. Add mushrooms and cook, stirring occasionally, about 5 minutes until limp and touched with brown.

3. Add shrimp and cook, tossing now and then, 3 to 5 minutes until pink. Mix in next seven ingredients (rice through broth), scoop into casserole, and cover with lid or foil.

4. Slide onto middle oven shelf and bake 25 to 30 minutes until all liquid is absorbed and rice is tender.

5. Mix in peas and parsley, re-cover, and bake 10 minutes longer.

6. Serve at table with oil-and-vinegar-dressed red-ripe tomato slices. For color, I often add thinnest ribbons (julienne) of fresh basil.

Baked chicken salad, a Southern classic I discovered years ago as an entry-level agricultural extension worker in Iredell County, NC, is perfect for family meals, perfect for potluck dinners. So, I thought, why not bake that other Southern favorite? Shrimp salad. Many of the ingredients are the same. Moreover, shrimp, like chickens, grow sweet and plump down South and are almost as plentiful. They cost more, true, but prepared this way, you can stretch a pound of shelled and deveined shrimp over six servings. *Note:* Frugal Southern cooks keep little jars of bacon drippings on hand for browning and seasoning all kinds of things. Still, bacon drippings may seem an odd choice for shrimp. Not at all. One popular Southern appetizer consists of two ingredients—bacon and shrimp—the first wrapped around the second, the two broiled until the bacon crisps. *Tip:* If fresh shrimp are unavailable, buy frozen, cooked, shelled, and deveined shrimp from a market you trust. Thaw and pat dry before using.

Baked Shrimp Salad

Makes 4 to 6 Servings

3 tablespoons bacon drippings or vegetable oil

8 large scallions, trimmed and thinly sliced (include some green tops)

2 large celery ribs, trimmed and moderately coarsely chopped

3 tablespoons all-purpose flour

1 can (12 ounces) evaporated milk (use "light," if you like) blended with ⅓ cup firmly packed mayonnaise-relish sandwich spread

¼ cup chicken or vegetable broth

1 pound cooked, shelled, and deveined medium-size shrimp (see Tip above)

1 package (10 ounces) frozen baby green peas, thawed and drained

1 jar (4 ounces) diced pimientos, well drained

⅓ cup coarsely chopped fresh parsley

¾ teaspoon salt, or to taste

½ teaspoon freshly ground black pepper, or to taste

1½ cups moderately fine soft white bread crumbs tossed with 1½ tablespoons melted butter (Topping)

1. Preheat oven to 350°F. Spritz shallow 1½-quart casserole with nonstick cooking spray and set aside.

2. Heat drippings in large heavy skillet over moderately high heat 1 minute, add scallions and celery, and cook, stirring often, 6 to 8 minutes until limp and golden.

3. Blend in flour and cook and stir 1 minute. Add evaporated milk mixture and broth and cook, stirring constantly, 3 to 5 minutes until thickened.

4. Remove from heat and mix in all remaining ingredients except Topping. Scoop mixture into casserole, spreading to edge, then scatter Topping evenly over all.

5. Slide onto middle oven shelf and bake uncovered 30 to 35 minutes until bubbling and lightly browned.

6. Serve at once as the main course of a casual lunch or supper, or make it your contribution to a potluck supper.

Of all the quick and easy ways to prepare shrimp, this one's a particular favorite. It was the specialty of my Mississippi friend, Jean Todd Freeman, whom I'd met in Beverly Hills, of all places. Jean, a senior editor at the Philadelphia headquarters of *Ladies' Home Journal*, was in Los Angeles to interview former movie starlet Dolores Hart, who'd become a nun. And I, a food editor at the *Journal*'s New York workshop, was in L.A. to profile Joan Fontaine for a major food feature (she, it turns out, was a gifted cook). Jean, staying at the Hotel Bel Air, left a message for me at my digs, the Beverly Hills Hotel, suggesting that we meet one evening for dinner. We did and hit it off at once. A few years later, when the magazine consolidated its two branches in New York, Jean's office was two doors down the hall from mine. Moreover, the West Village apartment she rented was just around the corner from me. Jean had two favorite party casseroles—chicken with artichoke hearts and shrimp with artichoke hearts. I asked for—and got—both recipes. This is my streamlined spin on Jean's shrimp casserole. For her chicken and artichoke recipe, see page 59.

Shrimp and Artichoke Hearts au Gratin

Makes 4 to 6 Servings

3 tablespoons extra-virgin olive oil

3 large garlic cloves, slivered

2 large whole bay leaves (preferably fresh)

2 packages (9 ounces each) frozen artichoke hearts, thawed, drained, and moderately thinly sliced

1 pound shelled and deveined raw medium-size shrimp

2 tablespoons fresh lemon juice

¼ teaspoon salt

¼ teaspoon hot red pepper sauce

4 ounces Gruyère cheese, coarsely grated

1 cup moderately fine soft white bread crumbs mixed with ¼ cup freshly grated Parmigiano Reggiano and 1½ tablespoons melted unsalted butter (Topping)

1. Preheat oven to 425°F. Spritz shallow 1½-quart casserole or au gratin pan with nonstick cooking spray and set aside.

2. Heat oil in large heavy nonreactive skillet over moderate heat 1½ to 2 minutes until ripples appear on pan bottom. Add garlic and bay leaves, cook 2 to 3 minutes, then scoop out and discard.

3. Add artichoke hearts to skillet, raise heat to moderately high, and stir-fry 2 to 3 minutes until beginning to brown. Add shrimp and stir-fry 3 to 5 minutes until pink.

4. Remove from heat, mix in lemon juice, salt, and hot red pepper sauce, then cheese. Scoop into casserole, spread to edge, and scatter Topping evenly over all.

5. Slide onto middle oven shelf and bake uncovered about 20 minutes until bubbling and nicely browned.

6. Serve at table with a tartly dressed salad of mixed greens or, if you prefer, perfectly ripened tomatoes.

As a riff on an old Southern classic, I've substituted plump red bell peppers for the green our grandmothers would have used, added rice (sometimes white, sometimes brown), seasoned with fresh dill and parsley, and used bottled mayonnaise-relish sandwich spread to bind. For Southerners, Duke's is the brand of choice but during my New York years, I used Hellmann's, Duke's being unavailable. Duke's ivory-hued mayo became famous back during World War I when to cheer the troops stationed at Fort Sevier, Eugenia Duke of Greenville, SC, served sandwiches spread with her own thick and creamy mayonnaise. It was such a hit that in no time Mrs. Duke was bottling it to sell at local groceries.

Baked Shrimp-Stuffed Red Bell Peppers

Makes 6 Servings

6 large red bell peppers

2 tablespoons extra-virgin olive oil or vegetable oil

6 large scallions, trimmed and moderately finely chopped (include some green tops)

1 medium celery rib, trimmed and finely diced

½ cup firmly packed mayonnaise-relish sandwich spread

½ cup firmly packed mayonnaise (see headnote)

1 pound shelled and deveined cooked medium-large shrimp, moderately coarsely chopped

2 cups cooked long-grain white or brown rice

2 tablespoons coarsely chopped fresh Italian parsley

2 tablespoons finely snipped fresh dill or ½ teaspoon dill weed

1 tablespoon fresh lemon juice

½ teaspoon salt, or to taste

¼ teaspoon freshly ground black pepper, or to taste

½ cup moderately fine soft white bread crumbs tossed with 1 tablespoon coarsely chopped fresh Italian parsley and 1 tablespoon olive oil (Topping)

1. Preheat oven to 375°F.

2. Slice about ½ inch off top of each bell pepper and set tops aside. Scoop seeds and veins from each pepper and discard. Stand peppers upside down on paper toweling. Remove and discard pepper stems, then coarsely chop pepper tops and reserve.

3. Heat oil in large heavy skillet over moderately high heat 1½ to 2 minutes until ripples appear on pan bottom. Add scallions, chopped bell pepper tops, and celery, and cook, stirring now and then, 5 to 6 minutes until limp.

4. Remove from heat and blend in sandwich spread and mayonnaise, then add all but final ingredient (Topping) and toss lightly to mix. Stuff peppers one by one, dividing shrimp mixture evenly. Sprinkle Topping over each stuffed pepper, again dividing total amount evenly.

5. Stand stuffed peppers shoulder to shoulder in shallow baking pan just big enough to hold them—peppers should touch and support one another. Then pour water into pan around peppers to depth of ¾ inch.

6. Slide stuffed peppers onto middle oven shelf and bake uncovered about 40 minutes until crisp-tender and lightly browned.

7. To serve, lift peppers to heated large round platter or to individual plates using two large spoons. I can think of no better accompaniment than a cool, crisp green salad.

Louisianans are as likely to stuff mirlitons with crawfish as shrimp and if available, by all means use them. The key here is not to overpower the mirliton's delicacy with a heavily seasoned stuffing. To learn more about mirlitons, see the headnote for Mirliton and Sausage Casserole (page 82). *Note:* Frozen, cooked, shelled, and deveined shrimp, a supermarket staple, save worlds of time. However, I insist on American shrimp and shy away from those netted elsewhere because I don't know how polluted the waters whence they came. *Tips:* To crumb bread zip-quick? Tear firm-textured white bread (crusts and all) into a food processor, then pulse till as coarse or fine as you like. One slice = ½ cup crumbs. Don't freak at the idea of using bacon drippings for sautéing but do use nitrite-free bacon. Pork fat is less saturated than butter.

Shrimp-Stuffed Mirlitons

Makes 6 Servings

3 large mirlitons (about 2 pounds), halved and seeded but not peeled (see headnote)

¼ cup bacon drippings, unsalted butter, or vegetable oil (see Tips above)

1 medium yellow onion, coarsely chopped

1 medium green bell pepper, cored, seeded, and coarsely chopped

1 medium celery rib, trimmed and coarsely chopped (include a few leaves)

1 large garlic clove, finely chopped

12 ounces cooked, shelled, and deveined shrimp, coarsely chopped (see Note above) or, if you prefer, crawfish tails

1½ cups soft white bread crumbs (see Tips above)

2 tablespoons coarsely chopped fresh Italian parsley

½ teaspoon salt, or to taste

¼ teaspoon freshly ground black pepper, or to taste

1 cup moderately fine soft white bread crumbs tossed with 2 tablespoons melted bacon drippings or unsalted butter (Topping)

1. Place mirlitons in large nonreactive saucepan, add just enough water to cover, and bring to a boil over moderately high heat. Adjust heat so water bubbles gently, cover pan, and simmer mirlitons about 25 minutes until not quite tender. Toward end of cooking, preheat oven to 350°F.

2. Meanwhile, melt drippings in large heavy skillet over moderate heat, add onion, bell pepper, and celery, and cook 8 to 10 minutes, stirring occasionally, until limp and lightly browned. Add garlic and cook and stir 1 to 2 minutes longer.

3. Remove from heat, add shrimp, bread crumbs, parsley, salt, and pepper, and toss lightly; set aside.

4. Drain mirlitons well, place upside down on several thicknesses paper toweling, and let stand several minutes. With tablespoon, scoop out mirliton halves leaving "shells" about ⅜ thick.

5. Drain scooped-out flesh, then coarsely chop. Add to shrimp mixture, and toss lightly.

6. Arrange mirliton shells side by side in ungreased shallow baking pan just large enough to hold them, fill with shrimp mixture, dividing amount evenly, pressing lightly, and mounding in center. Scatter Topping evenly over all.

7. Slide onto middle oven shelf and bake uncovered about 25 minutes until nicely browned.

8. Serve at once with a green vegetable or salad of your choice.

A frugal lunch or supper dish from the North Carolina Smokies that's nourished generations of mountain folk.

Baked Stuffed Eggs

Makes 4 Servings

6 large eggs, hard-cooked and peeled (see How to Hard-Cook Eggs, page 18)

3 tablespoons finely grated sharp Cheddar cheese

3 tablespoons melted bacon drippings or unsalted butter

1 tablespoon grated yellow onion

1 teaspoon cider vinegar

½ teaspoon salt

¼ teaspoon dry mustard

¼ teaspoon freshly ground black pepper

2 tablespoons all-purpose flour

1½ cups milk

1 cup moderately fine soft white bread crumbs tossed with 1 tablespoon melted unsalted butter (Topping)

1. Preheat oven to 350°F. Spritz shallow 8-inch round casserole with nonstick cooking spray and set aside.

2. Halve hard-cooked eggs lengthwise, scoop yolks into small bowl, and arrange whites in single layer in casserole. Mash yolks well with fork, blend in cheese, 1 tablespoon bacon drippings, onion, vinegar, ¼ teaspoon salt, mustard, and pepper. Shape into 12 balls of equal size and place in egg white halves.

3. Heat remaining bacon drippings in small heavy saucepan over moderate heat, blend in flour, and cook and stir 1 minute. Add milk and remaining salt and cook and stir 3 to 5 minutes until thickened and smooth. Spoon sauce evenly over eggs and scatter Topping over all.

4. Slide onto middle oven shelf and bake uncovered 25 to 30 minutes until bubbling and tipped with brown.

5. Serve hot as the main dish of a light lunch or supper. Best accompaniment? Steamed broccoli, asparagus, or other green vegetable. Or, if you prefer, a lightly dressed salad of mixed greens.

I've always adored deviled eggs but it would never have occurred to me to bake them until my father's department head invited our family to the Sunday dinner his very Southern wife had cooked. There, to the right of a roast capon, bubbled a casserole of deviled eggs. Barely 10 at the time, I was so taken by this unusual dish I still remember the details: rows of deviled eggs nested in chopped spinach, covered with cheese sauce, then buttered crumbs the color of caramel. From then on I've been dreaming up other deviled egg casseroles and think this one—created years later after weeks of traveling about India—one of the best. *Tip:* For hard-cooked eggs that peel neatly, choose those nearing their sell-by date.

Baked Curried Deviled Eggs

Makes 6 Servings

1½ cups white or brown converted rice, cooked according to package directions

EGGS

6 large eggs, hard-cooked, peeled, and halved lengthwise (see How to Hard-Cook Eggs, page 18)

¼ cup firmly packed mayonnaise or for more flavor, mayonnaise-relish sandwich spread

1 tablespoon finely grated yellow onion

2 teaspoons fresh lemon juice

2 teaspoons curry powder

2 teaspoons Dijon mustard

¼ teaspoon salt, or to taste

¼ teaspoon hot red pepper sauce, or to taste

SAUCE

¼ cup (½ stick) unsalted butter

2 medium yellow onions, moderately finely chopped

1 large garlic clove, finely chopped

1 tablespoon curry powder

¼ cup unsifted all-purpose flour

1½ cups chicken broth blended with 1¼ cups light cream

1 teaspoon salt, or to taste

¼ teaspoon freshly ground black pepper, or to taste

2 tablespoons mango chutney, pushed through a fine sieve

TOPPING

1½ cups moderately coarse soft white bread crumbs tossed with 2 tablespoons melted unsalted butter

1. Preheat oven to 350°F. Spritz a shallow 2-quart casserole or au gratin pan with nonstick cooking spray, spread rice over bottom, and set casserole aside.

2. *For Eggs:* Mash hard-cooked yolks with all remaining ingredients, mound in egg whites, and set aside.

3. *For Sauce:* Melt butter in medium-large heavy skillet over moderate heat, add onions, and sauté, stirring occasionally, about 12 minutes until nicely browned. Add garlic and curry powder and cook and stir 1 minute. Blend in flour, then cook, stirring, 1 minute. Add broth mixture, salt, and pepper and cook, stirring constantly, until thickened—about 3 minutes. Remove from heat and mix in sieved chutney.

continued on page 114

continued from page 112

4. Stir half of sauce into rice. Arrange deviled eggs side by side in rice and pour remaining sauce over deviled eggs. Scatter Topping evenly over all.

5. Slide casserole onto middle oven shelf and bake uncovered about 30 minutes until bubbling and tipped with brown.

6. Serve as the main course of a light lunch or supper. The perfect accompaniment? I like nothing better than olive oil–and-vinegar-dressed crisp-tender asparagus spears or broccoli florets.

It's said that Creole and Cajun cooks consider chopped onion, bell pepper, and celery the "holy trinity," that gumbos and jambalayas traditionally begin with these three, usually one part onion, two parts bell pepper, and three parts celery. But my Louisiana friend Alexis Touchet says, "There is no cut-and-dry rule about the proportion of onion, bell pepper, and celery. Each Louisiana cook does it his or her own way. I'm also not sure that everyone uses celery in jambalaya—that seems to vary—but onion, bell pepper, and celery are traditional in gumbo." As for Eggs Creole, Alexis says, "A delicious recipe—great for brunch!" *Tip:* To trim prep time, I processor-chop the onion and bell pepper together; scoop them out of the work bowl, then chop the celery rib solo. But each requires a bit of prep. Onion: Halve from stem to root end, peel, then quarter each half. Bell pepper: Slice about ½ inch off tops, halve pepper lengthwise, remove and discard seeds and pithy veins, then cut in 1½-inch chunks (don't forget top). Celery: Trim ribs and cut in 1- to 1½-inch chunks. For added flavor, include a few celery leaves.

Eggs Creole

Makes 6 Servings

7 tablespoons bacon drippings or unsalted butter

1 large yellow onion, moderately finely chopped (see Tip above)

1 medium green bell pepper, cored, seeded, and moderately finely chopped (see Tip above)

1 large celery rib, trimmed and moderately finely chopped (see Tip above)

1 can (14.5 ounces) diced tomatoes, with their liquid

¼ cup unsifted all-purpose flour

1½ cups half-and-half blended with 1 cup heavy cream, at room temperature

1 teaspoon salt, or to taste

¼ teaspoon freshly ground black pepper, or to taste

¼ teaspoon ground hot red pepper (cayenne), or to taste

10 large eggs, hard-cooked, peeled, and sliced about ¼ inch thick (see How to Hard-Cook Eggs, page 18)

¼ cup moderately coarsely chopped fresh Italian parsley

1 cup moderately coarse soda cracker crumbs

1. Preheat oven to 350°F. Spritz 2-quart shallow casserole or au gratin dish with nonstick cooking spray and set aside.

2. Melt 3 tablespoons drippings in large heavy nonreactive skillet over moderate heat, add onion, bell pepper, and celery, and cook, stirring occasionally, 15 to 18 minutes until soft and lightly browned.

3. Add tomatoes, bring to a boil, adjust heat so mixture barely bubbles, and cook uncovered at a bare simmer, stirring occasionally, about 15 minutes until tomatoes begin to disintegrate.

4. Meanwhile, melt remaining 4 tablespoons drippings in medium-size saucepan over moderate heat, blend in flour, and cook and stir 5 minutes. Whisking briskly, add cream mixture and cook, whisking constantly, 5 to 8 minutes until thickened and smooth. Season to taste with salt and black and cayenne peppers, then combine with skillet mixture.

6. Now layer ingredients into casserole this way: hard-cooked eggs, tomato sauce, parsley, and cracker crumbs—two layers of each should do it. Just be sure to end with crumbs.

7. Slide casserole onto middle oven shelf and bake uncovered about 30 minutes until bubbling and lightly browned.

8. Serve straightaway with a salad of crisp greens.

Who gave America macaroni and cheese? The frugal comfort food we love today? Would you believe that Thomas Jefferson served it at the White House in 1802? True, though most culinary historians agree that what this Virginia gentleman served was richer than the humble casserole we bake today. Jefferson imported a pasta-making machine from Italy in 1789, and soon after began serving two macaroni dishes at Monticello, his country estate near Charlottesville: a sweet macaroni pudding and a savory gratin dressed with equal amounts of butter and grated cheese. But the pasta Jefferson made was likely to have been flat strands, possibly short, possibly long strands broken in halves or thirds. Extruded elbow macaroni didn't exist then, at least not in young America. Our word "macaroni," by the way, descends from the Italian *maccheroni*, an "umbrella" word that embraces the whole huge pasta family. According to the late food historian Karen Hess, Mary Randolph, a Jefferson cousin and author of America's first Southern cookbook, *The Virginia Housewife* (1824), "likely gave Americans their first macaroni-and-cheese recipe." There was no pimiento in Jefferson's macaroni and cheese. Mary Randolph's either. Adding it is my own idea. And here's why: Southerners would rather eat a pimiento cheese sandwich than the best PB and J, in fact North Carolina novelist Reynolds Price called pimiento cheese "the peanut butter of my childhood."

Pimiento Mac 'n' Cheese

Makes 6 Servings

1 tablespoon unsalted butter

½ cup finely chopped yellow onion

¼ cup unsifted all-purpose flour

½ teaspoon salt, or to taste

¼ teaspoon freshly ground black pepper, or to taste

1½ cups milk

2 cups coarsely grated sharp Cheddar cheese

2 cups elbow macaroni, cooked according to package directions and well drained

2 jars (2 ounces each) diced pimientos, well drained

⅓ cup firmly packed mayonnaise or, if you prefer, mayonnaise-relish sandwich spread

1½ cups moderately fine soft white bread crumbs tossed with 1½ tablespoons melted unsalted butter (Topping)

1. Preheat oven to 350°F. Spritz shallow 2-quart casserole with nonstick cooking spray and set aside.

2. Melt butter in large heavy saucepan over moderate heat, add onion, and cook, stirring now and then, about 5 minutes until limp and golden.

3. Whisk flour, salt, and pepper into milk and when smooth, gradually whisk into onion and cook, stirring constantly, 3 to 5 minutes until thickened. Whisk in 1½ cups grated cheese and when melted, fold in macaroni, pimientos, and mayonnaise. Taste for salt and pepper and adjust as needed.

4. Scoop macaroni mixture into casserole; spreading to edge. Scatter remaining ½ cup cheese, then Topping, evenly over all.

5. Slide onto middle oven shelf and bake uncovered 30 to 35 minutes until bubbling and brown.

6. Serve as the main course of a simple lunch or supper. A tossed salad of crisp greens, tartly dressed, is all you need to accompany.

chapter three

Vegetables

& other sides

I've always wondered why Southerners are so partial to vegetable pies. Is it the crust they dote upon or the vegetables baked in a quiche-like custard? Of course vegetable pies were popular down South long before quiches caught our fancy. In olden days, cooks used canned asparagus spears for this pie, then came frozen asparagus, then, best of all, farmer's markets and homegrown asparagus. Instead of using the Cheddar integral to those early asparagus pies, I use an award-winning artisanal chèvre from the Celebrity Dairy near Siler City, NC. I particularly like the one they call "Silk Hope" because of its delicate blue-cheese flavor. But any fine chèvre will do. *Note:* If fresh asparagus is out of season, substitute one 10-ounce package frozen asparagus, cook according to package directions, drain dry, and cut in 1½-inch chunks.

Asparagus Pie

Makes 6 Servings

1½ pounds plump green asparagus (see Note above)

1 9-inch unbaked pie shell with a high fluted edge (see About Frozen Pie Shells, page 23)

2 ounces chèvre, finely crumbled

¼ cup freshly grated Parmigiano Reggiano

2 large eggs

1 cup milk

⅔ cup heavy cream

1 teaspoon salt

¼ teaspoon freshly ground black pepper

1. Set sturdy rimmed baking sheet on middle oven shelf and preheat oven to 400°F.

2. Working with one asparagus stalk at a time, bend until stalk breaks more or less in half. Save woody bottom halves to simmer into soup or discard. Peel top halves with swivel-bladed vegetable peeler, cut in 1½-inch lengths, and boil about 5 minutes in lightly salted water until crisp-tender. Drain well and pat dry on paper toweling.

3. Arrange asparagus in bottom of pie shell, sprinkle with chèvre, then Parmigiano Reggiano. Beat eggs with remaining ingredients until well combined and pour into pie shell.

4. Set pie on preheated baking sheet on middle oven shelf, reduce oven temperature to 350°F, and bake about 35 minutes until set. Transfer to wire rack and cool 30 minutes.

5. Cut pie into wedges and serve as the main course of a light luncheon or supper. To accompany? Wedged or sliced red-ripe tomatoes would be perfect. Ditto clusters of cherry or grape tomatoes.

This Southern spin on Yankee baked beans substitutes bourbon or sour mash whiskey for rum and to my mind is all the better for it (old-timers may prefer moonshine—lots of it back in the hills). Years ago a Raleigh friend, strolling the woods of a farm he'd just bought, came upon a stream the color of Orange Crush. Being a scientist, he knew what that meant: This was the rust-colored runoff of moonshining upstream. Later, my first job as assistant home agent in Iredell County, NC, was to drive into its nether reaches and persuade a farm woman to reinstate her two teenagers in the 4-H Club. "Tell her exactly when you'll arrive and be there on the dot," my boss warned. "Not one minute early, not one minute late. Otherwise, she'll think you're a revenuer and come out shooting." I did as I was told. Bourboned Beans may not be the fastest recipe in the South, but once in the oven, no "baby-sitting" needed. Low 'n' slow is what makes them extra-special. So does baking them on a raw wintry day when the warmth of an oven is welcome, not to mention the aroma of good things to come.

Bourboned Beans

Makes 6 Servings

1   pound dried navy or pea beans, washed and sorted

4   ounces richly smoky slab bacon, cut in ¼-inch dice

2   medium yellow onions, peeled and cut in slim wedges

⅓   cup molasses blended with 2 tablespoons spicy brown mustard

¼   cup firmly packed light brown sugar

2   teaspoons salt, or to taste

½   teaspoon freshly ground black pepper, or to taste

¼   teaspoon baking soda

¼   cup bourbon or sour mash whiskey

1. Place beans in large heavy saucepan, add 4 cups (1 quart) cold water, cover, and bring to a boil over moderately high heat. Adjust heat so water bubbles gently and simmer uncovered 2 minutes. Set pan off-heat, cover, and let beans stand 1 hour exactly.

2. Drain beans, rinse well, and return to pan. Add bacon and 6 cups (1½ quarts) cold water. Bring to a boil over moderately high heat, adjust heat so water barely bubbles, cover, and simmer 45 minutes. Toward end of cooking, preheat oven to 275°F.

3. Drain beans and bacon, reserving 1 cup cooking water. Place beans and bacon in ungreased 2½-quart bean pot, then push onion wedges deep into beans. Whisk reserved cooking water with remaining ingredients (molasses through bourbon) and stir into beans.

4. Cover bean pot, set in lower third of oven, and bake 6 to 6½ hours until beans are color of amber and richly glazed.

5. Serve with barbecue, roast pork, or grilled chicken. Or serve as a meat substitute. My favorite accompaniments? A tart but creamy coleslaw and crusty chunks of corn bread.

Riffling through my collection of Southern community cookbooks, those little spiral-bound paperbacks published as church or club fund-raisers, I am constantly struck by the number of vegetable casseroles, which appear as "scalloped" this and that. Even cookbooks printed a hundred or more years ago brim with them. The recipe that follows is an amalgam of several that caught my eye. *Note:* If using fresh limas, parboil 5 minutes in lightly salted water and drain well.

Scalloped Butter Beans (*limas*) and Corn with Bacon

Makes 6 Servings

3 tablespoons unsalted butter

1½ cups moderately coarse soft white bread crumbs (3 slices firm-textured white bread)

6 slices hickory-smoked bacon, snipped crosswise at ¼-inch intervals

1 medium yellow onion, coarsely chopped

¼ cup unsifted all-purpose flour

2 cups milk or for richer flavor, 1 cup each milk and evaporated milk

½ teaspoon salt, or to taste

½ teaspoon freshly ground black pepper, or to taste

2 cups fresh or thawed frozen baby lima beans (see Note above)

2 cups fresh or thawed frozen whole-kernel corn

¼ cup coarsely chopped, well-drained canned pimiento (optional)

1. Preheat oven to 350°F. Lightly coat 1½-quart casserole with nonstick cooking spray; set aside.

2. Melt 1½ tablespoons butter in large heavy saucepan over moderately low heat. Place bread crumbs in small bowl, drizzle in melted butter, toss lightly, and set aside.

3. Fry bacon in same pan about 15 minutes over moderately low heat until drippings cook out and only crisp brown bits remain. Drain browned bits on paper toweling, then mix ¼ cup into crumb mixture and set aside to use as topping. Reserve remaining bacon.

4. Pour bacon drippings from pan, then spoon 2 tablespoons back in. Add remaining 1½ tablespoons butter and melt over moderate heat. Add onion and cook and stir 5 to 7 minutes until lightly browned.

5. Blend in flour, then milk, and cook, stirring constantly, 3 to 5 minutes until thickened. Season with salt and pepper. Fold in limas, corn, reserved bacon, and pimiento, if desired.

6. Spoon into casserole, spreading to edge. Scatter crumb topping evenly over all, slide onto middle oven shelf, and bake uncovered about 25 minutes until bubbling and lightly browned.

7. Serve with grilled, roasted, or fried chicken. Equally good with roast turkey or baked ham.

I found this recipe in a little Natchez fund-raiser that I picked up years ago while on article assignment for *Food & Wine* magazine. It's a collection of antebellum Mississippi dishes that clearly have never been tested. The introductory headnote says, "This dish resembles cauliflower and is found by most to be very digestible and palatable." I also found it a tad bland and for that reason pumped up the flavor with two seasonings largely unknown to those long-ago mistresses of the house: finely grated Parmigiano Reggiano and hot red pepper sauce. Would they find the pepper sauce unladylike? I don't think so. They didn't object to a little cayenne in their sausage or head cheese—most of it made right at home.

Lady Cabbage

Makes 4 to 6 Servings

1 large green cabbage (about 3 pounds)

1 quart water mixed with 1 teaspoon salt (salted water)

2 large eggs

⅓ cup finely grated Parmigiano Reggiano

¼ cup heavy cream

1 tablespoon melted unsalted butter

½ teaspoon salt

¼ to ½ teaspoon hot red pepper sauce

¼ teaspoon freshly ground black pepper

1. Preheat oven to 350°F. Spritz shallow 1½-quart casserole with nonstick cooking spray; set aside.

2. Cut cabbage into eight wedges through the root end. Bring salted water to a boil in large heavy nonreactive saucepan, add cabbage, cover, and cook 10 minutes. Drain very well and set aside until cool enough to handle.

3. Meanwhile, whisk eggs in large bowl until frothy. Gradually whisk in cheese, heavy cream, butter, salt, hot red pepper sauce, and black pepper and continue whisking until well blended.

4. Slice off any cabbage core that is still firm and discard. Cut cabbage into ¾-inch pieces and toss with egg mixture. Transfer to casserole and spread evenly.

5. Slide onto middle oven shelf and bake uncovered 20 to 25 minutes until wisps of cabbage on top begin to brown.

6. Serve at once as an accompaniment to roast turkey, chicken, pork, beef, or lamb.

This recipe comes from Berkeley Plantation, one of the James River plantations I featured in an article I wrote for *Bon Appétit* some years ago. At the time, I was told that the recipe was a favorite both of Mrs. Malcolm Jamieson, the lady of the house, and her good friend Mrs. Paul Murphy, who lived in a dependency of "the big house." This dish is particularly good with roast turkey and that's altogether appropriate because America's first Thanksgiving was celebrated at Berkeley Plantation on December 4, 1619, well before the Pilgrims landed at Plymouth Rock.

Creamed Celery with Pecans

Makes 6 Servings

1 medium bunch celery, trimmed, leaves removed, and each rib cut crosswise and on the bias into slices ½ inch thick (you'll need 4 cups celery slices)

2 tablespoons unsalted butter

3 tablespoons all-purpose flour

2 cups milk

½ teaspoon salt

¼ teaspoon freshly ground black pepper

¾ cup coarsely chopped pecans

1 cup moderately fine soft white bread crumbs tossed with 2 tablespoons melted unsalted butter (Topping)

1. Preheat oven to 400°F. Butter 1½-quart casserole and set aside.

2. Cook celery in just enough lightly salted boiling water to cover for about 10 minutes until crisp-tender. Drain well.

3. Melt butter in medium-size heavy saucepan over moderate heat, blend in flour, and cook and stir 2 minutes. Whisk in milk and cook, whisking constantly, 3 to 5 minutes until thickened and smooth. Mix in drained celery, salt, and pepper.

4. Spoon celery mixture into casserole, spreading to edge. Scatter pecans evenly over all, then Topping.

5. Bake uncovered on middle oven shelf 40 to 45 minutes until bubbling and browned.

6. Serve hot with roast beef, lamb, veal, pork, turkey, or chicken.

If there's a way to bake a vegetable, trust a Southerner to find it. Who else, pray tell, would steam a head of cauliflower, sauce it, bread it, and bake it? *Note:* To save time, I nuke the cauliflower, adding no additional liquid. The drops of water clinging to the head after it's washed are quite enough. I simply put the cauliflower in a 2½-quart microwave-safe casserole deep enough to accommodate it, one with a tight-fitting domed lid. I then center the covered casserole in my microwave oven, set the cook-time at 14 minutes, and hit HIGH (full power). My microwave oven is a 650-watter; newer models of higher wattage will do the job faster—perhaps twice as fast. But you will know your particular model's prowess better than I. If you choose to steam the cauliflower instead, allow 8 to 10 minutes in a covered saucepan over moderate heat or until crisp-tender—there should be about ¾ inch of water in the pan. No steamer rack needed. While the cauliflower cooks, ready the sauce and bread crumb topping. That way no time wasted. *Tip:* For mellower flavor and smoother sauce, substitute freshly grated Parmigiano Reggiano cheese for the Cheddar our mothers and grandmothers would have used.

Baked Breaded Cauliflower

Makes 6 Servings

1 large cauliflower (about 3 pounds), trimmed of leaves and coarse bottom stem, then cooked until crisp-tender (see Note above)

2½ tablespoons unsalted butter

6 large scallions, trimmed and finely chopped (white part only)

3 tablespoons all-purpose flour

¾ teaspoon salt

½ teaspoon freshly ground black pepper

½ teaspoon freshly grated nutmeg

2 cups half-and-half, at room temperature

½ cup freshly grated Parmigiano Reggiano (see Tip above)

⅓ cup moderately coarse dry bread crumbs mixed with 2 tablespoons freshly grated Parmigiano Reggiano and 1 tablespoon melted unsalted butter (Topping)

1. Preheat oven to 375°F. Drain all liquid from cooked cauliflower, ease whole head into 9-inch pie pan generously coated with nonstick baking spray, and set aside.

2. Melt butter in small heavy saucepan over moderately low heat. Add scallions and cook, stirring occasionally, 2 to 3 minutes until limp. Blend in flour, salt, pepper, and nutmeg and cook and stir 3 minutes.

3. Whisking constantly, add half-and-half in slow, steady stream and continue whisking 5 to 8 minutes until thickened and no raw floury taste lingers. Add cheese and stir until melted. Carefully pour sauce over cauliflower and sprinkle with Topping.

4. Slide onto middle oven shelf and bake uncovered about 20 minutes until lightly browned.

5. Ease breaded cauliflower onto heated round platter and serve as an accompaniment to roast beef, lamb, or pork. Good, too, with roast chicken or turkey or baked ham.

The classic way to cook collards below the Mason-Dixon is to boil them "forever" with a piece of side meat. But why not bake them in a pie that can be served as the main course of a light lunch or supper as well as an accompaniment to grilled chicken, pork tenderloin, or even bluefish? As easy as it is yummy, this pie can also be made with kale, mustard, or turnip "sallet" (greens) as long as they're first sautéed until tender.

Collards and Bacon Pie

Makes 6 Servings

4 slices richly smoky bacon, snipped crosswise at ¼-inch intervals

1 large yellow onion, coarsely chopped

1 pound collards, washed, tough stems and ribs removed, and leaves coarsely chopped

1 9-inch unbaked pie shell with a high fluted edge (see About Frozen Pie Shells, page 23)

2 ounces Gruyère cheese, coarsely grated

2 large eggs

1½ cups half-and-half

3 tablespoons freshly grated Parmigiano Reggiano

½ teaspoon salt

¼ teaspoon freshly grated nutmeg

¼ teaspoon freshly ground black pepper

1. Set sturdy rimmed baking sheet on middle oven shelf and preheat oven to 350°F.

2. Brown bacon slowly in large heavy skillet over moderately low heat 12 to 15 minutes until all drippings cook out and only browned bits remain. Scoop to paper toweling and reserve.

3. Stir-fry onion in drippings over moderate heat about 5 minutes until limp and golden. Add collards, raise heat to moderately high, and stir-fry 8 to 10 minutes until tender. Set off-heat and cool 15 minutes, then spread skillet mixture over bottom of pie shell and sprinkle grated Gruyère evenly over all.

4. Beat eggs with remaining ingredients just enough to combine, pour into pie shell, and scatter reserved bacon bits on top.

5. Set pie on preheated baking sheet on middle oven shelf and bake about 35 minutes until set. Transfer to wire rack and cool 20 minutes.

6. Cut pie into wedges and serve as an accompaniment to grilled meat, fish, or fowl or as the main course of a light luncheon or supper along with a platter of tartly dressed sliced vine-ripened tomatoes.

Although I'm fond of old Southern recipes, I do use modern gadgets to prepare them—a Microplane to grate onion and a food processor to turn frozen kernels into cream-style corn. In fact, I mix the custard in the processor so it's in the oven in minutes. In my opinion, sweet corn is one of the few vegetables that freeze well. Moreover, by using frozen corn, I can enjoy corn custard right around the calendar. However, if sweet corn is in season, I'll use it (see Fresh Corn Custard variation that follows). *Note:* Introduced in 1885, unsweetened evaporated milk became popular down South because it required no refrigeration. I also think that its faintly caramel taste goes well with corn. And here's another plus: It's less likely to curdle than fresh milk.

Corn Custard

Makes 4 to 6 Servings

1 package (16 ounces) solidly frozen whole-kernel corn (preferably yellow)

2 tablespoons all-purpose flour

2 tablespoons raw or granulated sugar

1 teaspoon salt

½ teaspoon freshly ground black pepper

¼ teaspoon freshly grated nutmeg

1 can (12 ounces) evaporated milk

3 tablespoons melted unsalted butter

3 tablespoons finely grated yellow onion

3 extra-large eggs

1. Preheat oven to 325°F. Butter 2-quart casserole and set aside.

2. Alternately churn and pulse frozen corn in food processor 2 to 3 minutes until texture of cream-style corn. Pulse in flour, sugar, salt, pepper, and nutmeg, then with motor running, pour evaporated milk down feed tube. Pulse in melted butter, then grated onion, and finally, eggs, one by one.

3. Pour mixture into casserole, set in large shallow roasting pan, and slide onto middle oven shelf. Pour enough hot water into roasting pan to come halfway up sides of casserole.

4. Bake uncovered 1¾ to 2 hours until nicely browned and a cake tester inserted halfway between center and rim comes out clean.

5. Serve hot as an accompaniment to roast pork, turkey, or chicken. Good, too, with fried chicken or pork chops.

VARIATION

Fresh Corn Custard: After Step 1, shuck 8 medium-size ears of fresh sweet corn. Score each row of kernels down the middle—top to bottom—then using paring knife, scrape corn into large bowl. It will be cream-style. Measure out 4 cups, reserving any extra for pancakes, soups, or corn bread. Combine flour, sugar, salt, pepper, and nutmeg and mix into corn. Stir in evaporated milk, then melted butter and grated onion. Finally, beat eggs in one by one. To finish recipe, follow Steps 3 through 5 above. Makes 4 to 6 Servings.

A peppery spin on an old Southern favorite that acknowledges our growing appreciation of Mexican foods and takes advantage of the increased availability of things like queso fresco, a soft, snowy, lightly salty Mexican cow's milk cheese. And of course the now ubiquitous jalapeños and fresh cilantro. Though this pie contains bacon, there's precious little of it, so the pie can be served as an accompaniment to grilled or roasted chicken or pork, or, if you prefer, baked or boiled ham. It also serves nicely as the main course of a light lunch or supper in which case I would put out a platter of juicily ripe tomatoes, sliced and glossed with extra-virgin olive oil, or a tartly dressed toss of mixed salad greens.

Corn and Bacon Pie with Jalapeños

Makes 6 Servings

4 medium ears sweet corn (about 2½ pounds)

3 slices hickory-smoked bacon, cut crosswise at ¼-inch intervals

2 medium yellow onions, coarsely chopped

1 teaspoon finely minced fresh thyme or ¼ teaspoon dried leaf thyme, crumbled

½ teaspoon salt, or to taste

¼ teaspoon freshly ground black pepper, or to taste

1 9-inch unbaked pie shell with a high fluted edge (see About Frozen Pie Shells, page 23)

2 large eggs, lightly beaten

¼ cup coarsely chopped fresh cilantro or Italian parsley

¼ cup finely crumbled queso fresco, feta, or chèvre (see headnote)

2 to 4 tablespoons finely chopped, well-drained canned jalapeños (depending on how hot you like things)

1 cup light or heavy cream

1. Set sturdy rimmed baking sheet on middle oven shelf and preheat oven to 350°F.

2. Shuck corn, remove silks, then standing ears one by one in shallow pan, holding almost perpendicular, and using your sharpest paring knife, cut straight down freeing kernels several rows at a time. Pulse corn 8 to 10 times in food processor until you have cream-style corn (you should have about 2 cups). Set aside.

3. Brown bacon slowly in medium-size heavy skillet over moderately low heat 12 to 15 minutes until all drippings cook out and only browned bits remain. Scoop browned bits to paper toweling to drain and reserve.

4. Stir-fry onions in drippings over moderate heat 10 to 12 minutes until limp and nicely browned (this browned onion flavor is key). Mix in corn, thyme, salt, and black pepper and cook, stirring occasionally, about 5 minutes until corn no longer tastes raw. Remove from heat and cool 15 minutes.

5. Brush pie shell with a little beaten egg and allow to air-dry 15 minutes.

6. Mix cilantro, cheese, and jalapeños into cooled corn mixture, then beaten eggs and cream. Pour into pie shell and sprinkle reserved bacon evenly on top.

7. Set pie on preheated baking sheet on middle oven shelf and bake about 30 minutes or until set. Transfer to wire rack and cool 20 minutes.

8. Cut pie into wedges and serve as suggested in the headnote above.

In the South, "green" means young and sweet and fresh, not underripe. In most parts of the South, Silver Queen corn reigns, but I personally prefer "butter and sugar" corn with plump yellow and white kernels on each cob. When I lived in New York, I'd stroll down to the Union Square Greenmarket a few blocks south of Gramercy Park, my home for 20 years, and buy a dozen ears of "butter and sugar" at a clip, most of it fresh from Long Island. I keep looking for it at farmer's markets here, even tried to persuade some vendors to grow it. So far, no luck. Of course, the small white kernels of the beloved Silver Queen work just fine. *Note:* Pre–food processor, making creamy-style corn was both tedious and messy. How our grandmothers would have loved this "new-fangled" appliance.

Green Corn Pudding

Makes 6 to 8 Servings

6   large ears sweet corn (about 3½ pounds; see headnote)

3   large eggs

1   teaspoon salt

½   teaspoon freshly ground black pepper

¼   teaspoon freshly grated nutmeg or ¼ teaspoon ground mace

1   cup half-and-half

1   cup milk blended with about 2 tablespoons all-purpose flour

2   tablespoons melted unsalted butter

1. Preheat oven to 325°F. Lightly butter shallow 2½-quart casserole and set aside.

2. Shuck corn, removing all silks, then standing ears one by one in shallow pan, holding almost perpendicular, and using your sharpest paring knife, cut straight down freeing kernels several rows at a time (you should have about 8 cups). Pulse corn in two batches 8 to 10 times in food processor until you have cream-style corn (you should have about 5 cups); set aside.

3. With hand electric mixer, beat eggs, salt, pepper, and nutmeg in large bowl, first at low speed, then at high until thick and lemony—about 3 minutes. Whisk together half-and-half, milk mixture, and butter, beat into eggs, then fold in corn.

4. Turn into casserole, slide onto middle oven shelf, and bake uncovered about 1 hour until center is just set and top lightly browned.

5. Serve hot as an accompaniment to any roast—beef, veal, lamb, pork, turkey, or chicken. Delicious, too, with baked ham or fried chicken.

Eggplant, or Guinea squash as it's also called in the Deep South, has long been a favorite below the Mason-Dixon and recipes for it appear in some of our earliest cookbooks. What follows is an updated version of a recipe that appeared in a Virginia church cookbook nearly 125 years ago.

Eggplant Gratin

Makes 4 to 6 Servings

1 medium eggplant (about 1½ pounds)

1 large egg

¾ cup half-and-half

½ teaspoon salt

¼ teaspoon freshly ground black pepper

⅛ teaspoon ground hot red pepper (cayenne)

1 cup coarsely grated sharp Cheddar cheese

1 cup moderately fine soda cracker crumbs tossed with 2 tablespoons melted unsalted butter (Topping)

1. Preheat oven to 350°F. Spritz 5-cup au gratin pan or shallow casserole with nonstick cooking spray and set aside.

2. Peel eggplant, cut in ½- to ¾-inch dice, and place in ungreased 2-quart casserole that has a tight-fitting lid. Add enough boiling water to cover eggplant, put lid on casserole, slide onto middle oven shelf, and bake about 20 minutes until eggplant is tender. Drain very well.

3. Whisk egg until frothy in medium-size bowl. Whisk in half-and-half, salt, black pepper, and cayenne. Fold in drained eggplant and half of cheese. Transfer to au gratin pan, spreading to edge, and top with remaining cheese. Sprinkle Topping evenly over all.

4. Bake uncovered in upper third of oven 20 to 25 minutes until center is set and crumbs are nicely browned.

5. Serve oven-hot as an accompaniment to roast beef, lamb, veal, or pork. Good, too, with roast turkey or chicken.

My Illinois mother sliced and fried eggplant but never made a casserole of it. Good Mississippi cooks do and this easy recipe is especially good. Note that the eggplant is steamed whole, which prevents it from becoming waterlogged. My good friend and colleague Joanne Lamb Hayes who double-checked this recipe for me had this to say about it: "I don't usually like eggplant and I loved this. It would be a good vegetarian entrée."

Eggplant Casserole

Makes about 6 Servings

1 medium eggplant (about 1½ pounds), peeled but left whole

2 quarts water (about) mixed with 1 teaspoon salt

3 slices toast, broken into small pieces

½ cup milk or half-and-half

2 large eggs, lightly beaten

1 medium yellow onion, finely chopped

3 tablespoons melted unsalted butter

1 teaspoon salt

¼ teaspoon freshly ground black pepper

½ cup coarsely shredded sharp Cheddar cheese

1. Preheat oven to 350°F. Butter 1½-quart casserole well and set aside.

2. Place eggplant in a large nonreactive saucepan and add just enough salted water to float it; eggplant should be about 1 inch above bottom of pan. Bring to a boil over moderately high heat, then cover and steam for about 20 minutes until very tender. Meanwhile, soak toast in milk until soft.

3. Drain eggplant well, transfer to large bowl, and mash. Mix in toast and any residual milk, eggs, onion, melted butter, salt, and pepper.

4. Turn into casserole, spreading to edge, scatter cheese on top, and bake uncovered on middle oven shelf 30 to 35 minutes until lightly browned and center is set.

5. Serve hot as an accompaniment to any roast. Good, too, with fried chicken or fish.

As easy as it is elegant, this recipe dates back to the early 20th-century South—long before the super-sweet Vidalia onions came into our lives. First grown in Georgia during the Great Depression, they weren't known elsewhere until well after World War II. In fact, they seem not to have reached New York until the mid '70s, where I was living at the time. I feel certain that stronger-flavored yellow onions would have gone into those early onion puddings. They were all-purpose onions back then and remain supermarket staples today. To be honest, I think yellow onions are a better choice here than Vidalias because this onion pudding shouldn't be sweet. For me, it's the perfect accompaniment to roast pork, turkey, or chicken but have also served it with roast beef, veal, and lamb. On my Thanksgiving table, it's replaced the more traditional creamed white onions.

Onion Pudding

Makes 6 to 8 Servings

2 tablespoons melted unsalted butter

6 medium yellow onions (about 2¾ pounds), coarsely chopped

2 large eggs beaten with 1¼ teaspoons salt and ½ teaspoon freshly ground black pepper

1 cup milk whisked with 1 tablespoon all-purpose flour

1½ cups moderately fine soft white bread crumbs tossed with 1½ tablespoons melted unsalted butter (Topping)

1. Preheat oven to 350°F. Spritz 1½-quart shallow casserole with nonstick cooking spray and set aside.

2. Add 1 tablespoon melted butter to each of two large heavy skillets, add half of onions to each, and cook slowly over low heat, stirring frequently, 12 to 15 minutes until soft but not brown. Remove from heat and cool about 5 minutes.

3. Combine egg and milk mixtures in large bowl, whisking until well combined. Fold in onions, then transfer to casserole, spreading to edge and smoothing top. Scatter Topping evenly over all.

4. Slide onto middle oven shelf and bake uncovered 35 to 40 minutes until firm in center and nicely browned.

5. Serve as an accompaniment to almost any roast.

If Georgia's superbly mild Vidalia onions are unavailable, use Spanish or yellow onions for this unusual pie and serve it as the main course of a light luncheon or as an accompaniment to roast chicken, turkey, beef, veal, or pork.

Open-Face Vidalia Pie

Makes 6 to 8 Servings

3 tablespoons unsalted butter

2 large Vidalia onions (about 1½ pounds), halved lengthwise, then each half thinly sliced (about 4½ cups)

8 large scallions, trimmed and thinly sliced (include some green tops)

¼ teaspoon freshly grated nutmeg

¼ teaspoon dried leaf thyme, crumbled

3 tablespoons dry white wine such as Riesling, Chardonnay, or a gingery Gewürztraminer

1½ tablespoons all-purpose flour

3 large eggs

¾ cup half-and-half

½ teaspoon salt

¼ teaspoon freshly ground black pepper

1 9-inch unbaked pie shell with a high fluted edge (see About Frozen Pie Shells, page 23)

1. Set sturdy rimmed baking sheet on middle oven shelf and preheat oven to 350°F.

2. Melt butter in very large heavy nonreactive skillet over low heat, add onions, scallions, nutmeg, and thyme, and cook slowly, stirring often, about 10 minutes until soft and golden but not brown. Add wine and flour, stirring to coat onions evenly. Remove from heat and cool 10 minutes.

3. Meanwhile, vigorously whisk together eggs, half-and-half, salt, and pepper in large bowl. Fold in sautéed onion mixture and pour into pie shell.

4. Center pie on hot baking sheet in oven, and bake 30 to 35 minutes until set like custard.

5. Transfer pie to wire rack and cool 5 to 10 minutes before serving. The accompaniment I like best when the pie is served as the main course of a light lunch or supper? An oil-and-lemon-or-vinegar-dressed salad of mixed greens, some mild, some bitter (arugula, radicchio, nasturtium, dandelion, etc.).

Savory shortcakes are almost as popular south of the Mason-Dixon as those made with summer's best blackberries, blueberries, strawberries, and peaches. One of the more unusual—and best, I think—is this shortcake topped with Georgia's sweet Vidalia onions. I find it substantial enough to serve as the main course of a light luncheon or supper, though for a proper feast, it could join the parade of "sides." *Note:* If Vidalias are out of season, substitute almost-as-big-and-sweet fawn-skinned Spanish onions or pale, ivory-hued Bermudas. *Tip:* Because the eggs in the Vidalia sauce may not reach the temperature deemed safe, I use pasteurized eggs, which most supermarkets now routinely carry.

Vidalia Shortcake

Makes 6 Servings

SHORTCAKE

- 2 cups sifted all-purpose flour
- 1 tablespoon baking powder
- 1 teaspoon salt
- ½ teaspoon freshly ground black pepper
- ½ teaspoon dried leaf thyme, crumbled
- 8 tablespoons firmly packed lard (not vegetable shortening) or 1 stick refrigerator-cold unsalted butter, cut into pats
- ¾ cup milk

VIDALIA SAUCE

- 3 tablespoons bacon drippings or unsalted butter
- 2 medium-large Vidalia onions (about 1 pound), halved vertically, then each half thinly sliced (3 cups; see Note above).
- 1½ cups milk lightly beaten with 1 large pasteurized egg (see Tip above)
- 1 cup half-and-half blended with ¼ cup unsifted all-purpose flour
- 1 teaspoon salt
- ¼ teaspoon freshly ground black pepper

1. **For Shortcake:** Preheat oven to 450°F.

2. Whisk together flour, baking powder, salt, pepper, and thyme in large bowl. Add lard and cut in with pastry blender until texture of lentils. Forking briskly, scatter milk over all and continue forking until soft dough forms.

3. Turn dough onto lightly floured surface, knead gently 6 to 8 times, then pat over bottom of ungreased 9-inch pie pan.

4. Slide onto middle oven shelf and bake 15 to 20 minutes until nicely browned and hollow sounding when thumped.

5. **Meanwhile prepare Vidalia Sauce:** Melt drippings in large heavy skillet over moderate heat, add onions, and cook, stirring occasionally, about 15 minutes until limp and lightly browned.

6. Combine milk and half-and-half mixtures, salt, and pepper, add to onions, and cook, stirring constantly, 5 to 8 minutes until thickened and no floury taste lingers. Do not allow to boil or sauce may curdle.

7. To serve, cut fresh-from the-oven shortcake into wedges, split each, place bottom halves on heated luncheon plates, spoon on about half of Vidalia sauce, top with remaining biscuit halves, ladle on more sauce, and serve. The best accompaniment? Something light. A tossed salad of crisp greens would do nicely.

Favorite stuffings, or dressings as they're more commonly known below the Mason-Dixon, may contain sausage or shrimp or crab if they're to be served as a main dish, crumbled leftover corn bread or cooked rice if they're a side. In these rice-and-pecan-stuffed Vidalias, I've teamed three popular Southern staples in a single side dish and hope you like it as much as I do. Serve with roast pork, chicken, or turkey. *Note:* Choose round onions rather than flying-saucer-shaped ones, which are difficult to hollow out and stuff. If only saucer-ish Vidalias are available, use big round fawn-skinned Spanish onions instead.

Pecan-and-Rice-Stuffed Vidalias

Makes 6 Servings

6 softball-size Vidalia or Spanish onions (about 5 pounds; see Note above)

2 tablespoons unsalted butter

4 ounces (4 large) white or baby bella (cremini) mushrooms, stemmed, wiped clean, and coarsely chopped

½ teaspoon finely minced fresh thyme or ¼ teaspoon dried leaf thyme, crumbled

¼ teaspoon freshly grated nutmeg

1 cup cooked long-grain rice, preferably unseasoned (a good way to use up leftovers)

¾ cup lightly toasted pecans (8 to 10 minutes at 350°F), moderately finely chopped

1 large egg, lightly beaten

½ teaspoon salt

½ teaspoon freshly ground black pepper

1. Preheat oven to 350°F. Spritz 13 × 9 × 2-inch baking dish or pan with nonstick cooking spray and set aside.

2. Peel onions and, if necessary, trim bottoms so onions stand straight without wobbling. Slice off tops leaving onions 2 inches high, then parboil onions in about 1 inch lightly salted water in covered large saucepan 15 minutes until not quite tender.

3. Meanwhile, melt butter in small heavy skillet over moderate heat; add mushrooms, thyme, and nutmeg and sauté, stirring often, 5 to 8 minutes until mushrooms brown lightly and juices evaporate. Transfer to large mixing bowl.

4. With slotted spoon, lift onions to paper toweling, then with apple corer or teaspoon, scoop out centers leaving walls ½ to ¾ inch thick. Chop onion centers, measure out 1 cup, then save balance for soup, sauce, gravy, or stew.

5. Add 1 cup chopped onion to mushrooms along with rice, pecans, egg, salt, and pepper and mix well. Spoon into onion hollows, packing gently and mounding on top.

6. Stand stuffed onions in baking dish, not touching, cover loosely with foil, slide onto middle oven shelf, and bake 20 minutes. Remove foil and bake 10 to 15 minutes longer until very lightly browned.

7. Arrange onions on heated large platter and serve.

Parsley, green bell pepper, and scallion tops not only "green" the rice but also boost its nutritional value by contributing measureable amounts of vitamins A and C plus potassium. For "edge," I often add a fourth green—diced jalapeños—and offer them as an option. Serve Green Rice as an accompaniment to pork chops, roast pork, chicken, or turkey. Good, too, with broiled or fried chicken. *Note:* Which rice is best? It's a toss-up. Cooked according to package directions, long-grain white rice and converted (par-boiled) are equally good. but I don't recommend quick-cooking rice. And for sautéing the bell pepper, scallions, and garlic? I prefer bacon drippings because they add subtle meaty flavor. Before you freak, let me just say that pork fat is less saturated than beef or lamb fat, particularly that from heritage hogs like Ossabaws (see Sources, page 264). *Tip:* For better flavor and texture, grate the cheese yourself.

Gulf Coast Green Rice

Makes 6 Servings

2 tablespoons vegetable oil, unsalted butter, or bacon drippings (see Note above)

6 large scallions, trimmed and moderately thinly sliced (include green tops)

1 small green bell pepper, cored, seeded, and moderately coarsely chopped

2 large garlic cloves, finely chopped

1 cup converted or long-grain rice, cooked according to package directions (see Note above)

1 can (4 ounces) diced jalapeño peppers, well drained (optional)

½ cup moderately finely chopped fresh curly parsley

¾ cup milk blended with 1 tablespoon all-purpose flour

4 ounces sharp Cheddar cheese or 3 ounces Parmigiano Reggiano, moderately finely grated (see Tip above)

1 teaspoon salt, or to taste

½ teaspoon freshly ground black pepper, or to taste

1. Preheat oven to 350°F. Spritz 1½-quart casserole with nonstick cooking spray and set aside.

2. Heat oil in large heavy nonreactive skillet 1 to 1½ minutes over moderately high heat until ripples appear on pan bottom. Add scallions, bell pepper, and garlic and stir-fry 2 to 3 minutes until limp.

3. Remove from heat and mix in remaining ingredients. Scoop into casserole, spreading to edge.

4. Slide onto middle oven shelf and bake uncovered about 30 minutes until bubbly. Serve oven-hot with pork or poultry.

For many years a family favorite, this recipe comes from my stepmother's first cousin Ola Culpepper. Unlike many modern recipes, this one is distinguished by the delicacy of its flavor. Doubled, it is perfect for potluck dinners because it travels well. *Note:* In truth, this is more casserole than soufflé because the egg whites are not beaten and folded in at the end. Don't expect this soufflé to puff. It won't, but the flavor's wonderful! *Tip:* For better flavor, use crookneck squash.

Old Virginia Squash Soufflé

Makes 6 Servings

6   medium-small yellow squash (about 2 pounds), scrubbed, trimmed, and sliced ½ inch thick (see Tip above)

2   small yellow onions, coarsely chopped

2   cups water

3   tablespoons unsalted butter

2   large eggs

½   cup milk

¾   teaspoon salt

¼   teaspoon freshly ground black pepper

¼   teaspoon freshly grated nutmeg

1   cup moderately coarsely grated sharp Cheddar cheese

½   cup moderately coarse dry bread or soda cracker crumbs

1. Preheat oven to 350°F. Lightly butter 2-quart casserole or spritz with nonstick cooking spray and set aside.

2. Place squash, onions, and water in a medium-size heavy saucepan. Bring to a boil over moderate heat, adjust heat so water bubbles gently, cover, and cook 15 to 20 minutes until squash and onions are soft. Drain well, then return to moderate heat for a few minutes to drive off all excess moisture—mixture should be quite dry.

3. Mash with potato masher and mix in 2 tablespoons butter. Whisk eggs, milk, salt, pepper, and nutmeg in small bowl until foamy, stir in grated Cheddar, then add to squash and mix well.

4. Turn into casserole, top with crumbs, and dot with remaining butter. Slide onto middle oven shelf and bake uncovered about 45 minutes until bubbly and tipped with brown.

5. Serve at once as an accompaniment to roast chicken, turkey, or pork. Good, too, with fried chicken, roast beef, or lamb.

Few vegetables are more popular down South than baby yellow crookneck squash bursting with flavor and tender as a mother's love. Even young children who turn up their noses at "squush" soon come round when crooknecks are baked till delicately caramelized. *Tip:* You'll save worlds of time if you chunk the onion and crooknecks and processor-chop them in batches. To avoid overchopping, I pulse until about the size of chickpeas.

Casseroled Crooknecks

Makes 4 to 6 Servings

2 tablespoons bacon drippings

2 tablespoons unsalted butter

1 medium Vidalia, Spanish, or Bermuda onion, coarsely chopped (see Tip above)

1 teaspoon dried leaf marjoram, crumbled

½ teaspoon dried leaf thyme, crumbled

2½ pounds baby crookneck squash, scrubbed, trimmed, and coarsely chopped (see Tip above)

1 tablespoon raw sugar

1 teaspoon salt

½ teaspoon freshly ground black pepper

1. Heat bacon drippings and butter in large heavy nonreactive skillet over moderately high heat 1½ to 2 minutes until ripples appear on pan bottom.

2. Add onion, marjoram, and thyme and cook 10 to 12 minutes, stirring often, until richly browned—this browning is key for flavor.

3. Reduce temperature to moderately low and mix in squash, sugar, salt, and pepper. Cover and cook, stirring occasionally, 40 to 45 minutes until squash is soft and almost all skillet liquid evaporated. **Note:** Keep an eye on things and if squash is cooking too fast or threatening to stick, reduce heat to lowest point and slide a diffuser underneath skillet.

4. Toward end of cooking, preheat oven to 350°F. Also spritz 2-quart shallow casserole with nonstick cooking spray and set aside.

5. As soon as squash is done, scoop skillet mixture into casserole, spreading to edge.

6. Slide onto middle oven shelf and bake uncovered 1 to 1¼ hours until nicely browned.

7. Serve straight from the casserole as an accompaniment to any roast meat or poultry. I, myself, have been known to make a meal of Casseroled Crooknecks—no meat needed.

My stepmother Anne Lewis Anderson used to serve these often. They couldn't be easier to make and are perfect for dinner parties. Although Anne grew up in Lynchburg, VA (and descends from the Meriwether Lewis family), she insists that this recipe isn't an old one. No matter; it's delicious. Though she liked to serve these squash boats with roast lamb or grilled steaks, I think they're equally good with grilled, fried, or roast chicken. *Note:* You must use young and tender straight-neck squash for squash boats, otherwise they won't bake properly.

Yellow Squash Boats

Makes 6 Servings

6   young and tender straight-neck yellow squash (about 1¾ pounds), scrubbed and trimmed

¼   cup (½ stick) unsalted butter, at room temperature

½   cup fine dry bread crumbs (preferably homemade)

¾   teaspoon salt

¼   teaspoon freshly ground black pepper

¼   teaspoon dried leaf thyme, crumbled

1. Preheat oven to 350°F. Spritz 15½ × 10½ × 1-inch jelly roll pan with nonstick cooking spray and set aside.

2. Halve each squash lengthwise, then spread cut sides with butter. Quickly combine crumbs, salt, pepper, and thyme, and sprinkle on top of buttered halves, dividing amount evenly and pressing in lightly.

3. Arrange squash crumbed sides up in pan, slide onto middle oven shelf, and bake uncovered 45 to 50 minutes until fork-tender.

4. Serve hot as an accompaniment to roasts, steaks, chops, or grilled or fried chicken.

Always a fan of Austrian wiener schnitzel—those thin veal cutlets jacketed in crisp crumb coatings–I thought, why not sweet potatoes? To be honest, the idea came from some breaded yams I ate years ago on the Caribbean island of Grenada. I've tamed the sweetness and eliminated the nutmeg, which is grown commercially there. Though sweet potatoes are one of the South's principal crops, we've never been very creative about preparing them. "Schnitzel" gets us out of the marshmallow–crushed pineapple rut. Moreover, this recipe is as unusual as it is easy and delicious. *Note:* Choose round or oval sweet potatoes of about equal size so they'll be done at the same time.

Sweet Potato Schnitzel

Makes 4 Servings

1 cup moderately fine soft white bread crumbs (2 slices firm-textured white bread)

¼ cup freshly grated Parmigiano Reggiano

½ teaspoon salt

½ teaspoon freshly ground black pepper

½ cup buttermilk

2 large sweet potatoes (about 1 pound) of uniform size (see Note above)

1. Preheat oven to 350°F. Generously oil large rimmed baking sheet and set aside.

2. Combine crumbs, cheese, and ¼ teaspoon each salt and pepper in pie pan, then combine buttermilk and remaining salt and pepper in second pie pan.

3. Peel sweet potatoes, then cut each lengthwise into slices about ½ inch thick. Dip potato slices first in buttermilk mixture, then in crumbs, patting crumbs on firmly so slices are thickly coated.

4. Arrange breaded potato slices in single layer on baking sheet—not touching.

5. Slide onto middle oven shelf and bake uncovered 15 minutes. Remove from oven and carefully turn potato slices, patting on any loose crumbs. Return to oven and bake about 15 minutes more until potatoes are tender.

6. Serve as an accompaniment to roast turkey, chicken, or pork. Good, too, with baked ham.

If you're a frugal cook, you probably save bacon drippings for sautéing and seasoning. Nothing better for collards or turnip greens. This easy casserole, either, which I improvised one night to use up mushrooms and sweet potatoes nearing their "use-by" dates. I find this dish perfect for potluck dinners (even the Thanksgiving feast) because it travels well in its own baking dish and needs only a quick reheating by oven or microwave. *Tips:* Chunk and grate the cheese in a food processor until as coarse or fine as you like (I keep a jar of it in the refrigerator). Finally, processor-slice the potatoes exerting minimal pressure on the plunger—the harder you push, the thicker the slices.

Gratin of Sweet Potatoes and Mushrooms

Makes 6 to 8 servings

5 tablespoons bacon drippings or melted unsalted butter

3 bunches large scallions (about 20), washed, trimmed, and sliced ¼ inch thick (include some green tops)

3 packages (8 ounces each) sliced baby bella (cremini) or white mushrooms

2 teaspoons finely chopped fresh thyme or ¾ teaspoon dried leaf thyme, crumbled

3 tablespoons all-purpose flour

1 cup heavy cream

1 cup chicken broth

1 teaspoon salt

½ teaspoon freshly ground black pepper

2 tablespoons freshly grated Parmigiano Reggiano (see Tips above)

2½ pounds oval sweet potatoes of uniform size (about 5 medium), peeled and thinly sliced (see Tips above)

1 cup soft white bread crumbs mixed with 1½ tablespoons freshly grated Parmigiano Reggiano and 1 tablespoon melted unsalted butter (Topping)

1. Preheat oven to 425°F. Spritz shallow 2-quart casserole or au gratin dish with nonstick cooking spray and set aside.

2. Heat 3 tablespoons bacon drippings in large heavy skillet over moderately high heat 1 minute, add scallions, and sauté, stirring often, 2 minutes until beginning to soften. Mix in mushrooms and thyme and cook, stirring often, 10 to 12 minutes until mushrooms are limp, lightly browned, and their juices have evaporated. Scoop onto large plate and set aside.

3. Add remaining bacon drippings to skillet, set over moderate heat, blend in flour, then add cream, broth, salt, and pepper and cook, stirring constantly, 3 to 5 minutes until thickened and smooth. Remove from heat and mix in cheese.

4. Layer ingredients into casserole this way: one-third sweet potatoes, half mushroom mixture, one-third potatoes, half sauce, remaining mushroom mixture, remaining potatoes. Spread remaining sauce over potatoes, then rap casserole several times on counter—gently!—to level ingredients and distribute sauce.

5. Cover snugly with heavy-duty foil, slide onto middle oven shelf, and bake about 1 hour until bubbly and potatoes are nearly tender.

6. Remove casserole from oven and reduce temperature to 375°F. Lift off foil, scatter Topping evenly over potatoes, return to middle oven shelf, and bake uncovered about 15 minutes more until potatoes are tender and topping nicely browned.

7. Serve at once as an accompaniment to baked ham, roast pork, chicken, or turkey.

Whenever I thumb through Southern cookbooks printed a hundred or more years ago, I'm shocked by the amount of sugar recipes contain—main dishes and sides as well as sweets. Whatever for? My own theory is that back when there were no refrigerators, Southerners loaded all kinds of food with sugar—a natural preservative. The early recipe that inspired this one called for 1½ cups of it—more than many of today's desserts. A Thanksgiving favorite in some parts of the South, tomato pudding is equally delicious with roast or broiled chicken. I also like this updated, far less sugary version with baked ham, roast pork, and braised pork chops.

Tomato Pudding

Makes 6 Servings

1 can (28 ounces) diced tomatoes, with their liquid

¼ cup sugar

¼ cup (½ stick) melted unsalted butter

2 tablespoons cider vinegar

¼ teaspoon salt, or to taste

¼ teaspoon freshly ground black pepper

4 cups ¼-inch cubes firm-textured white bread (about 8 slices, crusts and all)

1 tablespoon coarsely chopped fresh parsley (optional)

1. Preheat oven to 325°F. Spritz 2-quart casserole with nonstick cooking spray and set aside.

2. Combine tomatoes, sugar, melted butter, vinegar, salt, and pepper in large bowl, then fold in bread cubes. Transfer to casserole, spreading to edge.

3. Slide onto middle oven shelf and bake uncovered 50 to 60 minutes until bubbling.

4. Sprinkle with parsley, if desired, and serve as an accompaniment to the main dish.

chapter four

Breads

(the yeast-raised & the quick)

Today a Moravian museum village on the south side of Winston-Salem, NC, Old Salem is known for its fresh-baked breads and buns, sugar cakes, and cookies. First stop for me is always the 200-year-old Winkler Bakery right on Old Salem's main street not only to stock up but also to watch yeast breads being shaped, then baked in wood-fired brick ovens. This chewy whole-wheat bread makes superb toast and even better sandwiches. Serve one loaf straightaway and freeze the second to enjoy another day. Snugly wrapped in foil and popped into a plastic zipper bag, it will keep "fresh" for about 3 months.

Old Salem Wheat 'n' Honey Bread

Makes Two 9 × 5 × 3-Inch Loaves

2½ cups warm water (105° to 115°F)

⅓ cup light golden honey

2 tablespoons raw sugar

2 envelopes (¾ ounce each) active dry yeast

1 cup nonfat dry milk powder

2 tablespoons lard (not vegetable shortening) or unsalted butter, at room temperature

1 large egg, well beaten

1 teaspoon salt

¼ teaspoon ground cumin

¼ teaspoon ground caraway or cardamom

¼ teaspoon freshly grated nutmeg

2 cups sifted unbleached all-purpose flour

6 to 6½ cups unsifted whole wheat flour

1. Combine warm water, honey, sugar, and yeast in large bowl and let stand about 10 minutes until frothy.

2. Add dry milk powder, lard, egg, salt, cumin, caraway, and nutmeg and beat until smooth. Mix in all-purpose flour, 1 cup at a time, then add just enough whole wheat flour to make stiff but workable dough.

3. Turn onto floured board and knead about 5 minutes until smooth and elastic. Shape into ball, place in well-buttered bowl, and turn buttered side up. Cover with clean dry cloth and let rise in warm spot away from drafts until doubled in bulk, about 1 hour.

4. Punch dough down, divide in half, and knead each half briskly 5 to 10 times. Shape into loaves and place in well buttered 9 × 5 × 3-inch loaf pans. Cover with clean dry cloth and again set in warm spot to rise until doubled in bulk, about 1 hour.

5. Toward end of rising period, preheat oven to 375°F. Slide risen loaves onto middle oven shelf—side by side but not touching—and bake until nicely browned and hollow sounding when thumped, 40 to 45 minutes.

6. Cool loaves in upright pans on wire racks 10 minutes, then loosen around edge with thin-blade spatula. Invert loaves on racks, turn right side up, and cool to room temperature before slicing.

This is an old, old recipe, old even when I picked it up decades ago in Iredell County, NC, where I'd arrived straight out of college to begin work as an assistant home demonstration agent. My mission? To teach 4-H club girls healthier ways to cook, safer ways to can and freeze food. To be honest, I learned more from them than they did from me. *Note: This bread slices more neatly if baked one day and served the next. It's particularly good spread with cream cheese and also makes delicious sandwiches.*

Peanut Butter Bread

Makes One 9 × 5 × 3-Inch Loaf

2¼ cups sifted all-purpose flour

1 cup lightly toasted coarsely chopped pecans (8 to 10 minutes at 350°F toasts them nicely)

½ cup firmly packed light brown sugar

2 teaspoons baking powder

½ teaspoon baking soda

1 teaspoon salt

¼ teaspoon freshly ground black pepper

1 cup buttermilk

⅔ cup firmly packed cream-style peanut butter

1 large egg, lightly beaten

1. Preheat oven to 325°F. Spritz 9 × 5 × 3-inch loaf pan with nonstick oil-and-flour baking spray and set aside. Spoon ¼ cup flour into small bowl, add pecans, and toss well; set aside.

2. Briskly whisk remaining flour, sugar, baking powder, baking soda, salt, and pepper in large bowl, then make a well in center of dry ingredients.

3. Whisk buttermilk and peanut butter in small bowl until smooth, then whisk in egg. Pour combined liquid ingredients into well in dry ingredients and stir only enough to combine. Fold in reserved pecans and all dredging flour. It's OK if a few floury specks show; they prove you haven't overbeaten the batter—it's quite thick. Scoop batter into pan, spreading to corners and smoothing top.

4. Rap pan on counter two or three times to expel large air bubbles, then slide onto middle oven shelf and bake 45 to 50 minutes until bread is browned and a cake tester inserted in middle of loaf comes out clean.

5. Cool loaf in upright pan on wire rack 15 minutes, loosen around edge with thin-blade spatula, and invert loaf on wire rack. Turn right side up and cool to room temperature before cutting. Better yet, wait until the next day to slice.

Always partial to quick breads, I've spent years dreaming up new recipes. This, my newest, puts three important Southern crops to good use: sweet potatoes, blueberries, and pecans. To boost the sweet potato flavor, I bake the potato (1 hour at 400°F), pricking it in several places before it goes into the oven. *Note:* Now that dried blueberries are widely available, I use them in this recipe. Fresh blueberries can be substituted but must be bone-dry. And frozen "blues" can be used as a last resort; they should be solidly frozen and bits of ice removed. If not, there'll be soggy spots in the bread. *Tip:* When making quick breads, I use a 2-quart, ovenproof glass measuring cup both to melt the butter (by microwave) and combine it with the sweet potatoes, OJ, molasses, and eggs. Saves dishwashing.

Sweet Potato Bread with Blueberries

Makes One 9 × 5 × 3-Inch Loaf

2 cups sifted all-purpose flour

¾ cup raw sugar

1½ teaspoons baking powder

½ teaspoon baking soda

1 teaspoon ground cinnamon

1 teaspoon ground ginger

½ teaspoon freshly grated nutmeg

½ teaspoon salt

1 cup coarsely chopped pecans, walnuts, black walnuts, or wild hickory nuts

¾ cup dried blueberries or 1 cup fresh or solidly frozen blueberries (see Note above)

1 cup firmly packed, puréed, cooked sweet potato (about 1 medium-large [8-ounce potato]; see headnote)

½ cup fresh orange juice

¼ cup molasses (not too dark)

¼ cup (½ stick) melted unsalted butter (see Tip above)

2 large eggs

1. Preheat oven to 350°F. Coat 9 × 5 × 3-inch loaf pan with nonstick oil-and-flour baking spray and set aside.

2. Whisk flour, sugar, baking powder, baking soda, cinnamon, ginger, nutmeg, and salt together in large mixing bowl. Add pecans and blueberries, toss well, then make a well in middle of dry ingredients.

3. Whisk sweet potato, orange juice, molasses, melted butter, and eggs until smooth in 2-quart measure (see Tip above) or small bowl. Pour into well in dry ingredients and stir only enough to combine. **Note:** It's good if a few floury specks show; they prove that you haven't overbeaten the batter.

4. Scoop batter into pan, spreading to corners, and bake on middle oven shelf about 1 hour until nicely browned and cake tester inserted in middle of loaf comes out clean.

5. Cool loaf in upright pan on a wire rack 15 minutes, loosen around edge with thin-blade spatula, then turn out on rack and cool completely before slicing.

This recipe comes from my thoroughly Southern niece Kim, who loves to bake. "This is a unique recipe," she says. "The bread smells exactly like green tomatoes and is one of the best sweet breads I have ever eaten. It's a great way to use up green tomatoes. To be honest, I don't remember where I got the recipe but it was from some obscure source." I've downsized Kim's recipe slightly and added a twist or two of my own. *Note:* Make sure the green tomatoes you use have heady green-tomato aroma, otherwise your bread will have no green tomato taste (it's delicate at best). You'll be pleased to know that there's no need to peel the tomatoes, in fact the skins add flavor and texture. Just core the tomatoes, chunk, and whiz in a food processor or electric blender—10 to 15 seconds should do it.

Green Tomato Bread

Makes One 9 × 5 × 3-Inch Loaf

2½ cups sifted all-purpose flour

1½ cups coarsely chopped pecans or ¾ cup each pecans and dark seedless raisins

1 teaspoon baking powder

¾ teaspoon baking soda

½ teaspoon salt

1 cup granulated sugar

⅓ cup raw sugar

2 large eggs

¾ cup corn, peanut, or other vegetable oil

1⅓ cups green tomato purée (about 2 medium tomatoes, ¾ to 1 pound; see Note above)

1½ teaspoons vanilla extract

1 teaspoon finely grated fresh ginger

1. Preheat oven to 350°F. Spritz a 9 × 5 × 3-inch baking pan well with nonstick oil-and-flour baking spray and set aside.

2. Spoon ¼ cup flour into small bowl, add pecans, and toss well; set aside. Whisk remaining flour with baking powder, baking soda, and salt in medium-size bowl and reserve.

3. Whisk remaining ingredients (granulated sugar though ginger) in large bowl until smooth. Add combined dry ingredients and fold in with a light touch—it's OK for a few floury specks to show. Fold in reserved pecans and dredging flour, taking care not to overmix. Scoop batter into pan, spread to edges, and smooth top.

4. Slide onto middle oven shelf and bake 50 to 60 minutes until richly browned and cake tester, inserted in middle of loaf, comes out clean.

5. Cool loaf in upright pan on wire rack 15 minutes, loosen around edge with small thin-blade spatula, then turn out on rack and cool right side up to room temperature before slicing.

I've always loved buttermilk biscuits pulled from a hissing-hot oven and crisply cooked, deeply smoky bacon almost as much. So why not, I thought, put these two Southern favorites together? I think you'll like the results. *Tip:* To save time, stack two slices bacon and snip crosswise with kitchen shears, then repeat with remaining four slices.

Bacon Biscuits

Makes 8 or 9

6	slices thickly sliced hickory-smoked bacon, cut crosswise at ¼-inch intervals (see Tip above)
2	cups sifted all-purpose flour
2	teaspoons baking powder
1	teaspoon salt
¼	teaspoon baking soda
⅓	cup firmly packed, well-chilled lard (not vegetable shortening) or 50-50 mix of lard and unsalted butter
¾	cup cold buttermilk

1. Preheat oven to 400°F.

2. Cook bacon in medium-size heavy skillet over moderate heat 10 to 12 minutes until all fat has rendered out and only crisp brown bits remain. With slotted spoon, lift bacon bits to paper toweling to drain. Pour drippings into small heatproof jar, cover, and refrigerate (use to make Casserole Corn Bread (page 162), Baked Shrimp Salad (page 105), and many other recipes in this book. I also use bacon drippings to dress spinach salads, collards, or turnip greens as well as to brown all manner of things).

3. Whisking briskly, combine flour, baking powder, salt, and baking soda in large mixing bowl. Add lard and with pastry blender, cut in until texture of lentils. Crumble in bacon and toss well. Forking briskly, add buttermilk and continue forking just until soft dough forms.

4. Turn onto lightly floured surface and knead 7 or 8 times—easy does it. With floured rolling pin, roll dough into circle ½ inch thick, then cut in rounds with lightly floured 2¾-inch biscuit cutter. Reroll scraps and cut.

5. Space biscuits 1 inch apart on ungreased baking sheet and bake in lower third of oven 12 to 15 minutes until nicely puffed and lightly browned.

6. Pile biscuits in napkin-lined basket, rush them to the table, and serve with plenty of butter.

Biscuits are the South's staff of life (with corn breads a close second) and clever cooks stir in everything from benne seeds to sweet potatoes to sharp Cheddar. Though cheese biscuits are usually baked full-size and served with meals, Southern hostesses sometimes make them bite-size, slip in slivers of Smithfield ham, and pass with cocktails. Tiny biscuits need less oven time—perhaps only 10 minutes; the recipe here should yield about three dozen 1-inch biscuits. *Note:* It's best to use one of the fine self-rising Southern flours for these biscuits; lard, too, because it produces flakier biscuits and adds subtle meat flavor. *Tip:* If self-rising flour is not available, use all-purpose and add 1½ teaspoons baking powder and ½ teaspoon salt.

Cheddar Biscuits

Makes About 1¼ Dozen

2 cups sifted self-rising flour (see Note and Tip above)

¼ teaspoon baking soda

¼ teaspoon ground hot red pepper (cayenne)

⅓ cup firmly packed cold lard (not vegetable shortening; see Note above)

½ cup coarsely shredded sharp Cheddar cheese (the sharpest you can find)

¾ cup cold buttermilk

1. Preheat oven to 425°F.

2. Whisk flour, baking soda, and cayenne together in large mixing bowl, then with pastry blender, cut in lard until texture of coarse meal. Add cheese and toss well. Make well in middle of dry ingredients, pour in buttermilk, then fork lightly to form soft but workable dough.

3. Turn dough onto lightly floured surface, knead 3 or 4 times, then using lightly floured rolling pin, roll to ½-inch thickness. Cut into rounds using floured 2½- to 2¾-inch biscuit cutter and space about 1½ inches apart on large ungreased baking sheet. Gather scraps, reroll, and cut as before.

4. Bake in lower third of oven 12 to 15 minutes until puffed and lightly browned.

5. Serve at once—no stinting on butter. Or, if you prefer, cool, split, and sandwich back together with slivers of Smithfield or country ham—the thinner, the better.

Not everyone—not even all Southerners—have a light hand when it comes to making biscuits. The most common problem? Two problems, actually: cutting the lard, butter, or shortening in too fine and overmixing the dough after the milk's added. For the biscuit-impaired, I offer this easy recipe in which heavy cream does double duty, substituting both for lard and milk. I think you'll find these biscuits supremely tender when served straight from the oven. Split them at once, tuck in pats of "sweet" (unsalted) butter, and let them melt before taking that first bite.

Feathery Four-Ingredient Biscuits

Makes 10 to 12

2 cups sifted all-purpose flour

1 tablespoon (3 teaspoons) baking powder

¼ teaspoon salt

1 cup heavy cream, whipped to soft peaks

1. Preheat oven to 450°F.

2. Sift flour, baking powder, and salt together into large bowl and make well in center. Scoop whipped cream into well and fork briskly to form a soft dough.

3. Turn dough onto lightly floured surface and knead 20 seconds. With lightly floured rolling pin, roll dough into circle ½ inch thick, then with floured 2- to 2½-inch biscuit cutter, cut into rounds.

4. Space biscuits about 1½ inches apart on ungreased baking sheet and bake on middle oven shelf 10 to 12 minutes until puffed and lightly browned.

5. Rush biscuits to the table and serve.

Pecans are of course the South's favorite nut, but hazelnuts, now available at high-end groceries, are increasingly popular, and I particularly like them in these biscuits. If fresh blanched hazelnuts are available, by all means buy them. Otherwise, toast the unblanched as directed below, then rub briskly in a clean dish towel to slake off the skins. Don't worry about any recalcitrant bits; they'll add color. Pick a dry sunny day for making these biscuits; in humid weather this soft dough will absorb atmospheric moisture and be difficult to shape. *Note:* Most biscuits are baked on ungreased baking sheets but because this dough's rich, I lightly spritz the pans with nonstick cooking spray. I also use bright aluminum baking sheets; darkly coated ones cause the biscuits to overbrown on the bottom.

Sweet Potato Biscuits with Toasted Hazelnuts or Pecans

Makes 1 Dozen

2 cups sifted all-purpose flour (not a soft Southern flour)

1 tablespoon (3 teaspoons) baking powder

½ teaspoon salt

½ teaspoon freshly ground black pepper

½ teaspoon freshly grated nutmeg

¾ cup finely chopped, richly toasted hazelnuts or pecans (12 to 14 minutes at 350°F)

6 tablespoons cold unsalted butter, diced

1 cup firmly packed puréed unseasoned baked sweet potato mixed with ½ cup milk

2 tablespoons light cream or half-and-half

1. Preheat oven to 400°F. Lightly spritz two baking sheets with nonstick cooking spray and set aside.

2. Combine flour, baking powder, salt, pepper, and nutmeg in large mixing bowl, add nuts, and toss well. Scatter pieces of butter over dry ingredients, then with pastry blender, cut in until size of lentils. Add sweet potato mixture and fork lightly just until soft dough forms.

3. Turn onto well floured pastry cloth and pat into circle about ¾ inch thick, flouring hands and dough as needed.

4. With well floured 2¾- to 3-inch round cutter, cut dough into rounds and space 1½ inches apart on baking sheets.

5. Bake, one sheet at a time, on middle oven rack about 20 minutes until golden brown.

6. Remove biscuits from oven, lightly brush with cream, then split while hot, tuck in pats of butter, and enjoy.

Such an easy recipe if you turn your food processor into a bread machine. Proof the yeast in the machine, mix and knead the dough there, even let it rise in the work bowl. But, make a note; you'll need a large (11- to 14-cup) processor with plenty of prowess. *Note:* For ¾ cup mashed sweet potato, you'll need one large sweet potato. Pierce with a fork and bake about 1 hour at 400°F.

Sweet Potato Focaccia

Makes 6 to 8 Servings

¾ cup firmly packed baked sweet potato blended with ⅓ cup hot water (mixture must be between 105° and 115°F; see Note above)

⅓ cup unsifted semolina (durum wheat or "pizza" flour—available in upscale groceries)

1 tablespoon active dry yeast (about 1½ envelopes, ¾ ounce each)

1 tablespoon raw sugar

2½ to 3 cups unsifted all-purpose flour

2 tablespoons extra-virgin olive oil

1 teaspoon salt

3 tablespoons extra-virgin olive oil mixed with 1 tablespoon coarsely chopped fresh rosemary (Topping)

1. Combine sweet potato mixture, semolina, yeast, and sugar in heavy-duty food processor work bowl fitted with chopping blade and pulse 4 or 5 times. Scrape work bowl, cover, and let stand 15 minutes.

2. With machine running, add 1¼ cups all-purpose flour (easier if you insert paper cone in feed tube). Scrape work bowl and taking care to dodge blade, redistribute dough so it's same height all round.

3. With motor running, add another 1¼ cups all-purpose flour, then olive oil and salt. Process 10 seconds. Dough should be soft and workable, not sticky, so add several more tablespoons flour, if necessary. Once again, carefully redistribute dough and process 20 seconds. Let dough rest 5 minutes, then process 20 seconds more.

4. Leaving blade in place, carefully redistribute dough and mark level on outside of work bowl. Let dough rise in sealed work bowl until doubled in bulk—about 40 minutes.

5. About 20 minutes before dough has risen fully, preheat oven to 425°F. Spritz 15 × 10 × 1-inch jelly-roll pan with nonstick cooking spray.

6. Pulse fully risen dough 4 or 5 times to "punch" down, then churn 20 seconds nonstop—dough will roll into a ball. Let dough rest 10 minutes in sealed work bowl. Carefully remove chopping blade and scrape dough onto lightly floured surface.

7. Quickly gather dough into ball, then greasing fingers lightly with Topping, pat dough over bottom of pan, pulling and stretching until pan is covered with thin, even layer.

8. Cover with wax paper and let rise until doubled in bulk—about 40 minutes. Again greasing fingers with Topping, dimple surface of dough at 2-inch intervals, then drizzle remaining Topping evenly over all.

9. Slide onto middle oven shelf and bake until focaccia is golden brown and sounds hollow when thumped—12 to 15 minutes.

10. Cool focaccia in upright pan on wire rack 15 minutes.

11. Cut into large squares or rectangles and serve. Give each person a little ramekin of fruity olive oil in which to dip chunks of focaccia.

The South is sweet potato country with my home state of North Carolina producing nearly 40 percent of America's crop and Louisiana and Mississippi not far behind. Tabor City in North Carolina's sandy coastal plains is known as the "Yam Capital of the World" though what it grows are sweet potatoes—yams aren't even botanical cousins. Perhaps this explains why Tar Heels are so fond of sweet potatoes and so inventive about using them. Does anyone else turn them into corn bread as good as this? If so, I've not tasted it. This is the recipe to try when you have leftover mashed sweet potato, preferably unseasoned. *Tip:* To measure mashed sweet potatoes for this recipe, pack lightly in a dry measure (the kind used to measure flour) and level off with the edge of a thin-blade spatula.

Sweet Potato Corn Bread
Makes One 9 x 9 x 2-Inch Loaf

2 cups unsifted stone-ground cornmeal (white or yellow)

2 tablespoons sugar

1 teaspoon baking powder

½ teaspoon baking soda

½ teaspoon salt

½ teaspoon freshly ground black pepper

¼ teaspoon freshly grated nutmeg

1 cup lightly packed mashed, cooked sweet potato (see Tip above)

1 cup buttermilk, at room temperature

2 large eggs, lightly beaten

¼ cup vegetable oil, melted lard (not vegetable shortening), or bacon drippings

1. Preheat oven to 400°F. Spritz 9 × 9 × 2-inch baking pan with nonstick cooking spray and set aside.

2. Combine all dry ingredients (cornmeal through nutmeg) in large mixing bowl and make well in center.

3. Scoop sweet potato into medium-size bowl, then with hand electric beater, gradually beat in—in this order—buttermilk, eggs, then oil, beating after each addition until smooth. Pour into well in dry ingredients and stir only enough to mix—it's OK if batter is lumpy. Scoop batter into pan, spreading to corners.

4. Slide onto middle oven shelf and bake about 25 minutes until nicely browned and cake tester inserted in middle of loaf comes out clean.

5. Serve straightaway with plenty of butter.

Has anyone ever counted the many types of corn bread popular down South? I wonder because I'm forever discovering ones I don't know, like this one from the Eastern Shore of Maryland. To be honest, it's more vegetable than bread, the perfect side dish for baked ham, roast pork, turkey, or chicken. *Note:* Old-time recipes called for a 1-pound can of cream-style corn—too sugary for my taste. I prefer the fresher flavor of frozen corn kernels. Moreover, they're a snap to "cream" in a food processor. *Tip:* In some parts of the country, I'm told, sour cream is no longer available in 8-ounce containers. No problem. Simply substitute 1 cup firmly packed sour cream.

Casserole Corn Bread

Makes 6 to 8 Servings

1 package (16 ounces) frozen whole-kernel corn, thawed but not drained (see Note above)

1 cup stone-ground white or yellow cornmeal

1½ teaspoons baking powder

½ teaspoon baking soda

½ teaspoon salt

½ teaspoon freshly ground black pepper

¼ teaspoon dried leaf thyme, crumbled (optional; not Southern but a welcome addition)

2 large eggs, well beaten

1 container (8 ounces) sour cream (see Tip above)

¼ cup each hissing-hot bacon drippings and vegetable oil, combined (½ cup in all)

1. Preheat oven to 375°F. Spritz 1½-quart casserole with nonstick cooking spray and set aside.

2. Alternately churn and pulse corn kernels in food processor until you have cream-style corn, then scoop into large mixing bowl. Whisk cornmeal with baking powder, baking soda, salt, pepper, and thyme, if desired, in second bowl and set aside.

3. Mix eggs and sour cream into corn, then fold in combined dry ingredients—easy does it. If you overmix at this point, your corn bread will be tough. Stirring lightly, drizzle in hot bacon drippings mixture. Scoop batter into casserole, spreading to edge and smoothing top.

4. Slide corn bread onto middle oven shelf and bake uncovered 25 to 30 minutes until nicely browned and cake tester inserted in center comes out clean.

5. Serve oven-hot. And don't forget to put out plenty of butter—room temperature, please—so that everyone can mix a little (or a lot) of it into their corn bread.

Not every Southern corn bread calls for stone-ground meal, in fact these corn sticks should be made with the granular yellow meal most supermarkets sell. Equally important are the pans you use. If corn sticks are to be crunchy-brown on the outside, you must use cast-iron corn stick pans and preheat them along with the oven. Call me old-fashioned, but I think the pans our grandmothers used make far better corn sticks than new ones with nonstick coatings. I bought mine at a tag sale but have seen them in country stores all over the South. They're also available online. *Note:* Lard is rendered hog fat, not vegetable shortening. Corn sticks, indeed all simple corn breads, have better flavor if made with lard and/or bacon drippings.

Crunchy Corn Sticks

Makes 12 to 14

1 cup sifted all-purpose flour

1 tablespoon sugar

2 teaspoons baking powder

½ teaspoon salt

¼ teaspoon baking soda

¼ teaspoon freshly ground black pepper

1 cup yellow cornmeal (see headnote)

½ cup boiling water

¼ cup melted lard (see Note above) or bacon drippings or 2 tablespoons of each

2 large eggs, beaten until frothy

1 cup milk, at room temperature

1. Rub two cast-iron corn stick pans generously with lard or bacon drippings, slide onto middle oven shelf, and preheat oven to 375°F.

2. Meanwhile, whisk flour, sugar, baking powder, salt, baking soda, and pepper together in small bowl and set aside.

3. Place cornmeal in large heatproof bowl, add water and melted lard, and stir until meal thickens somewhat. Beat in eggs, then milk. Finally, with the lightest of touches, fold in combined dry ingredients.

4. Remove hot corn stick pans from oven and spoon batter into each hollow, filling until level with rim.

5. Return pans to middle oven shelf and bake 25 to 30 minutes until corn sticks are nicely browned.

6. Serve straight from the oven and don't forget to put out plenty of butter.

To some Southerners batter bread is spoon bread, to others it's a thin cornmeal batter poured into a hissing-hot iron skillet and baked in the oven. The one here is spoon bread, a sort of cornmeal soufflé. Purists insist that there be no sugar, but many Southerners like a little sweetening in their corn bread, so I've made it optional. I've also added a bit of freshly grated nutmeg to the recipe—far from traditional but nice, I think. It, too, is optional. Batter bread is delicious with roast pork, chicken, or turkey and often takes the place of mashed potatoes (like them, it's served with plenty of butter). If batter bread is on the menu, I don't serve biscuits though many other Southerners do. Or perhaps a basket of fresh-baked yeast rolls.

Buttermilk Batter Bread

Makes 6 Servings

2 cups unsifted stone-ground cornmeal (yellow or white)

2 teaspoons sugar (optional)

1 teaspoon salt

¼ teaspoon freshly ground black pepper

¼ teaspoon freshly grated nutmeg (optional)

2½ cups boiling water

3 tablespoons unsalted butter

1 tablespoon bacon drippings

2 large eggs, separated

1 teaspoon baking soda

1½ cups buttermilk or sour milk

1. Preheat oven to 400°F. Lightly butter 2½-quart soufflé dish and set aside.

2. Combine cornmeal, sugar, if desired, salt, pepper, and if you like, nutmeg in large heatproof bowl. Add boiling water, butter, and bacon drippings and whisk hard until butter melts, mixture begins to thicken, and there are no lumps. Cool 10 minutes, whisking occasionally, then add egg yolks and again whisk until smooth.

3. Stir baking soda into buttermilk and the instant it foams, blend into cornmeal mixture. Beat egg whites to soft peaks and fold gently into batter till no streaks of white or yellow remain. Turn batter into soufflé dish and spread to edge.

4. Slide onto middle oven shelf, reduce oven temperature at once to 375°F, and bake uncovered about 45 minutes until puffy and delicately browned.

5. Serve oven-hot as an accompaniment to meat along with plenty of butter. **Note:** Like a soufflé, batter bread collapses soon after it leaves the oven, so waste no time serving it.

So old it's virtually forgotten, this quick bread is made with leftover rice and rice cooking water. Back when rice was "king" in the Carolina Lowcountry, Philpy was served with pride on polished plantation dining tables. But only cooks with a light touch could make it properly. *Note:* For me, the secret of mushy rice is to cook it like pasta, that is in plenty of boiling water until it's so tender you can mush the grains between your fingers. Drain the rice well, saving both rice and cooking water. The best rice to use? Long-grain white rice. Avoid quick-cooking or converted rice. Neither will have the proper texture or flavor. *Tip:* I've streamlined the method of mixing by using a food processor to mash the rice into a paste both soft and smooth. The mixing can be done by machine, too, even the flours can be pulsed in. Rice flour contains no gluten so no amount of beating will toughen a rice batter. There is all-purpose flour, yes, but this bread contains so little it doesn't matter. I do fold the beaten egg whites in by hand, however, lest they deflate and lose their power to leaven this delicate bread, which contains no baking powder, no baking soda, no yeast.

Philpy

Makes 6 to 8 Servings

1¼ cups very soft cooked long-grain rice (see Note above)

⅞ cup rice cooking water, at room temperature

¾ teaspoon salt

2 large eggs, separated

½ cup unsifted rice flour

⅓ cup sifted all-purpose flour

1. Preheat oven to 425°F. Butter 9-inch pie pan well and set aside.

2. Pulse rice several times in food processor, then with motor running, drizzle cooking water down feed tube. Add salt and alternately churn and pulse until smooth. Pulse in egg yolks.

3. Scatter rice flour over surface of rice paste, pulse gently to combine, then pulse in all-purpose flour just enough to combine—easy does it.

4. Transfer batter to large bowl. Beat whites with hand electric mixer in separate bowl to soft peaks, then using large rubber spatula, fold into batter gently but thoroughly. Scoop all into pie pan, spreading to edge.

5. Slide onto middle oven shelf and bake uncovered about 25 minutes until puffed and brown and cake tester inserted in center comes out clean.

6. Rush Philpy to table, cut into wedges, and put out a plate of unsalted butter. Like fresh-baked biscuits, Philpy should be split and buttered while hot enough to melt the butter.

Southerners have always had a light touch with breads and these oh-so-light muffins prove the point. They're delicious at any meal and need nothing more to accompany than fresh "sweet butter" though homemade jam or jelly wouldn't be amiss (my favorite's peach).

Yeast Muffins

Makes 1 Dozen

¾ cup milk

¼ cup (½ stick) unsalted butter

¼ cup sugar

1 teaspoon salt

½ teaspoon freshly grated nutmeg

1 envelope (¾ ounce) active dry yeast

2 large eggs, well beaten

2½ cups unsifted all-purpose flour

1. Heat milk, butter, sugar, salt, and nutmeg in small saucepan over moderate heat, stirring now and then, until butter melts. Pour into large mixing bowl and when mixture has cooled to between 105° and 115°F, stir in yeast and let stand several minutes until dissolved.

2. Mix in eggs, then flour, and beat hard until elastic; dough will be sticky. Transfer to large oiled bowl and lightly oil top of dough. Cover bowl with clean, dry cloth, and let rise in warm spot until doubled in bulk, about 35 minutes.

3. Preheat oven to 400°F. Coat 12 muffin pan cups with nonstick cooking spray and set aside.

4. Punch dough down, then using oiled ice cream scoop or two oiled spoons, scoop dough, a little bit at a time, into pans until each muffin pan cup is about two-thirds full.

5. Smooth tops with oiled fingers, cover with wax paper, and let rise in warm spot 20 to 25 minutes until slightly rounded above muffin pan cups.

6. Slide onto middle oven shelf and bake about 15 minutes until puffed, lightly browned, and hollow sounding when thumped.

7. Serve hot with butter and, if you like, fruit preserves, jam, or jelly.

The classic Southern Sally Lunn is a feathery yeast bread baked in an angel cake or Bundt pan, slightly sweet, slightly buttery. The first time I tasted it—years and years ago at the King's Arms Tavern in Colonial Williamsburg, VA—I thought it the best bread ever. I still do and include a recipe for it in my *Love Affair with Southern Cooking* (2007), which won a James Beard Best Cookbook Award. Equally rich, these muffins are leavened with baking powder instead of yeast—quicker to make and bake. Serve them right out of the oven with plenty of unsalted butter.

Sally Lunn Muffins

Makes About 1½ Dozen

3	cups sifted all-purpose flour
4	teaspoons baking powder
¾	teaspoon salt
½	cup (1 stick) unsalted butter, slightly softened
½	cup sugar
3	large eggs
1½	cups half-and-half

1. Preheat oven to 350°F. Coat 18 standard-size muffin pan cups with nonstick cooking spray and set aside.

2. Whisk flour, baking powder, and salt together in large bowl and set aside.

3. Cream butter at high electric mixer speed 1 to 2 minutes until fluffy, then with mixer at low speed, add sugar gradually. Raise mixer speed to high and continue beating 2 to 3 minutes more until nearly white.

4. Reduce mixer speed to moderately high, and add eggs one by one, beating well after each addition.

5. Add half-and-half to butter mixture alternately with combined dry ingredients, beginning and ending with dry and mixing by hand after each addition only enough to combine. It's good if a few floury specks show—they prove you haven't overbeaten the batter. Spoon batter into muffin pans so each cup is two-thirds full.

6. Slide onto shelf in lower third of oven and bake about 25 minutes until puffed and lightly browned.

7. Pile in napkin-lined bread basket and serve straightaway.

Bran muffins we all know, date muffins, blueberry muffins, raisin muffins, even apple muffins. But rice muffins? They're a specialty of the Deep South where rice plantations made men rich, especially in the Lowcountry where long-grain Carolina gold flourished. This particular recipe comes from farther south—the state of Mississippi, which to this day is one of America's leading producers of white rice along with Louisiana directly next door. This is the recipe to try when you have some leftover rice going begging. All you need is 1 cup.

Rice Muffins

Makes 10

1½ cups unsifted all-purpose flour
2 tablespoons sugar
2 teaspoons baking powder
½ teaspoon salt
1 large egg
⅔ cup milk
¼ cup (½ stick) melted unsalted butter
1 cup cooked long-grain rice, preferably unseasoned

1. Preheat oven to 375°F. Spritz 10 muffin pan cups with nonstick cooking spray and set aside.

2. Whisk together flour, sugar, baking powder, and salt in medium-size bowl and make well in center. Whisk egg in small bowl until frothy, then gradually whisk in milk and melted butter.

3. Add egg mixture to well in dry ingredients and with rubber spatula and scraping bowl often, mix only enough to combine. Do not overbeat—batter should be lumpy. Fold in rice. Spoon batter into muffin pan cups, dividing amount evenly.

4. Slide pan onto middle oven shelf and bake about 20 minutes until muffins are puffed, lightly browned, and centers spring back when gently pressed.

5. Serve hot with butter and, if you like, fruit preserves, jam, or jelly.

Peach cobbler most of us know well, peach pie, too, and of course peach ice cream. But in the South where peach orchards overrun the hills, good cooks stir tree-ripened fruits into a variety of breads and that includes muffins. Wait till local peaches are ripe before you bake these. To boost their flavor, I add a few coarsely chopped dried peaches, then glaze the muffins with unsieved peach preserves as soon as they come from the oven. *Tip:* To save time, I not only processor-purée the peaches but also mix the batter by food processor.

Peach Muffins

Makes 1 Dozen

2¼ cups sifted all-purpose flour

½ cup finely chopped pecans

¼ cup sugar

2½ teaspoons baking powder

½ teaspoon baking soda

¼ teaspoon freshly grated nutmeg

¼ teaspoon salt

1 cup firmly packed fresh peach purée (2 to 3 medium peaches—about 1 pound; see Tip above)

⅓ cup finely chopped dried peaches

1 large egg

3 tablespoons unsalted butter (no substitute), softened

1 tablespoon fresh lemon juice

½ teaspoon almond extract

⅓ cup peach preserves

1. Preheat oven to 400°F. Spritz 12 muffin pan cups with nonstick oil-and-flour baking spray and set aside. Whisk flour, pecans, sugar, baking powder, baking soda, nutmeg, and salt in medium-size bowl and set aside.

2. Combine peach purée, dried peaches, egg, butter, lemon juice, and almond extract in food processor and pulse 3 or 4 times to combine. Add flour mixture, pulse 3 or 4 times—only enough to combine, no more or your muffins will be tough. Scrape side of processor bowl and stir batter once. Spoon into muffin pan cups so each is two-thirds full.

3. Slide pan onto middle oven shelf and bake about 25 minutes until muffins begin to pull from sides of cups and cake tester inserted in middle of one muffin comes out clean.

4. Transfer pan of muffins to wire rack and brush immediately with peach preserves. Cool muffins in upright pan on wire rack 10 minutes, then loosen around edges with thin-blade spatula and lift muffins onto wire rack.

5. Serve warm or at room temperature with, or without, butter.

I have no idea why these "dainties" are called Mississippi Muffins although I do know they're popular in this Gulf state and have, in fact, eaten them in the home of good Hattiesburg friends. Usually baked as "minis," these show up at buffets and on tea tables. But I see no reason not to bake full-size Mississippi Muffins and serve as a snack or with dessert. Have you noticed that "muffin" has become a euphemism for "cupcake"? Even the method of mixing used here is one used for butter cakes. I'd be tempted to call these Mississippi Cupcakes and be done with it—less alliterative but more accurate.

Mississippi Muffins

Makes About 1 Dozen Full-Size Muffins, 3½ Dozen Mini Muffins

2 cups sifted all-purpose flour

¾ cup coarsely chopped pecans, walnuts, black walnuts, or hickory nuts

1 teaspoon baking soda

1 teaspoon ground cinnamon

¾ teaspoon ground allspice

½ teaspoon ground ginger

½ teaspoon salt

¼ teaspoon ground cloves

½ cup (1 stick) unsalted butter, slightly softened

1 cup granulated sugar

1 large egg

1 cup firmly packed applesauce (preferably homemade)

1 tablespoon confectioner's (10X) sugar (for dusting)

1. Preheat oven to 375°F. Spritz about 42 mini muffin pan cups or 12 standard muffin pan cups with nonstick cooking spray and set aside.

2. Spoon ¼ cup flour into small bowl, add pecans, and toss to dredge; set aside. Combine remaining flour, baking soda, cinnamon, allspice, ginger, salt, and cloves by whisking in large bowl, and set aside also.

3. Cream butter in large electric mixer bowl by beating at high speed 1 to 2 minutes until fluffy, add granulated sugar, and cream at high speed about 2 minutes until almost white. Beat in egg.

4. With mixer at low speed, add combined dry ingredients alternately with applesauce, beginning and ending with dry and beating after each addition only enough to combine. Fold in pecans and all dredging flour by hand.

5. Spoon batter into muffin pans so each cup is two-thirds full. Slide onto middle oven shelf and bake until puffed, browned, and springy when touched, 13 to 15 minutes for mini muffins and about 20 minutes for standard muffins.

6. Cool muffins in upright pans on wire racks 10 minutes, then remove from pans, turn muffins right side up, and cool to room temperature. Sift confectioner's sugar over muffins until lightly dusted.

Though not very sweet, shortbread is a tea party favorite throughout the South and none is better than that made in Carolina Lowcountry where rice is grown and milled. Here, cooks who pride themselves on their light and crumbly shortbreads will tell you that the secret is adding a little rice flour to the mix. If unavailable, use 1⅞ cup (2 cups minus 2 tablespoons) sifted all-purpose flour and 2 tablespoons unsifted cornstarch. *Note:* The key to making good shortbread is the temperature of the butter. It should be about the consistency of vegetable shortening but by no means substitute shortening—or one of those artificial soft butters—for real butter. Only old-fashioned stick butter—preferably unsalted—makes good shortbread.

Lowcountry Shortbread

Makes 6 to 8 Servings

½ cup (1 stick) unsalted butter, slightly softened (see Note above)

⅓ cup superfine sugar (not confectioner's sugar)

1½ cups sifted all-purpose flour combined with ½ cup unsifted rice flour (see headnote)

1. Preheat oven to 325°F.

2. Cream butter in medium-size bowl with hand electric mixer 1 to 1½ minutes at high speed until nearly white. With mixer at low speed, add sugar gradually, then beat at high speed about 2 minutes until fluffy and sugar is completely dissolved.

3. Work flour mixture in with fingers until uniformly crumbly. Squeeze a bit of dough; if it holds together, no further mixing needed.

4. Scoop dough into middle of ungreased baking sheet and pat into a round ¾ inch thick.

5. Bake on middle oven shelf 35 to 40 minutes until fairly firm and the color of ivory.

6. Transfer—baking sheet and all—to wire rack and cool shortbread to room temperature.

7. To serve, cut into slim wedges or break into chunks.

part 2

The
Sweets

I've always wondered why Southerners have such an insatiable sweet tooth and have come up with a couple of theories:

1. Old-timey cooks knew that sugar was a natural preservative and that recipes loaded with it weren't likely to spoil in sultry Southern climes. In my opinion, there's no better proof than our vast repertoire of achingly sweet "chest" or keeping pies—better known as chess.

2. Sugarcane was (and still is) grown in the Deep South and chunks of it were the lollipops of yesterday's children. I've even seen today's children sucking sugary shards in the cane fields of Louisiana. And not so long ago, either.

Either—or both—would give anyone a serious sweet tooth. I, myself, didn't discover chess pie until I was in the first grade (my parents being transplants from the Midwest). I'll never forget the day. As I made my way down the cafeteria line, I noticed clustered at the end among the desserts a wedge of pie unlike anything I'd ever seen. It was the color of amber, crackly on top, but jelly-like underneath as though caramels had softened on a sunny windowsill.

I grabbed a piece, shoved my pork chops and sweet slaw aside, and took my first bite of brown sugar pie. From that day forward, I was hooked—not only for brown sugar pie and lemon chess pie but also for

every other chess pie the school cafeteria served.

Before long, I was baking them myself as well as sampling every Southern sweet I encountered and, needless to add, developing a sweet tooth as ravenous as any Southerner's.

Over time, I discovered dozens of strictly Southern desserts—the crisps and cobblers, the puddings and pies, the cakes and cookies. The plain, the fancy, the classic, the contemporary. I learned to bake them all—or almost all. And now count them among my all-time favorites. Many appear in my *A Love Affair with Southern Cooking* (2007), but dozens more did not.

And these are the sweets you'll find in the pages that follow: Frankie Roach's Scuppernong Pie • Great Smokies Jelly Pie • Ruby Red Chess Pie • Pecan Tassies • Japanese Fruit Pie • Water Lily Pie • Key Lime Cheesecake • Praline Cheesecake • Right-off-the-Tree Peach Crisp • Appalachian Apple Crumble • Confederate Rice Pudding • Muscadine Mystery Cake • Bourbon-Glazed Sweet Potato Pound Cake • Lord Baltimore Cake • Smith Island Ten-Layer Cake • Red Velvet Cake • Hummingbird Cake • Wild Persimmon Bars with Lime Glaze • Grandmommy's Recipe for Moldy Mice • Angel Kisses • and many more.

chapter five

Pies

& pastries

I found this old Southern recipe in my mother's recipe file and to be honest, I don't believe she ever made it. Illinois born-and-bred, she was an inveterate (obsessive?) recipe collector constantly swapping recipes with Southern friends at various club meetings. Usually meticulous about noting recipe source in the upper right-hand corner of each index card, here she wrote simply "an old Southern recipe." I find this pie crust particularly good for juicy fruit pies as well as for savory pot pies. *Note:* If you need only a pie shell or pot pie top crust, halve the recipe but do add an entire egg yolk—a small one.

Old Hand Egg Pastry

Makes Enough for a 9-Inch Double-Crust Pie

2¼ cups sifted all-purpose flour

1 tablespoon sugar

½ teaspoon salt

½ cup (1 stick) unsalted butter (no substitute), cut into pats

3 tablespoons firmly packed lard (not vegetable shortening)

¼ cup cold water (about)

1 large egg yolk, lightly beaten

1 tablespoon fresh lemon juice or cider vinegar

1. Combine flour, sugar, and salt in large mixing bowl. Scatter butter pats and lard over combined dry ingredients and with pastry blender, cut in until texture of coarse meal.

2. Forking briskly, drizzle water, then egg yolk, then lemon juice over all and continue forking until you can gather mixture into a soft but manageable dough. If dough is too crumbly, fork in a little additional water.

3. Shape dough into ball, halve, then roll one half at a time or as individual recipes direct. **Note:** Dough can be made a day or so ahead of time, wrapped in plastic food wrap, and refrigerated. Let come to room temperature before rolling.

Why cover sunny peak-of-season peaches with a top crust? Why not showcase their beauty in an open-face pie? In Southern "peach country," many orchards hang out pick-your-own signs while others set up displays of just-off-the-trees peaches ready and waiting for a recipe like this. *Tip:* Freestone varieties are best, ditto peaches so ripe their skins slip right off—no blanching needed.

Open-Face Peach Pie

Makes 6 to 8 Servings

6	cups sliced, peeled, bursting-with-flavor medium-large peaches (about 3 pounds; see Tip above)
1½	tablespoons fresh lemon juice
1	teaspoon finely grated fresh ginger
1	cup sugar
6	tablespoons unsifted all-purpose flour
¼	teaspoon freshly grated nutmeg
¼	teaspoon salt
1	9-inch unbaked pie shell with a high fluted edge (see About Frozen Pie Shells, page 23)
1	cup heavy cream

1. Slide rimmed heavy-duty baking sheet onto middle oven shelf and preheat oven to 425°F.

2. Toss peaches with lemon juice and ginger in large nonreactive bowl and set aside. In second bowl combine sugar, flour, nutmeg, and salt and set aside.

3. Arrange one layer of peaches in pie shell and sprinkle generously with sugar mixture. Continue layering peaches into pie shell, sprinkling each with sugar mixture until pie shell is full, arranging top layer of peaches as artfully as possible. Drizzle cream evenly over all.

4. Set pie in oven on preheated baking sheet and bake 5 minutes. Reduce oven temperature to 350°F and bake pie 50 to 55 minutes longer until filling is bubbly and crust nicely browned. **Note:** If crimped edge is browning too fast, cover with strips of foil.

5. Transfer pie from oven to wire rack and cool to room temperature; this gives peach juices time to thicken a bit.

6. Cut pie into wedges and serve.

Also called Grape Hull Pie because the hulls (Southern-speak for skins) go into the filling, this old North Carolina recipe dates back to the days when everything was cooked from scratch and nothing was wasted. It came to me in a roundabout way. While I was researching this book, Kathi Purvis, food editor of *The Charlotte Observer*, answered my call for a Grape Hull Pie recipe. She knew a Charlotte lady who made an amazing scuppernong pie, skins and all. "Though I only met Babs Highfill when I joined St. Martin's Episcopal Church," Kathi explained, "I already knew her as 'the scuppernong pie lady'." Babs had given two pies to an *Observer* colleague of Kathi's who'd written an article on the historic neighborhood in which Babs lives—one pie to share at the office, another to take home. Kathi ate a slice, then "made a note of the pie for a possible future column. In no time I not only had 'the scuppernong pie lady's' famous recipe but also its back story." Frankie Roach, it turns out, was Babs Highfill's next-door neighbor in Lumberton, NC, in the early years of her marriage, a neighbor so kind she was "at the door with a chess pie the day our moving van arrived." The widow of a retired banker and well into her 80s at the time (late '70s), Frankie was a superb cook and skilled seamstress. "The scuppernong pie," Babs told me, "was one Frankie's mother had taught her to make, indeed with her mother working at the grist mill on the family farm, Frankie cooked most of the meals herself. She couldn't have been more than eleven and she never lost her enthusiasm for cooking." *Notes:* If scuppernong skins are to slip off easily, the grapes must be dead-ripe. For a rosy-red filling, use a 50-50 mix of scuppernongs and muscadines—but no other grapes, please (only these Southern grapes have the intense wild grape flavor needed). If a lattice top crust seems too fussy, cover the filling with a circle of pastry, crimp, then add a few decorative cuts to serve as steam vents. If pressed for time, use a prepared pie crust (see About Prepared Pastry Circles, page 23).

Frankie Roach's Scuppernong Pie

Makes 6 to 8 Servings

6 cups fully ripe scuppernong and/or muscadine grapes (about 2 pounds), washed well

2 tablespoons quick-cooking tapioca

1 tablespoon cornstarch

1 cup sugar, or to taste

1 large egg, lightly beaten

1½ tablespoons fresh lemon juice

Finely grated zest of 1 large orange

¼ teaspoon salt

Old Hand Egg Pastry (page 180)

1. Working over a large fine sieve set over a large bowl, halve grapes, then squeeze lightly to pop pulp from skins. Place pulp in small nonreactive saucepan and skins in medium-large nonreactive saucepan. Pour grape juice in bottom of bowl into 1-cup glass measure and set aside. Also set pan of grape skins aside.

2. Simmer grape pulp uncovered over moderately low heat, stirring often, about 15 minutes until seeds separate and float to top. Pour all into rotary food mill set over large heatproof bowl, and crank forcing pulp into bowl. Discard seeds and fibrous bits left behind.

3. Pour ⅓ cup reserved grape juice into small ramekin or custard cup and 2 tablespoons into second ramekin. Mix tapioca into juice in first ramekin and cornstarch into juice in second one. Set both aside.

4. Add grape pulp and remaining reserved juice to grape skins, set over moderately low heat, and simmer uncovered, stirring often, about 20 minutes until skins are tender but not mushy. **Note:** If skins are overly large, you may want to snip them into halves or quarters; using kitchen shears, I do this right in the pan.

5. Remove pan from heat, mix in reserved tapioca and cornstarch mixtures, and beat briefly to dissolve any large tapioca lumps. Blend in sugar, egg, lemon juice, orange zest, and salt; set aside.

6. Slide rimmed heavy-duty baking sheet onto middle oven shelf and preheat oven to 425°F.

7. Prepare pie crust as directed. With floured rolling pin, roll slightly more than half of pastry on lightly floured surface into circle about 3 inches larger than 9-inch pie pan. Fold pastry over rolling pin, ease into pie pan, and gently press over bottom and up sides of pan, taking care not to tear it. Trim overhang until 1 inch wider all around than pie pan. Roll remaining pastry into slightly smaller circle and cut into strips about ½ inch wide.

8. Scoop grape filling into pie shell.

9. *For lattice top:* Crisscross pastry strips on filling, spacing ½ inch apart. Trim strips so they lop over pan about 1 inch, then roll up with bottom crust overhang onto pan rim and crimp into high fluted edge.

10. Set pie in oven on preheated baking sheet and bake 5 minutes. Reduce oven temperature to 350°F and bake pie 45 to 50 minutes longer until filling is bubbly and crust nicely browned. **Note:** If crimped edge is browning too fast, cover with strips of foil.

11. Transfer pie from oven to wire rack and cool to room temperature before serving; this is to give the juices time to thicken a bit.

12. Cut pie into wedges and serve as is, or if you like, top each portion with whipped cream or scoops of vanilla ice cream. **Caution:** Though you make every effort to remove all grape seeds, a renegade or two may slip into the filling, so warn those at table to take care.

This filling, though made with cream and spiked with wine, is surprisingly light—a rarity among Southern pies.

Old Virginia Sweet Potato Pie

Makes 8 Servings

½ cup (1 stick) unsalted butter

¾ cup raw sugar

2 large eggs

Finely grated zest of 1 small lemon

1 tablespoon fresh lemon juice

1½ cups firmly packed unseasoned, mashed, cooked sweet potatoes (about 1½ pounds)

¼ cup light cream or half-and-half

2 tablespoons Malmsey (sweet Madeira wine) or cream sherry

1 9-inch unbaked pie shell (see About Frozen Pie Shells, page 23)

1. Preheat oven to 450°F.

2. Cream butter and sugar in large electric mixer bowl at high speed 2 to 3 minutes until fluffy-light. Beat in eggs, one by one, then lemon zest and juice. With mixer at low speed, blend in sweet potatoes, cream, and wine, then continue beating until smooth.

3. Pour filling into pie shell. Slide onto shelf in lower third of oven and bake 10 minutes. Reduce oven temperature to 350°F and bake pie 30 to 35 minutes longer until filling puffs and cake tester inserted midway between center and edge of pie comes out clean.

4. Transfer pie to wire rack and cool to room temperature before cutting. **Note:** The filling will fall somewhat as the pie cools, but this is exactly as it should be.

5. Cut into slim wedges and top, if you like, with whipped cream.

On one of many trips to Florida, I bought a copy of *Paths of Sunshine Cookbook*, a spiral-bound fundraiser published by the Florida Federation of Garden Clubs, Inc. A recipe in that appealing little volume inspired this orange pie that's blessed with a "just-picked" flavor. *Notes:* If you use a frozen pie shell, see About Frozen Pie Shells, page 23. Because this pie may not bake long enough to cook the eggs thoroughly, I call for pasteurized eggs, now available at many supermarkets. For more information about pasteurized eggs, see Eggs, page 18.

Orange Grove Pie

Makes 6 Servings

1 cup granulated sugar

¼ cup unsifted cornstarch

¼ teaspoon salt

1½ cups fresh orange juice

3 large pasteurized egg yolks, lightly beaten (see Notes above)

2 tablespoons fresh lemon juice

2 teaspoons finely grated orange zest

2 tablespoons unsalted butter, at room temperature

1 9-inch baked pie shell (see Plantation Days Custard Pie, page 198)

MERINGUE

3 large pasteurized egg whites

¼ teaspoon cream of tartar

3 tablespoons granulated sugar

3 tablespoons confectioner's (10X) sugar

1 teaspoon coarsely grated orange zest (optional)

1. Preheat oven to 425°F.

2. Combine sugar, cornstarch, and salt in a large nonreactive saucepan, then blend in orange juice. Set over moderate heat and cook and stir about 3 minutes until thickened and clear.

3. Remove from heat, blend about ½ cup hot orange mixture into egg yolks, then stir back into the pan, return to moderate heat, and cook and stir 2 minutes longer. Remove from heat, add lemon juice, orange zest, and butter and stir until butter melts. Pour into pie shell, smoothing to edge.

4. *For Meringue:* Beat egg whites and cream of tartar at medium speed in small electric mixer bowl until frothy, then add granulated and confectioner's sugars gradually, beating all the while. Raise mixer speed to high and beat 3 to 5 minutes until meringue peaks softly. **Note:** Pasteurized egg whites whip more slowly than the unpasteurized. Swirl meringue over filling, making sure that it touches crust all around.

5. Slide pie onto a baking sheet and bake on middle oven shelf 8 to 9 minutes or just until meringue is tipped with brown.

6. Cool pie to room temperature before cutting. But first, garnish, if you like, by scattering grated orange zest over meringue. **Note:** Refrigerate any leftover pie.

Throughout Appalachia, frugal mountain folk never let wild blackberries or grapes, apples, crabapples, or plums go to waste, turning them into jellies that could be spread on fresh-baked biscuits and also be used as a sweetener when precious sugar ran short. Calling for only half a cup of sugar, this chess-like Tennessee pie is a perfect example of making do. The best jelly to use? Old-timers preferred apple, crabapple, or plum but would of course have grabbed whatever they had on hand.

Great Smokies Jelly Pie

Makes 6 to 8 Servings

⅔ cup (10½ tablespoons) unsalted butter, at room temperature

½ cup sugar

2 tablespoons stone-ground cornmeal (white or yellow)

¼ teaspoon salt

1⅓ cups firmly packed jelly (preferably apple, crabapple, or plum)

4 large eggs

1 9-inch unbaked pie shell with a high fluted edge (see About Frozen Pie Shells, page 23)

1. Slide rimmed heavy-duty baking sheet onto middle oven shelf and preheat oven to 425°F.

2. Cream butter, sugar, cornmeal, and salt in large electric mixer bowl 2 to 3 minutes at high speed until light and fluffy. With mixer at low speed, add jelly, then beat at moderately high speed until well combined with no flecks of jelly visible. Add eggs one by one, beating well after each addition.

3. Pour filling into pie shell, spreading to edge. Set pie in oven on preheated baking sheet and bake 10 minutes. Reduce oven temperature to 350°F and bake pie 25 to 30 minutes longer until filling is softly set. Filling will barely jiggle when you nudge the pan and a cake tester inserted halfway between the edge and middle should come out clean. **Note:** If crimped edge is browning too fast, cover with strips of foil.

4. Transfer pie to wire rack and cool to room temperature before cutting. **Note:** The filling will fall somewhat but this is the nature of chess pies.

5. Cut pie into smallish wedges and top, if you like, with whipped cream, "to cut the richness," Southerners say.

Here is another chess pie I've developed to salve the South's sweet tooth—and not least, my own. Use a top-quality bittersweet chocolate for this pie, one that melts smoothly. *Tip:* I melt the chocolate and butter at the outset so they've time to cool a bit before being mixed with the other ingredients. If too hot, they may "cook" the eggs meaning lumps in a filling that should be jelly-smooth.

Chocolate Chess Pie

Makes 6 to 8 Servings

6 tablespoons (¾ stick) unsalted butter, diced (see Tip above)

3 squares (1 ounce each) bittersweet chocolate, coarsely chopped

1 cup granulated sugar

¼ cup firmly packed light brown sugar

2 tablespoons all-purpose flour

¼ teaspoon salt

4 large eggs, lightly beaten

2 tablespoons heavy cream

1 tablespoon vanilla extract

1 9-inch unbaked pie shell (see About Frozen Pie Shells, page 23)

1. Preheat oven to 325°F.

2. Melt butter and chocolate slowly in small heavy saucepan over lowest heat, stirring often.

3. Meanwhile, combine both sugars, flour, and salt in medium-size bowl, pressing out any lumps with your fingers. Add eggs, cream, and vanilla, and whisk until smooth. Add melted butter and chocolate and again whisk until smooth. Pour filling into pie shell.

4. Slide pie onto rimmed baking sheet and bake on middle oven shelf 50 to 55 minutes or just until top puffs and filling barely jiggles when you nudge pan.

5. Transfer pie to wire rack and cool to room temperature before cutting. **Note:** Filling will fall somewhat but this is the nature of chess pies.

6. Cut into slim wedges and serve as is or top with whipped cream or ice cream—vanilla, dulce de leche, butter pecan, or hazelnut gelato.

Beloved since plantation days, chess pies have evolved over the years. Although the classic chess pies remain popular, they're being challenged by newcomers. This one—my own improvisation—teams chocolate with Southern bourbon and pecans. Rich as all-get-out, it's dedicated to chocolate lovers everywhere.

Chocolate-Bourbon-Pecan Pie

Makes 6 to 8 Servings

½ cup (1 stick) unsalted butter, diced

4 squares (1 ounce each) semi-sweet chocolate, coarsely chopped

1 cup firmly packed light brown sugar

2 tablespoons all-purpose flour

4 large eggs

¼ cup light corn syrup

2 tablespoons bourbon or sour mash whiskey

1 teaspoon vanilla extract

¼ teaspoon salt

1 cup coarsely chopped, lightly toasted pecans (8 to 10 minutes in a 350°F oven)

1 9-inch unbaked pie shell (see About Frozen Pie Shells, page 23)

1. Preheat oven to 325°F.

2. Melt butter and chocolate slowly in small heavy saucepan over lowest heat, stirring often.

3. Meanwhile, combine sugar and flour in medium-size bowl, pressing out any lumps with your fingers. Add eggs and whisk until smooth.

4. Quickly whisk corn syrup, bourbon, vanilla, and salt together in 1-cup measure, pour into brown sugar mixture, and whisk until smooth. Add melted chocolate mixture and again whisk until smooth. Fold in pecans and pour filling into pie shell.

5. Slide pie onto rimmed baking sheet and bake on middle oven shelf about 1 hour until top puffs and forms a crust (it will crack in several places the way a macaroon cracks). The filling should barely jiggle when you nudge pan and cake tester inserted halfway between edge and middle should come out clean.

6. Transfer pie to wire rack and cool to room temperature before cutting. **Note:** Filling will fall somewhat—always the way with chess pies.

7. Cut into slim wedges and serve as is or top with whipped cream or vanilla ice cream.

What's unusual about this Southern fund-raiser favorite? It bakes in a well-greased pie pan—sans crust. My good friend Moreton Neal told me that her Mississippi grandmother often made this killer dessert. Did she ever add nuts? "Absolutely not," Moreton said. "If she had, the nuts would have been pecans from her own backyard, but then this would have been a completely different dessert." Meaning, no longer one so moist it's the texture of not-quite-set fudge (it reminds me of that once-so-trendy flourless chocolate cake but I like fudge pie better). For edge, I've added a little instant espresso. After I finished testing this recipe, I phoned Moreton. We'd bumped into one another at the supermarket earlier in the day and Moreton told me she was having a gang of young people over for dinner. Not daring to have that rich pie tempt me, I asked if she'd like it. And how. Here's what Moreton e-mailed me the day after the dinner party:

"Jean, thanks so much for the recipe and especially the delicious pie. It was a big hit with all of us and we loved the dulce de leche ice cream with it. I grew up eating fudge pie with whipped cream (cream was way better back in the old days). My grandmother's recipe used ⅓ cup flour and she separated the eggs, then folded in the beaten whites at the end. Glad to know that's not necessary, which makes this the easiest recipe ever."

Serve fudge pie as is or top with whipped cream or ice cream—vanilla, dulce de leche (which I'd suggested to Moreton), or my new absolute favorite: hazelnut gelato. *Note:* I microwave-melt the butter and chocolate together in an uncovered 1-quart ovenproof glass measuring cup (a spouted one). Takes about 8 minutes on DEFROST in my 650-watt model. It's best to melt the butter and chocolate first so they have time to cool while you prepare the other ingredients. *Tip:* Use a silver-colored pie pan—aluminum or stainless steel—for this recipe, not a darkly coated pan, which absorbs heat so fast the fudge pie may overbrown.

Fudge Pie

Makes 6 to 8 Servings

½ cup (1 stick) unsalted butter (no substitute)

2 squares (1 ounce each) unsweetened chocolate (see Note above)

¾ cup granulated sugar

¼ cup firmly packed light brown sugar

¼ cup unsifted all-purpose flour

1½ teaspoons instant espresso powder or granules

¼ teaspoon salt

2 large eggs, lightly beaten with 1½ teaspoons vanilla extract

1. Preheat oven to 350°F. Coat 9-inch pie pan well with nonstick cooking spray and set aside (see Tip above).

2. Melt butter and chocolate together as described in Note above, then set aside to cool, whisking occasionally, while you proceed with recipe.

3. Combine both sugars, flour, espresso, and salt in mixing bowl and make well in center.

4. Whisking briskly, slowly add melted butter-chocolate mixture to egg mixture. It will thicken a bit but this is as it should be. Pour mixture into well in dry ingredients and gently fold in until batter is smooth and uniformly dark brown. Scoop into pie pan, spreading to edge. Slide pan onto middle oven shelf and bake uncovered about 30 minutes until cake tester inserted in middle of pie comes out clean.

5. Cool pie 20 minutes in pan on wire rack or, if you prefer, cool to room temperature.

6. Cut pie into slim wedges and serve—as is or topped with whipped cream or ice cream (see headnote for suggestions).

Lemon chess pie is a classic, descended some say from the English lemon "cheese" or curd. In fact, the very name "chess" may be a corruption of "cheese," in olden days spelled "chese." I've always considered other citrus fruits good candidates for chess pie and decided to develop a recipe using Ruby Red grapefruit—a particular favorite down South. This pie is more delicate than lemon chess, less tart, too, though adding grapefruit zest injects welcome tang. I make this pie entirely by food processor, even grating the grapefruit zest. If you mix by hand, substitute 1 tablespoon finely grated grapefruit zest for the strips called for here—a Microplane does it perfectly in jig time. *Tip:* To gloss clementine segments, place in a plastic zipper-bag along with the corn syrup mixture, close, and gently invert the bag—several times—until segments glisten.

Ruby Red Chess Pie

Makes 6 to 8 Servings

1   cup sugar

3   (3-inch) strips Ruby Red grapefruit zest, removed with a vegetable peeler (see headnote above)

¼   teaspoon salt

¾   cup freshly squeezed Ruby Red grapefruit juice

1   tablespoon fresh lemon juice

5   large eggs

⅓   cup melted unsalted butter

1   9-inch unbaked pie shell with a high, fluted edge (see About Frozen Pie Shells, page 23)

OPTIONAL GARNISHES

4   clementines (mandarin oranges) or small tangerines, peeled, sectioned, and glossed with 2 tablespoons light corn syrup mixed with 1 tablespoon warm water (see Tip above)

8   small sprigs lemon geranium or lemon verbena

1. Preheat oven to 325°F.

2. Alternately whiz and pulse sugar, grapefruit zest, and salt in food processor 1 to 2 minutes until zest is finely grated.

3. Pulse in grapefruit and lemon juices, then add eggs one by one, pulsing briefly after each addition. Finally, drizzle in melted butter, pulsing lightly all the while—easy does it. If you beat filling mixture too long or hard, the eggs will lose their power to thicken.

4. Pour filling into pie shell, set on baking sheet, and bake on middle oven shelf about 50 minutes until puffed and lightly browned. Filling should jiggle slightly when you nudge pan.

5. Remove pie from oven and cool on wire rack to room temperature.

6. Cut into small pieces and if you like, spoon a few glossed clementine segments alongside each portion and tuck in a sprig of lemon geranium. **Note:** Refrigerate any leftover pie.

To be honest, I didn't discover this particular chess pie until fairly recently when the recipe began surfacing in those little spiral-bound cookbooks published by clubs and churches to raise funds for worthy local causes. Japanese Fruit Pie appears to be wholly Southern and as for its name, I haven't a clue except that this version contains three ingredients integral to the South's beloved Japanese Fruitcake—coconut, orange, and raisins. This much I can tell you: Japanese Fruit Pie has nothing to do with Japan.

Japanese Fruit Pie

Makes 8 Servings

½ cup raw sugar

½ cup granulated sugar

3 large eggs

1 tablespoon fresh lemon juice

1½ teaspoons vanilla extract

1 teaspoon finely grated orange zest

¼ teaspoon salt

½ cup (1 stick) melted unsalted butter

1 cup lightly toasted, coarsely chopped pecans (8 to 10 minutes at 350°F)

1 cup grated coconut (preferably unsweetened)

1 cup dark seedless raisins

1 9-inch unbaked pie shell with a high fluted edge (see About Frozen Pie Shells, page 23)

1. Place heavy-duty baking sheet on middle oven shelf and preheat oven to 350°F.

2. Combine first seven ingredients (raw sugar through salt) in large bowl, whisking until smooth. Blend in melted butter, then fold in pecans, coconut, and raisins.

3. Pour into pie shell, center on preheated baking sheet, and bake 40 to 45 minutes until puffed and nicely browned. Filling should jiggle slightly when you nudge the pan.

4. Remove pie from oven and cool to room temperature on wire rack. **Note:** Filling will fall slightly as it does with every chess pie.

5. Cut into small pieces and if you like, top with whipped cream.

To be honest, this is more cake than pie. One friend said it reminded her of a one-layer spice cake with plenty of nuts. Yet Southerners persist in calling this recipe a pie as they do many desserts that are more cake than pie, even more pudding than pie. When serving Mirliton Pie, I like to scoop vanilla ice cream aboard or drift with whipped cream though it's also delicious "straight up." *Note:* To learn more about mirlitons, see page 20. *Tip:* For the 1 cup firmly packed, puréed, cooked mirlitons this recipe calls for, you'll need about 2 medium-large mirlitons (approximately 1 pound). To shortcut cooking time, I microwave peeled 1-inch mirliton cubes with ¼ cup water in a covered, microwave-safe container until very tender. In my 650-watt microwave oven this takes 8 to 10 minutes on HIGH (full power). More powerful models may do the job faster but you know your particular microwave best. Once cooked, drain mirlitons very well, then purée in a food processor or electric blender.

Mirliton Pie

Makes 6 to 8 Servings

1¾ cups sifted all-purpose flour

1½ cups coarsely chopped pecans, walnuts, or black walnuts

½ teaspoon baking powder

½ teaspoon baking soda

½ teaspoon ground cinnamon

½ teaspoon freshly grated nutmeg

¼ teaspoon salt

½ cup (1 stick) unsalted butter, at room temperature

1 cup sugar

1 large egg

1 cup firmly packed, puréed cooked mirlitons, at room temperature (see Note and Tip above)

1. Preheat oven to 350°F. Coat 9 × 9 × 2-inch baking pan well with nonstick oil-and-flour baking spray and set aside.

2. Place ¼ cup flour in small bowl, add pecans, toss well, and set aside. Whisk remaining 1½ cups flour with baking powder, baking soda, cinnamon, nutmeg, and salt in separate bowl and set aside.

3. Cream butter in electric mixer at high speed 1 minute until fluffy-light. With mixer at low speed, add sugar gradually, then beat about 2 minutes at high speed until nearly white.

4. At moderate speed, beat in egg, then add combined dry ingredients alternately with mashed mirlitons, beginning and ending with dry and beating after each addition only enough to combine. By hand, fold in dredged pecans and all dredging flour. Scoop batter into pan and spread to corners.

5. Slide onto middle oven shelf and bake 35 to 40 minutes until "pie" begins to pull from sides of pan, is springy to touch, and a cake tester inserted in middle comes out clean.

6. Transfer at once to wire rack, cool to room temperature in upright pan.

7. To serve, cut into 6 or 8 squares of equal size and top, if you like, with vanilla ice cream or whipped cream.

For a recipe that's said to have been secret for years, this one's all over the place. You'll find one version or another in dozens of community cookbooks both Southern and non-Southern, as well as online. Everyone has a pet recipe for this buffet favorite, but mine, I think, is particularly good because I lightly toast the pecans to bring out their flavor and also brown the butter that goes into the filling. *Note:* These mini pecan tarts freeze so well they taste just-baked after 3 months "on ice." So is it any wonder savvy Southern hostesses bake quantities of them well before Christmas and stash them in their freezers? *Tips:* To toast pecans, spread in a pie pan and bake uncovered on middle shelf of a preheated 350°F oven for 8 to 10 minutes. Stir once or twice and watch closely—nuts burn easily. To brown butter, melt in a small heavy saucepan over low heat, then let bubble and brown, shaking pan often, until the color of topaz. This will take about 15 minutes, but watch closely.

Pecan Tassies

Makes About 4 Dozen

PASTRY

- 1 cup (2 sticks) unsalted butter, slightly softened
- 2 packages (3 ounces each) cream cheese, at room temperature
- ¼ teaspoon salt
- 2¼ cups sifted all-purpose flour

FILLING

- ½ cup granulated sugar
- ¾ cup firmly packed light brown sugar
- 2 large eggs
- 1 teaspoon vanilla extract
- 1 tablespoon bourbon
- ¼ teaspoon salt
- 6 tablespoons unsalted butter, browned until color of topaz (see Tips above)
- 1¼ cups coarsely chopped, lightly toasted pecans (see Tips above)

1. *For Pastry:* Beat butter, cream cheese, and salt together until smooth, then mix in flour, about half of total amount at a time, until soft dough forms. Divide dough in half and roll each into "snake" about 12 inches long. Wrap in foil and chill 2 to 3 hours or overnight.

2. When ready to proceed, preheat oven to 350°F. Remove chilled dough, one piece at a time, slice ½ inch thick, and press into ungreased mini muffin pan cups forming little tart shells—you will need 48 shells in all. Set aside.

3. *For Filling:* Combine first six ingredients (granulated sugar through salt) by pulsing in food processor until smooth or by beating in small electric mixer bowl at moderately high speed. With machine running, drizzle in browned butter. By hand, fold in pecans.

4. Spoon filling into tart shells dividing total amount evenly—you'll need about 1 heaping teaspoon per shell.

5. Slide muffin pans onto middle oven shelf and bake tassies until filling bubbles and browns lightly, 20 to 25 minutes.

6. Cool tassies in pans on wire racks to room temperature, then gently remove from pans, using a thin-blade spatula or poultry pin, if necessary, to unstick any recalcitrant spots.

7. Serve tassies at once or layer in freezer containers between sheets of foil or wax paper and store in freezer. They only need to be thawed before they're served.

Despite its popularity, not much is known about this Southern pie. It's said to come from Arkansas, said, too, to have been named in honor of an Osgood, but which Osgood remains a mystery as do exactly when and where. Others say Osgood's simply a slang-y contraction of "Oh, so good." Maybe so. Maybe no. Needless to add there are countless variations of Osgood Pie, some of them heavily spiced, some with raisins only, some with a 50-50 mix of raisins and lightly toasted pecans (8 to 10 minutes in a 350°F oven is all it takes). This is the version I like best. And this critique from a friend who baked this pie proves why: "I wasn't going to eat any of it because my hips don't need any more padding, but over 1½ days I ate three-quarters of the pie—½ inch at a time!"

Osgood Pie

Makes 8 Servings

1½ cups sugar

½ cup (1 stick) melted unsalted butter

3 large eggs

1 cup dark seedless raisins, plumped about 10 minutes in warm water and drained well or ½ cup each drained, plumped raisins and coarsely chopped lightly toasted pecans (see headnote)

2 tablespoons cider vinegar

1 teaspoon vanilla extract

¼ teaspoon salt

1 9-inch unbaked pie shell (see About Frozen Pie Shells, page 23)

1. Slide a heavy-duty baking sheet on middle oven shelf and preheat oven to 325°F.

2. Beat sugar and melted butter in small electric mixer bowl for about 1 minute, first at low speed, then at moderate, until well blended.

3. With mixer at low speed, beat in eggs one by one and continue beating about 30 seconds until light. Combine raisins, vinegar, vanilla, and salt in separate small bowl, then gently fold into egg mixture and pour into pie shell.

4. Slide pie onto preheated baking sheet on middle oven shelf and bake 50 minutes to 1 hour or until nicely browned and cake tester inserted midway between edge and center comes out clean.

5. Cool pie on wire rack 30 minutes and serve warm. Or cool to room temperature before serving. Cut the pieces small—this pie is super-rich.

Both George Washington and Thomas Jefferson were connoisseurs of fine Madeiras, and when the founding fathers toasted the Declaration of Independence, they did so with glasses of Malmsey. Forty-four years earlier, Englishman James Oglethorpe, New World–bound to found a settlement at the mouth of the Savannah River, arrived with five tons of Madeira, thanks to a port-of-call at the Portuguese island of Madeira. Soon Madeira wines—from dry to sweet—were the favorite tipple among Lowcountry gentry and remained so for years. Spurred, perhaps, by nostalgia for those long-gone-with-the-wind days, a group of distinguished Savannah gentlemen founded the Madeira Club in 1950, a series of exclusive formal dinners at which fine Madeiras were served, savored, and discussed. Though that club no longer exists, Savannah remembers its Madeira tradition with an annual month-long event—"Potable Gold"—held at the historic Davenport House Museum. This supremely rich custard pie offers both a taste of and tribute to the Colonial South and its love affair with Madeira. *Tip:* Thickened with egg yolks only, this pie will leave you with orphaned whites. I like to use them up in Coconut Kisses (page 263). *Note:* This recipe makes a bit more filling than needed to fill a 9-inch pie shell, but because it's so exquisite, I decided to bake the extra filling in two buttered 6-ounce ramekins in a hot water bath 15 to 20 minutes at 325°F until they jiggle slightly when nudged. Cool these lovely little Madeira custards and consider them "lagniappe" for the cook.

Antebellum Madeira Pie

Makes 8 Servings

1   9-inch baked pie shell (see Plantation Days Custard Pie, page 198)
1½ cups light cream
1   cup heavy cream
¾   cup sugar
2   strips (each 3 inches long and ½ inch wide) orange zest
¼   teaspoon salt
8   jumbo egg yolks (see Tip above)
2   tablespoons dark corn syrup or light unsulfured molasses
¼   cup sweet Madeira wine such as Malmsey or Bual

1. Make, bake, and cool pie shell as directed. Leaving baking sheet in place on middle oven shelf, reduce oven temperature to 325°F.

Heat both creams, sugar, orange zest, and salt about 15 minutes in medium-size nonreactive saucepan over moderately low heat just until they simmer.

2. Meanwhile, whisk egg yolks briskly in small bowl until smooth, then whisk in about ½ cup hot cream mixture. Stir back into pan, and cook and stir 1 minute. Off-heat, mix in corn syrup and Madeira. Strain mixture through small, fine sieve into 1- or 2-quart heatproof glass measuring cup. You should have 3⅔ cups custard filling.

3. Pull middle oven shelf out, center cooled pie shell on baking sheet, and pour in 2⅓ cups filling. **Note:** At end of recipe headnote, I tell how to bake the 1⅓ cups remaining filling—it's the cook's reward.

4. Carefully slide shelf back into oven and bake pie 25 to 30 minutes until table knife inserted midway between center and rim comes out clean. **Note:** If crimped crust is overbrowning at any point, cover with strips of foil. When done, custard filling will be soft in middle and jiggle slightly when pan is nudged. But it will firm up on cooling.

5. Transfer pie to wire rack and cool to room temperature before serving. Or, if you prefer, cover loosely and chill well before cutting.

6. When serving, make the pieces small—this pie is rich, rich, rich.

The problem with custard pies is that unless the pie shell is blind-baked (i.e. before it's filled) the crust will be soggy. But for pies baked low 'n' slow that presents another problem: overbrowned crust, the crimped rim, in particular. Skilled bakers solve both problems by making a "slipped" custard pie, meaning they bake the filling in a well-buttered pie pan—sans crust—then when done, ease it into a baked pie shell. I've tried it a time or two with disastrous results, so don't recommend this technique. For me, this recipe works well if you follow it to the letter. *Note:* Make no substitutions and most of all, do not use a frozen prepared pie crust or refrigerated pastry that you unfurl and fit into the pan. *Tip:* Save leftover egg whites and add to your next omelet or batch of scrambled eggs.

Plantation Days Custard Pie

Makes 6 Servings

PASTRY

1⅓ cups sifted all-purpose flour

½ teaspoon salt

4 tablespoons well-chilled lard (not vegetable shortening)

2 tablespoons well-chilled unsalted butter

4 to 6 tablespoons ice water (about)

CUSTARD

3 large egg yolks (see Tip above)

2 large whole eggs

⅓ cup sugar

1½ teaspoons vanilla extract

⅛ teaspoon salt

1¼ cups half-and-half

½ cup heavy cream

⅛ teaspoon freshly grated nutmeg

1. Place heavy-duty baking sheet on middle oven shelf and preheat oven to 450°F.

2. *For Pastry:* Whisk flour and salt together in large mixing bowl, add lard and butter, and with pastry blender, cut in until size of lentils. Forking briskly, drizzle ice water evenly over all and continue forking until soft dough forms.

3. Pat dough into ball, place on lightly floured pastry cloth, then with lightly floured stockinette-sleeved rolling pin, roll dough into 13-inch circle. Lay rolling pin across center of pastry circle, lop half over rolling pin, and ease into pie pan. With fingers, gently press pastry over bottom and up sides of pan, then trim overhang until 1 inch larger all around than pan rim. Rolling pastry edges under, shape into high fluted edge on rim of pan. Prick bottom and sides of pie shell lightly with table fork.

4. Line pie shell with double thickness of foil, then to help pie shell keep its shape, pour in about 1½ cups uncooked rice or dried beans.

5. Slide pie shell onto baking sheet on middle oven shelf, and bake 10 minutes. Remove pie shell from oven, lift out foil and rice or beans; discarding foil but saving rice or beans to weight pie shells in future. Return pie shell to baking sheet on middle oven shelf and bake 3 to 5 minutes longer until pale golden. Transfer pie shell to wire rack. Leaving baking sheet in place, lower oven temperature to 350°F.

6. For Custard: At low electric mixer speed, beat egg yolks, whole eggs, sugar, vanilla, and salt until frothy. Raise mixer speed to moderately high, and beat 3 to 5 minutes until thick and pale yellow. With mixer again at low speed, add half-and-half, then gradually add heavy cream and continue beating only enough to combine.

7. Pull middle oven shelf out and center cooled pie shell on baking sheet. Pour custard through large fine sieve directly into pie shell, then sprinkle with nutmeg.

8. Gently slide shelf back into oven (easy does it—this is a full pie) and bake 30 to 35 minutes or until table knife inserted midway between center and rim comes out clean. **Note:** If crimped crust is overbrowning at any point, cover with strips of foil. When done, custard filling will be soft in middle and jiggle slightly when pan is nudged. But it will firm up on cooling.

9. Transfer pie to wire rack and cool to room temperature before serving. Or, if you prefer, cover loosely and chill well before cutting. **Note:** Refrigerate leftovers.

When I was a little girl growing up in Raleigh, I loved grocery shopping with my mother at the Piggly-Wiggly—our only supermarket and compared to the vast sprawl of today's supermarkets, not very "super." In that long-gone era of everything from scratch, preshredded coconut was unheard of. So if you wanted to bake a coconut cake or pie, you had to buy a coconut. In our house, cracking the coconut open and prying out the "meat" was Daddy's job, peeling off the tough brown skin was Mama's job, and feeding the coconut piece by piece through a clamp-to-the-counter meat grinder was my job. Oh, for a food processor back then. Though most classic Southern coconut pies begin with a good basic custard, I prefer the buttermilk-tang of this one. The good news is that it's a little less sweet, a little less caloric. *Note:* If you use sweetened flaked coconut instead of fresh, reduce the amount of sugar to ¾ cup.

Coconut Buttermilk Pie

Makes 6 Servings

1   9-inch baked pie shell (see Plantation Days Custard Pie, page 198)
1   cup sugar
3   tablespoons all-purpose flour
½   cup (1 stick) melted unsalted butter
2   teaspoons vanilla extract
¼   teaspoon salt
3   large eggs
1½ cups buttermilk
1¼ cups moderately finely grated coconut (preferably fresh; see Note above)

1. Make, bake, and cool pie shell as directed. Leaving baking sheet in place on middle oven shelf, reduce oven temperature to 325°F.

2. Beat sugar, flour, melted butter, vanilla, and salt in small electric mixer bowl at moderate speed about 1 minute to combine. Beat eggs in one by one, then with mixer at low speed, add buttermilk in slow steady stream. By hand, gently stir in 1 cup grated coconut.

3. Pull middle oven shelf out and center cooled pie shell on baking sheet. Pour buttermilk filling directly into pie shell and scatter remaining ¼ cup grated coconut evenly on top.

4. Carefully slide shelf back into oven and bake pie 40 to 45 minutes until table knife inserted midway between center and rim comes out clean. **Note:** If crimped crust is overbrowning at any point, cover with strips of foil. When done, buttermilk filling will be soft in middle and jiggle slightly when pan is nudged. But it will firm up on cooling.

5. Transfer pie to wire rack and cool to room temperature before serving. Or, if you prefer, cover loosely and chill well before cutting. I personally prefer this pie refrigerator-cold.

This particular recipe was inspired by one that appeared in *Coastal Cookery*, a slim spiral-bound volume first published in 1937 by the Cassina Garden Club of St. Simon's Island, GA. It's an unusual pie, one I've seen nowhere else, but like most Southern sweets, doesn't lack for richness. The crust is meringue, but it is not baked à la angel pie. The uncooked meringue is shaped into a sort of nest and the rich chess-like filling spooned in. Then something magical happens in the oven: The outer portion of the meringue crisps while the inner one merges with some of the filling and drifts to the top leaving a buttery golden layer underneath. If you cool Water Lily Pie to room temperature before serving—or better yet, refrigerate several hours—you can cut it into neat wedges although the point of each may be thin. If so, scrape some of the buttery filling off the pie plate using a spatula and plop on top. Or even easier, serve Water Lily Pie in dessert bowls—almost as attractive and equally delicious. "To cut the richness," as Southerners are fond of saying, drift each portion with unsweetened whipped cream.

Water Lily Pie

Makes 8 Servings

3 large eggs, separated

¼ teaspoon cream of tartar

1 cup sugar

½ cup (1 stick) unsalted butter, at room temperature

1 teaspoon vanilla extract

½ teaspoon rum extract

¼ teaspoon salt

1. Preheat oven to 300°F. Generously butter 9-inch pie plate, dust bottom and sides well with flour, tip out excess, and set pie plate aside.

2. Beat egg whites with cream of tartar in large electric mixer bowl at high speed until frothy. With motor running, add ½ cup sugar gradually and continue beating about 3 minutes at high speed until meringue peaks stiffly when beaters are withdrawn. Spread meringue over bottom and up sides of pie plate, leaving hollow in middle for filling.

3. With same mixer bowl and beaters, beat egg yolks with remaining ½ cup sugar, butter, vanilla and rum extracts, and salt about 1 minute at moderately high mixer speed until smooth. Spoon egg yolk filling into hollow in meringue and spread evenly.

4. Slide onto middle oven shelf and bake uncovered 45 to 55 minutes until meringue shell is pale tan and filling softly set.

5. Cool to room temperature before serving.

Everyone loves Florida's famous Key Lime Pie. Everyone loves cheesecake. So why not merge the two? That's what I've done here and I think the results "powerful good," as old-time Southerners would say. *Note:* Once again I call for pasteurized eggs to eliminate any risk of salmonella (see Eggs, page 18). *Tips:* If 8-ounce containers of sour cream are no longer available in your area, simply substitute 1 cup firmly packed sour cream. Do not use "light" or low-fat sour cream or cream cheese in this recipe. Both contain thickeners that may break down when baked making filling and topping look curdled. Finally, because Key limes aren't widely available as well as being the very devil to juice—even with an electric juicer—I often use bottled Key lime juice (see Sources, page 264).

Key Lime Cheesecake

Makes 10 Servings

CRUST

1½ cups graham cracker crumbs (you'll need about twelve 5 × 2¼-inch double crackers)

¼ cup sugar

5 tablespoons melted unsalted butter (no substitute)

FILLING

1 package (8 ounces) cream cheese, at room temperature (see Tips above)

1 package (3 ounces) cream cheese, at room temperature

1 can (14 ounces) sweetened condensed milk

⅔ cup Key lime juice, fresh or bottled (see Tips above)

2 large pasteurized eggs (see Note above)

2 large pasteurized egg yolks

¼ teaspoon salt

TOPPING

1 carton (8 ounces) sour cream, at room temperature (see Tips above)

2 tablespoons sugar

Few shreds Persian (green) lime zest (optional decoration)

1. Position shelf in lower third of oven and preheat oven to 375°F.

2. *For Crust:* Combine all ingredients, press over bottom and halfway up sides of ungreased 9-inch springform pan, and set aside.

3. *For Filling:* Beat all ingredients in large electric mixer bowl about 1 minute at moderate speed until smooth. Pour filling into crumb crust.

4. Center pan on shelf in lower third of oven and bake uncovered 20 minutes. Remove cheesecake from oven and cool 15 minutes. Meanwhile, raise oven temperature to 475°F.

5. *For Topping:* Blend sour cream and sugar and carefully spread over filling.

6. Return cheesecake to lower third of oven and bake uncovered 10 minutes longer.

7. Transfer at once to wire rack and cool to room temperature in upright pan. Cover with foil and refrigerate 10 to 12 hours or overnight before serving

8. To serve, carefully loosen cheesecake around sides with small thin-blade spatula, release and remove springform sides, then slide cheesecake (still on pan bottom) onto large, colorful round platter. Scatter grated lime zest over cheesecake, if you like, cut into slim wedges, and serve.

How would our grandmothers have described this dessert? "Smooth as a peeled peach and richer than sin." What makes it so? A pound of cream cheese, ½ cup firmly packed light brown sugar plus 2 large eggs plus pecans in both the crumb crust and on top. My advice: Forget about calories and enjoy. *Note:* Why pasteurized eggs? Because the eggs may not cook thoroughly and with salmonella being an ongoing problem, I'd rather be safe than sorry (see Eggs, page 18). *Tip:* In some parts of the country, I'm told, sour cream is no longer available in 8-ounce containers. No problem. Simply substitute 1 cup firmly packed sour cream. Do not use "light" or low-fat sour cream or cream cheese in this recipe—their thickeners may break down or curdle as the cheesecake bakes.

Praline Cheesecake

Makes 10 Servings

CRUST

1⅓ cups graham cracker crumbs (you'll need about ten 5 × 2¼-inch double crackers)

2 tablespoons moderately finely chopped pecans

2 tablespoons each granulated sugar and light brown sugar

4½ tablespoons melted unsalted butter (no substitute)

FILLING

2 packages (8 ounces each) cream cheese, at room temperature (see Tip above)

½ cup firmly packed light brown sugar

1½ teaspoons vanilla extract

¼ teaspoon salt

2 large pasteurized eggs (see Note above)

TOPPING

1 carton (8 ounces) sour cream, at room temperature (see Tip above)

2 tablespoons each granulated sugar and light brown sugar

1 teaspoon vanilla extract

¼ cup moderately finely chopped pecans

1. Position shelf in lower third of oven and preheat oven to 375°F.

2. **For Crust:** Combine all ingredients, press over bottom and halfway up sides of ungreased 9-inch springform pan, and set aside.

3. **For Filling:** Beat all ingredients in large electric mixer bowl about 2 minutes at moderate speed until smooth. Scoop filling into crumb crust, spreading to edge and smoothing top.

4. Center pan on shelf in lower third of oven and bake uncovered 20 minutes. Remove cheesecake from oven and cool 15 minutes. Meanwhile, raise oven temperature to 475°F.

5. **For Topping:** Blend all ingredients except pecans and carefully spread over filling. Scatter pecans evenly on top.

6. Return cheesecake to lower third of oven and bake uncovered 10 minutes longer.

7. Transfer at once to wire rack and cool to room temperature in upright pan. Cover with foil and refrigerate 10 to 12 hours or overnight before serving.

8. To serve, carefully loosen cheesecake around sides with small thin-blade spatula, release and remove spring form sides, then slide cheesecake (still on pan bottom) onto large, colorful round platter. Cut into slim wedges and serve with freshly brewed coffee.

chapter six

Puddings,

cobblers, crisps, crumbles & more

The South isn't usually associated with apples, yet orchards run up the Smokies and Blue Ridge foothills and ripple across Virginia's vast Shenandoah Valley. Virginia is in fact America's sixth largest apple grower (after Washington, New York, Michigan, Pennsylvania, and California). And North Carolina ranks number eight—just behind Oregon. Dozens of apple varieties grow in the Southern highlands but the best-sellers are Red Delicious, Golden Delicious, Rome Beauty, and Gala with Granny Smith not far behind. Henderson County, NC, one of this nation's top ten apple-producing counties, has been hosting the state's Apple Festival every Labor Day Weekend for more than 65 years. This crumble, an old Smokies staple, calls for Golden Delicious apples, which hold their shape when baked. Old-timers add wild hickory nuts or black walnuts to the topping—me, too, if I can find them (see Sources, page 264). But plump, sweet Georgia pecans are equally delicious. *Note:* It's best to make the topping first and let it stand at room temperature while you proceed with the recipe. This gives the butter time to soften—then a last-minute toss is all it needs.

Appalachian Apple Crumble

Makes 8 Servings

TOPPING

- 1 cup quick-cooking rolled oats
- 1 cup coarsely chopped wild hickory nuts, black walnuts, or pecans
- ½ cup firmly packed light brown sugar
- ⅓ cup unsifted all-purpose flour
- ¼ teaspoon salt
- 6 tablespoons (¾ stick) refrigerator-cold unsalted butter, cut into small dice

FILLING

- 6 large Golden Delicious apples (about 3½ pounds), peeled, cored, and sliced about ¼ inch thick
- ⅓ cup apple cider
- 2 tablespoons fresh lemon juice
- 1 tablespoon good bourbon or sour mash whiskey (optional)

- ¼ cup firmly packed light brown sugar mixed with ¼ cup unsifted all-purpose flour
- 1 teaspoon ground cinnamon
- ½ teaspoon ground ginger
- ½ teaspoon freshly grated nutmeg
- ¼ teaspoon salt

1. Preheat oven to 400°F. Spritz 13 × 9 × 2-inch baking dish with nonstick cooking spray and set aside.

2. *For Topping:* Place all ingredients in medium-size bowl, toss well, and set aside.

3. *For Filling:* Place all ingredients in large nonreactive bowl, toss well to combine, and let stand at room temperature 5 minutes. Toss well again, scoop into baking dish, and spread to corners.

4. Toss Topping ingredients well again, distributing butter throughout, then scatter evenly over filling.

5. Slide onto middle oven shelf and bake uncovered 40 to 45 minutes until bubbling and brown.

6. Dish up at table, adding a trickle of heavy cream to each portion, if you like. Or top with whipped cream or scoops of vanilla ice cream.

As a child, I loved to go "blackberrying" in the fields around our West Raleigh house and as long as I focused on cobbler to come, didn't even mind the inevitable scratches. The only thing I didn't like about blackberries? The seeds. Always too many and always too big. Today's cultivated varieties have fewer seeds and by teaming the South's best blueberries and blackberries, I've not only enriched the cobbler but also reduced the number of seeds. What further distinguishes this cobbler is its drop biscuit topping made with equal parts whole wheat and all-purpose flours.

Blackberry-Blueberry Cobbler with Whole Wheat Biscuit Topping

Makes 6 Servings

FILLING

2   cups fresh blackberries, washed and stemmed

2   cups fresh blueberries, washed and stemmed

½   cup raw or granulated sugar blended with 3 tablespoons cornstarch

1   teaspoon each finely grated orange and lemon zest

1   tablespoon unsalted butter, diced

TOPPING

1   cup unsifted whole wheat flour

1   cup sifted all-purpose flour

¼   cup sugar

1   tablespoon (3 teaspoons) baking powder

¼   teaspoon salt

⅓   cup firmly packed lard (not vegetable shortening)

5   tablespoons unsalted butter

½   cup milk

1   cup light or heavy cream (optional), to drizzle over each portion

1. Preheat oven to 400°F.

2. *For Filling:* Combine blackberries, blueberries, sugar mixture, and orange and lemon zest in large nonreactive bowl and set aside.

3. *For Topping:* Combine both flours, sugar, baking powder, and salt in large shallow bowl, add lard and butter, and with pastry blender, cut in until texture of coarse meal. Forking briskly, drizzle milk over surface and continue forking into soft dough.

4. Scoop berry mixture into ungreased 2-quart casserole and dot with diced butter. Drop dough on top in clumps, then spread to edge, covering berries completely.

5. Slide onto middle oven shelf and bake uncovered 10 minutes. Reduce oven temperature to 350°F and bake 25 to 30 minutes longer until bubbly and tipped with brown.

6. Cool 30 minutes, then spoon cobbler into dessert dishes and, if you like, trickle a little cream over each portion.

This elegant but easy dessert uses the South's freshest blueberries and pecans to best advantage and to the hilt.

Blueberry-Pecan Crisp

Makes 6 Servings

TOPPING

⅔ cup unsifted unbleached all-purpose flour

⅓ cup firmly packed light brown sugar

2 tablespoons rolled oats (not quick-cooking)

½ teaspoon ground cinnamon

¼ cup (½ stick) chilled unsalted butter, cut in ½-inch dice

½ cup coarsely chopped, lightly toasted pecans (8 to 10 minutes in a 350°F oven)

2 tablespoons honey

FILLING

5 cups fresh blueberries, washed and stemmed

½ cup granulated sugar

1½ tablespoons cornstarch

1 tablespoon fresh lemon juice

FINISHING TOUCH

1 cup heavy cream softly whipped with 2 tablespoons confectioner's (10X) sugar and ½ teaspoon vanilla extract

1. Preheat oven to 375°F. Butter a shallow 1½-quart casserole and set aside.

2. *For Topping:* Pulse flour, brown sugar, oats, and cinnamon briskly several times in food processor to combine. Scatter diced butter evenly on top and pulse just until mixture begins to clump. Remove chopping blade and mix in pecans. Wrap Topping in wax paper and set in freezer.

3. *For Filling:* Bring 1 cup blueberries, sugar, cornstarch, and lemon juice to a boil in medium-size nonreactive saucepan over moderately high heat, stirring all the while, then cook and stir 2 to 3 minutes until juices thicken and clear. Mix in remaining blueberries and scoop into casserole, spreading to edge.

4. Remove Topping from freezer and crumble over berry mixture, distributing evenly. Slide onto middle oven shelf and bake uncovered about 30 minutes until bubbly. Drizzle honey evenly over Topping and bake 5 minutes more until golden.

5. Cool crisp 15 to 20 minutes, then for a finishing touch, drift with sweetened whipped cream, and serve.

*Back in the 1950s, the North Carolina Federation of Home
Demonstration Clubs published a little cookbook, now long out of
print, filled with family favorites, among them this beloved rice
pudding, dated 1850. It was submitted by Mary Ivey of Wayne County
southeast of Raleigh and introduced with this headnote:
"This recipe was my great grandmother's. It was used by my
grandmother who at one time lived in and helped operate the Seven
Springs resort hotel when it was famous . . . and noted for its Saturday
night square dances, which sometimes lasted all night, my grandfather
playing the violin and his sister the piano." Here's that 1850 recipe:*

Heirloom Antebellum Rice Pudding

Makes 4 to 6 Servings

2 cups cooked rice
½ cup sugar
1 cup sweet milk
Grated rind of ½ lemon
½ cup raisins
½ teaspoon nutmeg

Mix ingredients, place in buttered dish, and bake in a slow
oven until the rice has absorbed the milk and is brown.

My updated version, written in greater detail for cooks who may never have made old-fashioned rice pudding, contains a little cream because the "sweet milk" of 1850 was richer than ours today. *Note:* The Seven Springs Hotel, famous for its "healing" mineral waters, opened toward the end of the 19th century and didn't close until after World War II. The town of Seven Springs, devastated by Hurricane Floyd in 1999, now has fewer than 100 residents. *Tip:* Do not use converted rice for this recipe; the pudding will not be as creamy, indeed will be crunchy if refrigerated.

Antebellum Rice Pudding

Makes 4 to 6 Servings

¾ cup long- or short-grain rice (see Tip above)

½ teaspoon salt

¾ cup light or heavy cream

¾ cup milk

½ cup sugar

½ cup dark seedless raisins

1 teaspoon vanilla extract

½ teaspoon finely grated lemon zest

½ teaspoon freshly grated nutmeg

1. Preheat oven to 325°F. Butter 1½-quart casserole and set aside.

2. Combine rice and ¼ teaspoon salt with 1¾ cups cold water in medium-size saucepan and bring to a boil over moderate heat. Cover, reduce heat to low, and simmer 12 to 15 minutes just until all liquid has been absorbed.

3. Mix remaining ingredients including final ¼ teaspoon salt into cooked rice and transfer to casserole.

4. Slide onto middle oven shelf and bake uncovered 25 to 30 minutes just until rice absorbs most of the liquid.

5. Serve hot, at room temperature, or chilled.

Having felt sugar-deprived as a little girl during World War II, I was surprised to discover that the Deep South suffered few sugar shortages during the War Between the States (Civil War) because sugarcane was widely grown there. But with Charleston, Savannah, Mobile, New Orleans, and other major seaports blockaded, the seasonings so dear to Southern cooks—vanilla beans, cinnamon sticks, whole nutmegs webbed with mace—disappeared. Earlier rice puddings contained vanilla and/or spices like cinnamon or freshly grated nutmeg and often raisins as well (see Antebellum Rice Pudding, page 213). Not so this 1860s version, which compensates for their loss with a healthy splash of Madeira, sherry, or bourbon. *Note:* Begin this pudding a day ahead of time because it must be served refrigerator-cold. For me, there's nothing better when summer turns sultry.

Confederate Rice Pudding

Makes 8 Servings

2 cups half-and-half

2 cups milk

1 cup sugar

¼ teaspoon salt

4 large eggs, well beaten

1 cup long-grain rice, cooked according to package directions and still hot

⅓ cup sweet Madeira (Malmsey), cream sherry, top-quality bourbon, or sour mash whiskey

1. Preheat oven to 325°F. Lightly butter 2-quart casserole and set aside.

2. Bring half-and-half, milk, sugar, and salt to simmering in large heavy saucepan over moderate heat, stirring often. Whisking hard, pour about 1 cup hot milk mixture into eggs, stir back into pan, and cook and stir 1 minute—no longer or eggs may curdle. Remove from heat and mix in cooked rice.

3. Pour into casserole. Place in small roasting pan and center on pulled-out middle oven shelf. Pour enough hot water into pan to come about halfway up casserole.

4. Slide oven shelf into oven and bake pudding uncovered 35 to 40 minutes until set like custard and cake tester inserted in middle of pudding comes out clean.

5. Transfer pudding to wire rack and cool to room temperature. With small thin-blade spatula, carefully pull pudding away from sides of casserole and pour Madeira into space now circling casserole.

6. Cover pudding with plastic food wrap and refrigerate at least 24 hours before serving.

An old, old Southern recipe that may or may not have come from **Martha Washington**. It was particularly popular early last century, a place-of-pride dessert served at the end of an elegant meal. "It reminds me a bit of mince pie," a friend remarked, "at least the bread pudding part underneath that cloud of meringue." But Martha Washington pudding—or rather my slightly less caloric version—is easier to make than mince pie. *Notes:* If raisins are to plump nicely, steep them overnight in the port. The reason for using pasteurized eggs? The baking time and temperature may not be sufficient to cook the eggs thoroughly and in this Age of Salmonella, it's always best to play it safe.

Martha Washington Pudding

Makes 6 to 8 Servings

1 cup dark seedless raisins (see Notes above)

1 cup ruby or vintage Port or sweet Madeira wine (Malmsey)

3 cups 1/4-inch cubes firm-textured white bread (no need to remove crusts)

1 cup heavy cream

1/2 cup granulated sugar

3 large pasteurized eggs, separated (see Notes above)

1/4 teaspoon salt

1/4 teaspoon cream of tartar

1/3 cup unsifted confectioner's (10X) sugar

1. Place raisins and Port in small nonreactive bowl, cover, and let stand overnight on kitchen counter.

2. Next day, preheat oven to 350°F. Butter 2 1/2-quart casserole and set aside. Place bread cubes in medium-size bowl, add cream, and let stand 10 minutes.

3. Whisk granulated sugar, egg yolks, and salt in large bowl until smooth. Mix in cream-soaked bread cubes along with unabsorbed cream, plumped raisins, and unabsorbed wine. Pour into casserole.

4. Slide pudding onto middle oven shelf and bake uncovered 40 to 45 minutes until almost set—pudding should quiver slightly when you nudge casserole.

5. When pudding has baked 35 minutes, beat egg whites with cream of tartar in large electric mixer bowl at moderately high speed until fluffy. With machine running, gradually beat in confectioner's sugar; then continue beating 1 to 2 minutes until soft peaks form when beater is raised.

6. Remove pudding from oven and carefully spread meringue on top, swirling into peaks and valleys. Return pudding to middle oven shelf and bake uncovered 15 minutes more until meringue is set and tipped with brown.

7. Serve Martha Washington Pudding hot or, if you prefer, at room temperature—it's delicious either way. If there should be any pudding left—not likely—cover and refrigerate.

Southerners are especially clever about using up breads, raisins, and other dried fruits going stale. This frugal bread pudding—elegant enough for a party—is a case in point. The bread to use is firm-textured white bread (a.k.a. farm-style bread). I think raisin bread would be equally delicious though I've never tried it. And if I do, I'll omit the raisins or use half the amount called for. *Tip:* Only top-quality bourbon or sour mash whiskey will do for the sauce. Cheap brands lack flavor.

Favorite Bread and Butter Pudding with Bourbon Sauce

Makes 6 Servings

4 stale slices firm-textured white bread, crusts and all (see headnote)

2 tablespoons unsalted butter, softened

½ cup dark seedless raisins (see headnote)

3 large eggs, lightly beaten

⅓ cup granulated sugar

½ teaspoon vanilla extract

½ teaspoon ground cinnamon

¼ teaspoon freshly grated nutmeg

1¼ cups milk

1 cup half-and-half

BOURBON SAUCE

¼ cup firmly packed light brown sugar

1½ tablespoons cornstarch

¼ teaspoon freshly grated nutmeg

¼ teaspoon salt

1 cup water

⅓ cup bourbon (see Tip above)

2 tablespoons unsalted butter

1 tablespoon fresh lemon juice

1. Butter 1½-quart casserole or spritz with nonstick cooking spray and set aside.

2. Spread one side of each slice of bread with butter, cut each slice into four pieces of equal size, spread half of them in casserole, and sprinkle half of raisins on top. Repeat layers and set aside.

3. Beat eggs, sugar, vanilla, cinnamon, and nutmeg at high electric mixer speed about 2 minutes until creamy. With mixer at low speed, add milk gradually, then half-and-half.

4. Pour over bread and raisins in casserole and let stand uncovered at room temperature 1 hour. After 40 minutes, preheat oven to 350°F.

5. When pudding has stood 1 hour, set in large shallow pan, and place on pulled-out middle oven shelf. Pour hot water into pan to depth of 1 inch, slide shelf into oven, and bake pudding uncovered about 1 hour until cake tester inserted in center comes out clean.

6. Transfer casserole to wire rack and cool 20 minutes.

7. *Meanwhile, prepare Bourbon Sauce:* Combine sugar, cornstarch, nutmeg, and salt in small nonreactive saucepan. Whisk in water and bourbon and continue whisking until smooth. Add butter, set over moderate heat, and cook, whisking constantly, 2 to 3 minutes until thickened and translucent. Remove from heat, mix in lemon juice, and transfer to heated sauceboat.

8. Serve pudding warm at table, trickle a little sauce over each portion, and pass the rest.

Was this Arkansas classic the forerunner of Charleston's famous Huguenot Torte? According to South Carolina Lowcountry food historian John Martin Taylor ("Hoppin' John"), no question. A careful researcher, he traced Huguenot Torte to Evelyn Florance, who baked it for Charleston's Huguenot Tavern back in the 1940s—a tweaked version, indeed, of Ozark Pudding. Featured in *Charleston Receipts*, Huguenot Torte caught the eye of *New York Herald Tribune* food columnist Clementine Paddleford, whose praise put it on the map—though not the Ozark Pudding that inspired it. If you compare the two recipes, you'll find few differences: brown sugar only for Ozark Pudding plus more cinnamon and fewer nuts. Of course, Ozark pudding recipes vary from cook to cook. I picked this one up nearly forty years ago while on assignment in the Ozarks.

Ozark Pudding

Makes 6 Servings

¾ cup unsifted all-purpose flour

1½ teaspoons baking powder

½ teaspoon ground cinnamon

¼ teaspoon freshly grated nutmeg

¼ teaspoon salt

1 large egg, well beaten

¾ cup firmly packed brown sugar (preferably light)

1½ teaspoons vanilla extract

¾ cup finely chopped peeled and cored apple (about 1 large Golden Delicious or Granny Smith)

½ cup moderately finely chopped wild hickory nuts or pecans

1 cup heavy cream whipped with 2 tablespoons confectioner's (10X) sugar (optional)

1. Preheat oven to 350°F. Coat a 9-inch round, 2-inch-deep pie pan or au gratin dish with nonstick oil-and-flour baking spray and set aside.

2. Sift flour, baking powder, cinnamon, nutmeg, and salt onto wax paper and reserve. Beat egg, sugar, and vanilla well in small mixing bowl to combine, mix in reserved flour mixture, then apple and nuts.

3. Scoop into pan, spreading to edge and smoothing top. Slide onto middle oven shelf and bake uncovered 25 to 30 minutes until richly browned.

4. Cool pudding 20 minutes, then cut into wedges and top each portion, if you like, with whipped cream.

Back when I was growing up on the fringes of Raleigh, the road running past our house was red clay and fields and forests outnumbered houses. Every October we'd head for a grove of wild persimmon trees and fill our buckets with sticky, prickly fruits, swatting flies and yellow jackets the whole enduring time. Never having heard of persimmon pudding, my Midwestern mother baked what we'd gathered into cobblers. I, myself, never tasted wild persimmon pudding until I went to work, right out of college, as an assistant home demonstration agent in Iredell County some 150 miles west of Raleigh. August was Picnic Month for the Home Demonstration Clubs to which the 4-Hers' mothers all belonged. These huge potluck suppers gave each woman a chance to showcase her best recipes: fried chicken, sweet slaw, yellow squash pudding, and so forth. Desserts invariably included three or four different wild persimmon puddings—old family recipes—with club members waging a friendly competition year after year. This particular recipe is an amalgam of several old Iredell County recipes.

Iredell County Wild Persimmon Pudding

Makes 4 Servings

1 cup unsifted all-purpose flour

½ teaspoon baking soda

½ teaspoon salt

¼ teaspoon freshly grated nutmeg

¼ teaspoon ground ginger

¼ teaspoon ground cinnamon

⅛ teaspoon ground allspice

2 extra-large eggs

¼ cup firmly packed light brown sugar

1 teaspoon vanilla extract

1 cup firmly packed wild persimmon purée (see Persimmons, page 22)

1 cup milk minus 2 tablespoons

2 tablespoons melted unsalted butter

1. Preheat oven to 350°F. Spritz 1-quart casserole with nonstick cooking spray and set aside.

2. Sift flour, baking soda, salt, nutmeg, ginger, cinnamon, and allspice onto wax paper and set aside.

3. Beat eggs, sugar, and vanilla at moderately high electric mixer speed 1½ to 2 minutes until thick and pale yellow. Reduce mixer speed to low and beat in persimmon purée and milk. Add sifted dry ingredients and mix by hand until well blended. Finally, stir in melted butter, mixing only enough to combine.

4. Pour batter into prepared casserole, spreading to edge, then set in baking pan on pulled-out middle oven shelf. Pour hot water into pan to come halfway up sides of casserole and slide middle shelf back into oven.

5. Bake pudding—uncovered—in water bath about 1 hour until it pulls from sides of casserole and cake tester inserted in middle comes out clean. Transfer to wire rack and cool to room temperature.

6. Serve topped with whipped cream or vanilla ice cream.

Southerners are lucky because peach orchards abound and peak-of-flavor peaches are as near as the nearest farmers' market. Even some supermarkets showcase the homegrown in season and these are the peaches to buy for this quick and easy dessert—preferably freestone peaches that require little time and effort to peel, pit, and slice. *Tip:* How do you tell if a peach is ripe? Look for creamy-gold color (the amount of red blush varies from species to species and isn't a true indicator of ripeness). Sniff the peach (it should smell like a peach—sweet and fragrant), then press it ever so gently. A ripe peach will yield to light palm pressure but still feel fairly firm. Reject any peaches that seem mushy, bruised, or have split or shriveling skin. Also reject any that smell musty, sour, or vinous.

Right-off-the-Tree Peach Crisp

Makes 4 to 6 Servings

FILLING

- 4 large firm-ripe peaches (about 2½ pounds), peeled, pitted, and sliced about ¼ inch thick (see Tip above)
- 2 tablespoons fresh lemon or lime juice
- ¼ teaspoon finely grated lemon zest
- ¼ teaspoon almond extract
- ¼ cup granulated sugar

TOPPING

- 1 cup firmly packed light brown sugar
- ¾ cup unsifted all-purpose flour
- 1 teaspoon ground cinnamon
- ½ teaspoon ground ginger
- ¼ teaspoon freshly grated nutmeg
- ¼ teaspoon salt
- ½ cup (1 stick) unsalted butter, cut into pats and softened to room temperature

1. Preheat oven to 350°F.

2. *For Filling:* Place peaches, lemon juice and zest, almond extract, and sugar in large bowl, toss well to mix, then scoop into ungreased deep 9-inch pie plate and spread to edge.

3. *For Topping:* Place all ingredients in same bowl—now wiped clean—and toss well to mix, making sure softened butter is well distributed. Scatter topping evenly over peaches.

4. Slide pie plate onto rimmed baking sheet and bake on middle oven shelf about 45 minutes until bubbly and lightly browned.

5. Cool peach crisp in pie plate on wire rack to room temperature.

6. Serve "straight up," or if you prefer, top with whipped cream or scoops of vanilla ice cream.

VARIATION

Two-Kinds-of-Apple Crisp: Prepare as directed substituting 2 large Golden Delicious apples and 2 large Granny Smith apples peeled, cored, and thinly sliced for peaches, finely grated orange zest for lemon zest, and omit almond extract. Also add ¼ teaspoon finely grated orange zest to Topping. Bake as directed. Makes 4 to 6 Servings.

There's a microclimate in south-central North Carolina called the Sandhills where peaches grow plump and sweet and where, come June, families arrive by the carload to buy just-off-the-tree Redhavens or other golden-fleshed freestones that peel, pit, and slice neatly. Soon there will be biscuit-crowned peach cobblers cooling, sugary crisps (see page 220), and pies both open-face (see page 181) and closed. Much as I adore crisps, cobblers, and pies, I like peach soufflé even better IF the peaches are dead-ripe and bursting with flavor. Don't let soufflés intimidate you. Most fail simply because the egg whites have been whipped until stand-up stiff. If beaten only till soft and billowing, your soufflé will rise majestically—and along with it, your reputation.

Peak Season Peach Soufflé

Makes 4 to 6 Servings

1 cup firmly packed fresh peach purée (about 3 medium-size peaches)

2 tablespoons fresh lime or lemon juice

⅓ cup granulated sugar blended with 3 tablespoons cornstarch

¼ teaspoon freshly grated nutmeg

¼ teaspoon salt

Pinch ground ginger

4 large egg yolks lightly beaten with ¼ cup light or heavy cream

1 tablespoon bourbon or sour mash whiskey

6 large egg whites

2½ tablespoons confectioner's (10X) sugar

Pinch cream of tartar

1. Preheat oven to 375°F. Butter a 1½-quart soufflé dish well, add 2 tablespoons granulated sugar, then tilt dish this way and that to coat bottom and sides; tap out excess sugar and set dish aside.

2. Combine peach purée, lime juice, sugar-cornstarch mixture, nutmeg, salt, and ginger in medium-size heavy nonreactive saucepan, set over moderate heat, and cook, stirring constantly, about 3 minutes until mixture bubbles, thickens, and clears.

3. Remove from heat, whisk a little hot peach mixture into beaten egg yolk mixture, stir back into pan, and cook, stirring constantly, over low heat 2 minutes; do not boil or mixture may curdle.

4. Transfer to ice bath to quick-chill, stirring often to prevent mixture from "skinning." When cool, blend in bourbon.

5. Beat egg whites until frothy in large electric mixer bowl at moderately high speed, then with mixer at low speed, add 2 tablespoons confectioner's sugar and cream of tartar. Continue beating until whites are soft and billowing and peaks lop over when beater is withdrawn.

6. Fold about one-third beaten whites into peach mixture to lighten it, then add remaining two-thirds and fold in until no streaks of white or yellow remain—easy does it.

7. Pour into soufflé dish, set on heavy-duty rimmed baking sheet, slide onto middle oven shelf, and bake uncovered 20 minutes.

8. Carefully open oven, sift remaining ½ tablespoon confectioner's sugar over soufflé, gently close oven door, and bake soufflé 10 to 15 minutes longer until puffed and tipped with brown. It should quiver slightly when dish is nudged.

9. Rush soufflé from oven to table and serve straightaway—being softly set, it will collapse as it cools. But this is the nature of all good soufflés.

My good friend Fran McCullough, who spent some of her early childhood in the South Carolina Lowcountry and who now lives in North Carolina's historic Hillsborough after a distinguished New York career as cookbook author/editor, suggested a brilliant way to use my leftover "recipe-testing" muscadines: create a clafoutis. It you don't know this French dessert, it's a sort of cherry cobbler from the Limousin. Fran even wondered if clafoutis recipes might have come to South Carolina with the French Huguenots (Protestants fleeing religious persecution) more than 325 years ago. Among those landing in Charleston was the Reverend Elie Prioleau of Pons, a town maybe 100 miles west of the Limousin. He became pastor of this country's first Huguenot church (it's still there in Charleston and still active). After riffling through early Southern cookbooks, I find no recipes for—or mentions of—clafoutis. So I e-mailed food historian Damon Lee Fowler, who replied, "I don't think clafoutis is an old thing in the Lowcountry." There's no denying, however, that today's Southern chefs are doing magic tricks with the original clafoutis, substituting our best blackberries, blueberries, even figs for the *cerises* (cherries) of Limousin. I think muscadines even better. *Note:* By mashing the grapes, then macerating in lemon juice, I managed to halve the cooking time needed to soften the leathery muscadine skins.

Muscadine Clafoutis

Makes 6 Servings

4 cups dead-ripe muscadines (about 1½ pounds), washed, halved, and seeded (see headnote, Muscadine Mystery Cake, page 224)

Juice (from grapes above)

¼ cup fresh lemon juice

Finely grated zest of 1 large lemon

2 tablespoons granulated sugar

2 tablespoons all-purpose flour

BATTER

½ cup granulated sugar

⅓ cup unsifted all-purpose flour

¼ teaspoon salt

4 large eggs, at room temperature

2 tablespoons melted unsalted butter

1½ cups milk, at room temperature

1½ teaspoons vanilla extract

¼ teaspoon salt

1 to 2 tablespoons confectioner's (10X) sugar (Topping)

1. Place grapes and their juice in large nonreactive bowl and mash with potato masher. Mix in lemon juice and zest, cover, and macerate overnight at room temperature.

2. When ready to proceed, transfer grape mixture to medium-size nonreactive saucepan and simmer, stirring often, 10 to 15 minutes until grape skins are tender. Drain well, setting grapes aside and returning juice to pan.

3. Boil grape juice uncovered over high heat 5 to 7 minutes, stirring often, until reduced to ⅓ cup. Set off-heat and reserve.

4. Preheat oven to 375°F. Lightly butter shallow 2-quart round or oval baking dish; set aside.

5. *For Batter:* Combine sugar, flour, and salt in large bowl. Beat eggs until frothy in second bowl, then whisk in melted butter, milk, vanilla, and salt. Whisking constantly, gradually add egg mixture to dry ingredients, and continue whisking until as smooth and thin as crêpe batter.

6. Spread drained grapes over bottom of baking dish, sprinkle with granulated sugar, then flour. Drizzle with reserved ⅓ cup reduced muscadine juice and pour batter over all.

7. Slide onto middle shelf and bake uncovered about 40 minutes until billowing and brown. Transfer to wire rack and cool 30 to 40 minutes.

8. Before serving, sift confectioner's sugar over clafoutis and, if you like, sift a little more over each portion.

Having a quart of muscadines going begging, I dreamed up this layered affair with muscadines on the bottom, custard in the middle, and yellow cake on top—a spin, if you will, on the lemon pudding cake we loved as kids. There are hundreds of muscadine grape varieties, some with tougher skins than others. Mine, to use an old Southern saying, "were tough as old Nick." So to keep their chewiness from eclipsing the cake's delicacy, I simmered them into submission, then gave them a good chop. *Note:* If grapes are truly ripe (soft) and halved from stem to blossom end, you can thumb out the seeds. Most muscadines have two lentil-size seeds—both often in one of the two halves. Seed the grapes over a sieve-topped bowl to catch the precious juice. A nimble-fingered colleague of mine says she can seed a quart of muscadines in 5 minutes. It takes me 15.

Muscadine Mystery Cake

Makes 6 Servings

4 cups dead-ripe muscadines (about 1½ pounds), washed, halved, and seeded (see Note above)

Juice (from grapes above)

⅓ cup sugar

1 tablespoon fresh lemon juice

1½ teaspoons finely grated lemon zest

BATTER

2 large eggs, separated

1½ tablespoons unsalted butter, at room temperature

1½ teaspoons finely grated lemon zest

¼ teaspoon salt

½ cup sugar

2 tablespoons all-purpose flour

½ cup milk

2 tablespoons fresh lemon juice

1. Simmer halved grapes and juice in uncovered medium-small nonreactive saucepan over moderate heat, stirring now and then, about 25 minutes until skins are soft. Mix in sugar, lemon juice, and zest, and cook uncovered, stirring occasionally, 5 minutes.

2. Scoop into large sieve over heatproof bowl and press as dry as possible, discarding any "missed" seeds. Transfer pressed-dry grapes to cutting board and chop till size of cornflakes.

3. Boil sieved grape juice uncovered over moderately high heat about 5 minutes until as thick as corn syrup. Mix 1 tablespoon grape syrup into grapes and set aside. Use remaining grape syrup to decorate mystery cake plates. Or save to spread on fresh-baked biscuits or muffins.

4. Set 13 × 9 × 2-inch baking pan on middle oven shelf, add water to depth of ¼ inch, and preheat oven to 325°F. Lightly butter 8 × 8 × 2-inch baking dish and set aside.

5. *For Batter:* With hand electric mixer, beat egg yolks, butter, lemon zest, and salt at high speed about 1 minute until as smooth as lemon curd. Add ¼ cup sugar and beat 2 minutes until mayonnaise-like. By hand, mix in flour, milk, and lemon juice.

6. With clean beaters, whip egg whites until frothy, then at high speed, add remaining $\frac{1}{4}$ cup sugar gradually and beat until consistency of boiled icing. Fold into batter—gently.

7. Scoop grape mixture into baking dish, spreading to corners, and pour batter evenly over all.

8. Set baking dish in water bath water on middle oven shelf and bake uncovered 45 to 50 minutes until top is springy and lightly browned.

9. Cool cake on wire rack to room temperature before cutting. **Note:** To "paint" dessert plates with grape syrup, thin with 1 to 2 teaspoons hot water. Pour into a small squirt bottle, then make squiggles or dots around plate rims. Easy once you get the hang of it.

chapter seven

Cakes & Cookies

It's said to be the state of Maryland's "official cake" and I admit that it takes a bit of doing not to mention a mother lode of 9-inch layer cake pans. Send the call out among friends and neighbors. Most will have at least two 9-inchers and be happy to lend them (maybe for a taste of this amazing cake?). Or you could do what my resourceful friend and colleague Joanne Lamb Hayes has done and that's to fashion foil pan liners using a turned-upside-down 9-inch layer cake pan as a template. Tear off ten 12-inch pieces of aluminum foil. Invert a 9-inch round layer cake pan on the counter, then one at a time, press foil pieces over the bottom and side of the pan fashioning a liner, then trim until sides of the liners are no more than an inch high. Fit the liners into as many 9-inch round pans as you have—pie pans, springform pans, whatever—then spritz each with nonstick oil-and-flour baking spray and set aside. *Note:* If you manage to commandeer ten 9-inch pans, line the bottom of each with baking parchment and spritz well with nonstick oil-and-flour baking spray—a small price to pay to keep those thin layers of cake from sticking to the pans and tearing. No matter how many pans you round up, you will have to bake the layers in batches, so keep the batter in a cool spot in the kitchen. Fortunately, the layers are thin and bake fast.

Smith Island Ten-Layer Cake

Makes One 9-Inch, 10-Layer Cake

3⅓ cups sifted all-purpose flour

4 teaspoons baking powder

½ teaspoon salt

2 cups sugar

1 cup (2 sticks) unsalted butter, softened (no substitute)

1 tablespoon vanilla extract

4 large eggs

1 cup evaporated milk (do not use reduced-fat or fat-free)

FROSTING

3 cups (18 ounces) semisweet chocolate chips

1¼ cups heavy cream

1. Preheat oven to 375°F.

2. Whisk flour, baking powder, and salt together in medium-size bowl and set aside. Prepare layer cake pans or foil pan liners as directed in the Note and headnote above, making sure each is well spritzed with nonstick oil-and-flour baking spray. Set aside.

3. Beat sugar, butter, and vanilla in large electric mixer bowl, first at low speed, then at high, about 3 minutes until fluffy, scraping sides of bowl frequently. Add eggs, one by one, beating well after each addition.

4. With mixer at low speed, add combined dry ingredients alternately with milk, beginning and ending with dry, and beating between additions only enough to combine.

5. Ladle ⅔ cup batter into each foil liner or parchment-lined pan, spreading to edge and smoothing top. Slide 2 or 3 pans onto middle oven shelf, more if your oven can accommodate them without touching one another or oven walls.

6. Bake about 10 to 12 minutes until layers begin to pull from sides of pans and centers spring back when gently pressed—tops will not be brown.

7. Cool layers in upright pans or foil liners on wire racks 2 minutes. Gently lift cake layers from pans and set aside to cool still in liners or on parchment. **Note:** If you don't have 10 cake pans, as soon as

several layers are baked, cooled briefly, and removed from pans, run cool water over bottoms of pans and wipe dry. Insert new foil liners in pans or quickly wash and dry pans and reline with baking parchment. Spritz liners or parchment with nonstick oil-and-flour baking spray. Spoon ⅔ cup batter into each liner or pan and bake as before. Repeat until you have baked 10 layers.

8. *For Frosting:* While final layers bake, melt chocolate in double-boiler top over barely simmering water. Heat cream in small saucepan over low heat until bubbles begin forming around edge of pan. Lift double-boiler top to counter, add cream, and whisk until smooth.

9. To assemble cake, place one layer, right side up, on large round cake plate. Add about 2 tablespoons frosting and spread to edge. Continue layering the same way until all 10 layers are in place. Frost top and sides of cake with remaining frosting.

10. Let frosted cake stand about 20 minutes before cutting. If there are leftovers, cover and refrigerate, if you like. I personally would do so only in torrid weather—the chocolate filling and frosting is so rich it's not likely to spoil.

No one knows who created Lord Baltimore Cake, when or where, though there are myths, one of them dating back to the original Lord Baltimore who, piqued at the extravagant use of egg whites in his wife's favorite cake, spent a tipsy night with the head cook dreaming up a way to use the orphaned yolks. A later but similar story is that the cake was invented to use up the yolks left over from Lady Baltimore Cake. Trouble is, the original Lady B. Cake was yellow (for the story behind this beloved Southern classic as well as the recipe for it, see my *Love Affair with Southern Cooking*, 2007). In truth, that recipe comes from a tea room in Charleston, SC, not Baltimore, and was immortalized in Owen Wister's 1906 best-selling romantic novel, *Lady Baltimore*). *Note:* Because the egg whites in the frosting never reach the temperature the U.S. Department of Agriculture deems safe, I specify pasteurized eggs, which many supermarkets now sell. If unavailable, buy eggs from a local source you trust to minimize the risk of salmonella food poisoning.

Lord Baltimore Cake

Makes One 9-Inch, 3-Layer Cake

3 cups sifted cake flour

1 tablespoon baking powder

½ teaspoon salt

1⅓ cups sugar

¾ cup (1½ sticks) unsalted butter, softened (no substitute)

1 tablespoon vanilla extract

6 large pasteurized egg yolks (see Note above)

¾ cup milk

FROSTING

1½ cups sugar

2 large pasteurized egg whites (see Note above)

¼ cup cold water

1 tablespoon light corn syrup

¼ teaspoon cream of tartar

½ teaspoon vanilla extract

¼ teaspoon almond extract

⅓ cup coarsely chopped pecans

⅓ cup coarsely chopped blanched almonds

⅓ cup coarsely chopped candied red cherries

⅓ cup coarsely chopped almond macaroons

1 teaspoon finely grated lemon zest

1. Preheat oven to 350°F. Spritz three 9-inch round layer cake pans with nonstick oil-and-flour baking spray, line pan bottoms with parchment, spritz again, and set aside. Whisk flour, baking powder, and salt together in medium-size bowl and set aside also.

2. Beat sugar, butter, and vanilla in large electric mixer bowl, first at low speed, then at high, about 3 minutes, scraping sides of bowl frequently, until fluffy. Add egg yolks two at a time, beating well after each addition to combine.

3. Add combined dry ingredients alternately with milk, beginning and ending with dry and beating after each addition only enough to combine. Further beating will toughen the cake. Divide batter evenly among the three pans, spreading to edge and smoothing tops.

4. Slide pans onto middle oven shelf, touching neither one another nor oven sides, and bake about 25 minutes until layers begin to pull from sides

continued on page 232

continued from page 230

of pans and cake tester inserted in middle of one layer comes out clean.

5. Cool layers in upright pans on wire rack 15 minutes, loosen around edges with thin-blade spatula, then invert on racks, turn right side up, and cool to room temperature.

6. *For Frosting:* With hand electric beater, beat sugar, egg whites, water, corn syrup, and cream of tartar in double-boiler top at moderate speed until smooth. Set over simmering water and beat about 7 minutes at high speed until thick and fluffy. Stir in vanilla and almond extracts. Place pecans, almonds, cherries, macaroon bits, and lemon zest in small bowl, toss well, and set aside.

7. Invert one cake layer in middle of large round cake plate. Spread with ½ cup frosting and sprinkle with ⅓ cup nut mixture. Place second layer right side up on top; spread with ½ cup frosting and sprinkle with ⅓ cup nut mixture. Center third layer right side up on top, then frost top with remaining frosting. Wreathe remaining nut mixture around top of cake.

8. Let cake stand about an hour, then cut into wedges and serve. Cover any leftover cake and store in the refrigerator.

The high country of Virginia, Tennessee, and North Carolina is apple country, indeed North Carolina's Henderson County claims to grow more apples than any other county in America. Most popular varieties? Delicious (both the red and the golden), Rome Beauty, and Gala. Any good pie apple works well in this recipe, but I prefer those on the tart side—Granny Smiths, for example, or Greenings. This is what Southerners call a "snacking cake," an unfussy loaf that can be eaten on the run. Riffling through my collection of Southern community cookbooks, I find many recipes for fresh apple cake. Some call for a heavy boiled glaze that begins with a pound of brown sugar. This cake is plenty rich without it, so I skip the glaze and extra calories. *Note:* You can now buy prediced dates—a major time-saver. I sometimes substitute raisins or dried blueberries for dates. Neither is traditional but both are delicious.

Fresh Apple Cake

Makes One 13 × 9 × 2-Inch Loaf Cake

3 cups sifted all-purpose flour

1 cup coarsely chopped pecans, black walnuts, or wild hickory nuts

1 cup diced dates or, if you prefer, dark seedless raisins or dried blueberries

1 teaspoon baking powder

½ teaspoon baking soda

½ teaspoon salt

½ teaspoon ground cinnamon

½ teaspoon ground ginger

½ teaspoon freshly grated nutmeg

2 cups sugar

¾ cup corn oil or vegetable oil

2 extra-large eggs

3 cups moderately finely chopped, peeled and cored tart apples (about 1½ pounds; see headnote)

1. Preheat oven to 350°F. Coat a 13 × 9 × 2-inch baking pan with nonstick oil-and-flour baking spray and set aside.

2. Spoon ½ cup flour into medium-size bowl, add pecans and dates, and toss well; set aside. Sift remaining flour, baking powder, baking soda, salt, and spices onto wax paper and set aside.

3. Using hand electric mixer, beat sugar and oil at high speed about 1 minute until thick and smooth. Beat eggs in one by one. By hand, fold in apples, then sifted dry ingredients, then pecans and dates and all dredging flour.

4. Scoop batter into pan, spreading to corners. Slide pan onto middle oven shelf and bake about 45 minutes until cake tester inserted in middle of loaf comes out clean.

5. Cool cake in upright pan on wire rack, then cut into squares and serve.

Several Southern friends—excellent bakers all—have asked about a long-lost recipe, something called Orange Cake. Descriptions vary but most remember it as a yellow layer cake filled and glossed with an orange glaze or syrup. My food friend Bob Holmes of Greensboro, NC, a devout and accomplished hobby cook, described the orange cake of his childhood Christmases this way:

"I remember it being the family Christmas cake (along with a fresh coconut cake). It had pure orange flavor—no fluffy boiled or seven-minute frosting. And certainly no buttercream. In fact it had no 'icing' at all with the same orange filling being used between the layers, on the sides, and top. The layers were not much thicker than a pancake, and the cake was never eaten the day it was made so it had time to mellow. I remember grating the orange zest ever so carefully on one of those old box graters to avoid getting any of the bitter white. And I remember it took an incredible number of oranges to get enough juice. I think our Orange Christmas Cake had six, maybe seven, layers so my grandmother and aunt must have doubled the filling for that many layers."

When I asked Bob if his folks might have baked three layers and halved them crosswise, he said, "My aunt never used more than three pans to cook the six layers. She would take the first three out of the oven, turn them out of her well-seasoned pans immediately, and into the still hot pans went the next batch of batter. We always thought the Orange Christmas Cake got better the longer it sat. But it never sat for long." Bob could kick himself for not getting this old family recipe and when he called a cousin to see if she might have it, she said she never learned to make the cake because she never liked it. What follows is my stab at Bob's family's Orange Christmas Cake, which he says looks like the real thing except that it's a three-layer cake instead of a six. Next time I bake this Orange Christmas Cake, I'll invite Bob to drive over from Greensboro for a taste (and a big "doggie bag"). *Note:* Use oranges with robust flavor for this cake. I like Valencias.

Orange Christmas Cake

Makes One 9-Inch, 3-Layer Cake

3 cups sifted all-purpose flour

1 tablespoon baking powder

½ teaspoon salt

2 cups sugar

1¼ cups (2½ sticks) unsalted butter, softened (no substitute)

2 teaspoons finely grated orange zest (see Note above)

1 teaspoon vanilla extract

4 large eggs, separated

1 cup milk

ORANGE SYRUP

1½ cups strained fresh orange juice (see Note above)

1 cup sugar

4 teaspoons finely grated orange zest

OPTIONAL GARNISH

Orange zest curls

1. Preheat oven to 350°F. Spritz three 9-inch round layer cake pans with nonstick oil-and-flour baking spray, line bottoms of pans with parchment, spritz again, and set aside.

2. Whisk flour, baking powder and salt together in large mixing bowl and set aside also.

3. Cream sugar, butter, orange zest, and vanilla in large electric mixer bowl about 3 minutes at high speed until fluffy, pausing frequently to scrape sides of bowl. Add egg yolks and beat only enough to combine. At low mixer speed, add combined dry ingredients alternately with milk, beginning and ending with dry and beating after each addition just until combined.

4. With clean bowl and beaters, beat egg whites to soft peaks and fold gently into batter. Divide batter among pans, spreading to edges and smoothing tops.

5. Slide pans onto middle oven shelf (they should not touch one another or walls of oven) and bake about 25 minutes until layers begin to pull from sides of pans and cake tester inserted in middle comes out clean.

6. Cool layers in upright pans on wire racks 15 minutes, loosen around edge with thin-blade spatula, then invert on racks, turn right side up, and cool to room temperature.

7. *For Orange Syrup:* Combine orange juice and sugar in small nonreactive saucepan and bring to a boil over low heat. Adjust heat so mixture bubbles gently and simmer 1 minute. Remove from heat and stir in half of orange zest.

8. To assemble, place one cake layer right side up on large round cake plate, pierce top 12 to 15 times with toothpick, and gradually spoon on one-third of orange syrup, allowing it to soak in. Set second layer right side up on top, pierce, and soak with another one-third syrup. Stir remaining orange zest into remaining syrup. Top cake with third layer, again placing right side up, then pierce, and spoon on remaining syrup. Garnish with orange zest curls, if desired.

9. Let cake stand at room temperature about an hour before cutting.

I found this recipe in *Coastal Cookery*, a slim spiral-bound volume first published in 1937 by the Cassina Garden Club of St. Simon's Island, GA. It has now gone through at least eight editions, the last printed in 1972 and the one I have. This is my updated version of that long-ago recipe. Unlike many Southern cakes, this one is not very sweet—perfect, I think, for an afternoon tea or open house.

Marmalade Tea Cake

Makes One 9 × 5 × 3-Inch Loaf

2¾ cups sifted all-purpose flour

2½ teaspoons baking powder

½ teaspoon baking soda

½ teaspoon salt

1 cup orange marmalade

2 tablespoons unsalted butter, slightly softened (no substitute)

1 large egg

¾ cup fresh orange juice

¾ cup finely chopped pecans, black walnuts, or English walnuts

GLAZE

¼ cup fresh lemon juice

¼ cup sugar

1. Preheat oven to 325°F. Line 9 × 5 × 3-inch pan with baking parchment or aluminum foil leaving an overhang on both sides, then spritz with nonstick oil-and-flour baking spray. Set pan aside.

2. Whisk flour with baking powder, baking soda, and salt in medium-size mixing bowl and set aside.

3. Beat marmalade and butter at high electric mixer speed about 1 minute to combine. Scrape sides of bowl, add egg, and beat 2 minutes until light.

4. At low mixer speed, add combined dry ingredients alternately with orange juice, beginning and ending with dry and mixing after each addition only enough to combine. By hand, fold in nuts. Scoop batter into pan, spreading to corners.

5. Slide pan onto middle oven shelf and bake 1 to 1½ hours until nicely browned, loaf begins to pull from sides of pan, and cake tester inserted in middle comes out clean.

6. Transfer loaf to wire rack, placing right side up.

7. *For Glaze:* Combine lemon juice and sugar in small nonreactive saucepan, set over moderate heat, and cook, stirring constantly, about 1 minute until sugar dissolves. Pierce cake 10 to 12 times with toothpick, spoon hot glaze slowly over cake, letting it soak in and dribble down sides. Let stand 15 minutes in upright pan on wire rack.

8. Grasping edges of parchment, gently lift cake from pan to wire rack and cool to room temperature before removing parchment.

9. To serve, cut tea cake into slices about ⅜ inch thick using your sharpest serrated knife and a gentle see-saw motion. **Note:** Some Southern hostesses halve or quarter each slice—easier to eat while balancing a cup of tea or coffee.

In our grandmothers' day, this cake was baked in a large tube pan, which meant that it was in the oven for 1½ hours, maybe more. I use a faster-baking shallow loaf pan—standard equipment in today's kitchens. There's another bonus: Cakes baked in shallow pans are less likely to fall.

Gran's Sweet Potato Cake

Makes One 13 × 9 × 2-Inch Loaf Cake

2½ pounds sweet potatoes (about 4 medium-large), scrubbed but not peeled

3 cups sifted all-purpose flour

1½ teaspoons baking powder

1 teaspoon ground cinnamon

1 teaspoon ground ginger

1 teaspoon freshly grated nutmeg

½ teaspoon baking soda

¼ teaspoon salt

1½ cups firmly packed light brown sugar

1 cup coarsely chopped pecans

1 cup (2 sticks) melted unsalted butter (no substitute)

4 large eggs, lightly beaten

1 teaspoon finely grated orange zest

1 teaspoon vanilla extract

3 tablespoons granulated sugar mixed with ½ teaspoon ground cinnamon (Topping)

1. Preheat oven to 400°F.

2. Pierce each sweet potato with a skewer, then arrange potatoes, not touching, on baking sheet; slide onto middle oven shelf and bake for about 1 hour or until very soft. Cool until easy to handle. Meanwhile, coat 13 × 9 × 2-inch loaf pan with nonstick cooking spray and set aside. Also lower oven temperature to 350°F.

3. Sift next 7 ingredients (flour through salt) into a large mixing bowl. Add brown sugar and work in with your fingers, pressing out all lumps. Add pecans, toss well, then make a well in middle of dry ingredients. Set aside.

4. Halve cooled sweet potatoes lengthwise and scoop flesh into a second large mixing bowl. Mash until fluffy, add melted butter, and whisk until smooth. Add eggs, orange zest, and vanilla, and whisk to combine.

5. Pour sweet potato mixture into well in dry ingredients, then with large rubber spatula, fold in gently but thoroughly. Don't beat or you'll toughen the cake.

6. Scoop batter into pan, spreading to corners and smoothing surface. Sprinkle Topping evenly on top.

7. Slide cake onto middle oven shelf and bake 45 to 50 minutes until springy to touch and cake tester inserted in middle comes out clean.

8. Cool cake to room temperature in upright pan on wire rack, then cut into large squares and serve. **Note:** I think this cake so rich and moist it needs nothing more, but I know cooks who add a scoop of vanilla ice cream or cloud of whipped cream.

I find this a delicious way to use up leftover sweet potato; a large one, puréed, will give you about what you need here. You can make this cake in advance, wrap in foil, and freeze. But don't glaze it until an hour or two before serving. Though this pound cake can be served "straight up," it's better still when topped by a scoop of vanilla ice cream or drift of whipped cream.

Bourbon-Glazed Sweet Potato Pound Cake

Makes One 10-Inch Tube Cake

4 cups coarsely chopped, richly toasted pecans (10 to 12 minutes at 350°F)

4 cups sifted all-purpose flour (not a soft Southern flour)

1½ teaspoons freshly grated nutmeg

1 teaspoon baking powder

¼ teaspoon baking soda

¼ teaspoon salt

2 cups (4 sticks) cold unsalted butter (no substitute)

2 cups granulated sugar

6 extra-large eggs

1 cup firmly packed, puréed, unseasoned baked sweet potato, at room temperature (see headnote)

½ cup milk

2 tablespoons bourbon

1 teaspoon vanilla extract

1 teaspoon finely grated orange zest

BOURBON GLAZE

¾ cup unsifted confectioner's (10X) sugar

1½ tablespoons each bourbon and cold water

1½ teaspoons vanilla extract

1. Preheat oven to 300°F. Coat 10-inch tube pan with nonstick oil-and-flour baking spray and set aside.

2. Dredge pecans in ½ cup flour in large bowl; set aside. Whisk remaining flour, nutmeg, baking powder, baking soda, and salt together in second large bowl and set aside.

3. Cream butter at low electric mixer speed 3 minutes, scraping bowl at halftime, then with mixer at highest speed and without pausing to scrape mixing bowl, cream butter 3 minutes longer until light. Scrape bowl well, then beating at low speed, add granulated sugar gradually. Raise speed to high and beat 5 minutes until fluffy and almost white, pausing often to scrape bowl.

4. At low mixer speed, add eggs one by one, beating well after each addition. Combine sweet potato, milk, bourbon, vanilla, and orange zest in a spouted 1-quart measure, then with mixer at low speed, add dry ingredients alternately with sweet potato mixture, beginning and ending with dry and beating only enough to partially incorporate—no more or you'll toughen the cake. Four additions of the dry and three of sweet potato mixture are about right.

continued on page 240

continued from page 239

5. By hand, fold in pecans and dredging flour, scooping down to bottom of bowl to make sure they're distributed evenly. This is a stiff batter; handle it with a light touch

6. Scoop batter into pan, smooth top, and rap sharply once or twice on counter to release large air bubbles.

7. Slide cake onto middle oven shelf and bake $1\frac{1}{2}$ hours until it begins to pull from sides of pan and cake tester inserted midway between central tube and edge of pan comes out clean.

8. Cool cake in upright pan on wire rack 20 minutes. Carefully loosen around edge and central tube with small, thin-blade spatula and invert cake on rack. Cool cake to room temperature.

9. Transfer cake (rack and all) to wax-paper-covered counter. Quickly combine all Bourbon Glaze ingredients, then drizzle glaze decoratively over cake, letting it run down sides. **Note:** Scoop up any glaze that lands on wax paper and continue spooning over cake. Allow cake to stand at least an hour before cutting.

10. To serve, cut cake into wedges and top each portion, if you like, with a scoop of vanilla ice cream or billow of whipped cream.

I'm forever trying new ways to use the South's beloved pecans, the latest being this flourless European-style torte. I've always adored the hazelnut torte in *The New German Cookbook*, which I coauthored with my Bavarian friend Hedy Würz, so I thought, why not rework it substituting pecans? And here's the beauty of this recipe: You can bake the layers ahead of time, wrap them individually, and freeze. When ready to serve, thaw the layers, fill and frost with sweetened whipped cream, and garnish with lightly toasted pecan halves. How easy is that? *Note:* To prepare pecans, spread 4 cups (about 1 pound) broken pecans on an ungreased baking sheet, slide onto middle shelf of a preheated 350°F oven, and toast 10 to 12 minutes, stirring at halftime, until nuts are nicely browned and smell irresistible. Cool to room temperature, then pulse in two or three batches in a food processor until texture of kosher salt—perhaps a little finer. Easy does it. You don't want "pecan butter." *Reminder:* Don't forget that you'll also need 12 perfect pecan halves, lightly toasted, to garnish the torte. Toast them just as you do the broken pecans.

Toasted Pecan Torte

Makes One 10-Inch, 2-Layer Torte

10   extra-large eggs, separated

1½   cups granulated sugar

 2   teaspoons vanilla extract

 4   cups finely ground toasted pecans (about 1 pound; see Note above)

¼   teaspoon salt

FILLING, FROSTING, & DECORATION

3½   cups refrigerator-cold whipping cream

¼   cup confectioner's (10X) sugar

 1   teaspoon vanilla extract

12   perfect pecan halves, lightly toasted (see Reminder above)

1. Preheat oven to 350°F. Liberally coat bottom and sides of two 10-inch springform pans with nonstick oil-and-flour baking spray and set aside.

2. Beat egg yolks, 1¼ cups granulated sugar, and vanilla in large electric mixer bowl at high speed 3 to 5 minutes until color and consistency of mayonnaise, pausing several times to scrape mixer bowl. At low speed, mix in pecans. Transfer to large shallow mixing bowl.

3. With clean beaters and bowl, beat egg whites and salt until frothy, then with machine at low speed, add remaining ¼ cup sugar gradually. Raise mixer speed to high and continue beating until whites glisten, peak softly, but are stiff enough to hold their shape. **Note:** If you beat longer at this point, you'll knock the air out of whites and that's what leavens the torte.

4. Mix about one-third of beaten whites into pecan mixture in shallow bowl to lighten it, then carefully fold in remaining whites until no streaks of white or brown show.

5. Divide batter evenly between two springform pans, spreading to edge and smoothing surface.

6. Bake layers in lower third of oven 35 to 40 minutes until they begin to pull from sides of pans and cake tester inserted in middle comes out clean.

7. Cool layers in upright pans on wire racks 15 minutes, then loosen carefully around edge with small thin-blade spatula. Release and remove springform sides, then gently loosen layers from pan bottoms and invert on wire racks. Cool to room temperature.

8. *For Filling, Frosting & Decoration:* Whip cream with confectioner's sugar and vanilla to soft peaks (tips should just lop over when beater is withdrawn but cream should be stiff enough to hold its shape).

9. Center one layer right side up (wire rack marks will show) on large round cake plate and spread with half of whipped cream. Set second layer on top—rack marks facing down—and swirl remaining whipped cream on top. Do not frost sides of torte. The finishing touch? Twelve toasted pecan halves arranged in a decorative ring on top.

10. Cut this rich torte into slim wedges and serve at the end of an elegant dinner party.

I love nothing more than taking homegrown Southern sweet potatoes and developing new recipes for them—like these amazingly tender dump-and-beat electric-mixer cupcakes. Because I like to slip finely chopped fresh ginger into recipes both sweet and savory, I keep it on hand and processor-chop until fairly fine. If tightly covered, chopped ginger will keep for about 2 weeks in the refrigerator. Add a little of it to marinades and salad dressings, to cooked carrots, green beans, and broccoli along with a drizzle of soy sauce. Delicious!

Gingery Sweet Potato Cupcakes with Walnuts and Dried Cranberries

Makes 2 Dozen

2¼ cups sifted all-purpose flour

¾ cup dried cranberries, blueberries, or dark seedless raisins, coarsely chopped

¾ cup walnuts, black walnuts, or pecans, moderately coarsely chopped

1½ teaspoons baking powder

1 teaspoon ground cinnamon

½ teaspoon freshly grated nutmeg

½ teaspoon baking soda

½ teaspoon salt

1½ cups firmly packed, puréed, unseasoned baked sweet potato, at room temperature

¼ cup finely chopped fresh ginger

1¼ cups raw sugar

¾ cup (1½ sticks) unsalted butter, at room temperature (no substitute)

⅓ cup milk

2 large eggs

3 tablespoons granulated sugar mixed with ½ teaspoon ground cinnamon (Topping)

1. Preheat oven to 350°F. Line 24 muffin pan cups with crinkly foil or paper liners and set aside. Place ¼ cup flour, dried cranberries, and walnuts in a small bowl and toss well to dredge. Set aside.

2. Combine remaining flour, baking powder, cinnamon, nutmeg, baking soda, and salt in large electric mixer bowl. Add next six ingredients (puréed sweet potato through eggs) and beat at low speed 20 to 30 seconds to combine; scrape mixing bowl well. Raise mixer speed to high and beat 2 minutes more. By hand, fold in dried cranberries, walnuts, and dredging flour.

3. Scoop into muffin pans, about half filling each cup, then sprinkle a little Topping over each cupcake.

4. Bake on middle oven shelf 25 minutes or until puffed and a toothpick inserted in center of cupcake comes out clean.

5. Transfer at once to wire racks and cool to room temperature before serving—IF you can wait!

As Southern classics go, this one is fairly new. According to my e-mail pal Donna Florio, senior writer at Birmingham-based *Southern Living*, her magazine was the first to print a Hummingbird Cake recipe. Submitted by Mrs. L. H. Wiggins of Greensboro, NC, it appeared in the February 1978 issue in an article devoted to bananas. "The cake's won numerous blue ribbons at county fairs," Donna told me. "No one knows what hummingbirds have to do with it, but the cake is so moist and delicious no one cares! It's still our most requested recipe." Today Hummingbird Cake is popular all over the country. In 2002, Elizabeth Schatz of the *New York Sun* devoted an article to Hummingbird Cake, which had begun "popping up at popular baking boîtes around town with little fanfare." Calling it "the sweetest import from below the Mason-Dixon," Schatz wrote: "To many Southerners living in New York, the concoction of mashed banana, pineapple, pecans, and cream cheese icing weighing more than your average one-year-old serves as a sweet, immediate reminder of home." Four years later, New York–based *Family Circle* magazine reprinted its own two-layer version of Hummingbird Cake; it remains a reader favorite. But as Schatz noted in the *New York Sun*, even the more impressive three-tiered cake "is, in fact, quite easy; it can be whipped up in little more than an hour." What follows is my own version.

Hummingbird Cake

Makes One 9-Inch, 3-Layer Cake

3 cups sifted all-purpose flour (not a light Southern flour)

2 cups granulated sugar minus 2 tablespoons (1⅞ cups)

1 teaspoon baking soda

1 teaspoon ground cinnamon

¾ teaspoon freshly grated nutmeg

½ teaspoon salt

Pinch ground allspice

1⅓ cups vegetable oil

3 large eggs, well beaten

1½ teaspoons vanilla extract

¼ teaspoon almond extract

2 cups finely chopped bananas (about 1 pound)

1 can (8 ounces) crushed pineapple, with all liquid

1 cup coarsely chopped, lightly toasted pecans (8 to 10 minutes in a 350°F oven)

FROSTING

2 packages (8 ounces each) cream cheese, at room temperature (use "light" Neufchâtel, if desired)

¾ cup (1½ sticks) unsalted butter, at room temperature (no substitute)

2 boxes (1 pound each) confectioner's (10X) sugar

1½ teaspoons vanilla extract

¼ teaspoon almond extract

Pinch salt

⅔ cup coarsely chopped lightly toasted pecans

1. Preheat oven to 350°F. Spritz three 9-inch round layer cake pans with nonstick oil-and-flour baking spray and set aside.

2. Sift flour, sugar, baking soda, cinnamon, nutmeg, salt, and allspice into large mixing bowl and make well in center. Add oil, eggs, vanilla and almond extracts, and stir only enough to moisten dry ingredients. Do not beat. Fold in bananas, pineapple and all liquid, and pecans.

3. Divide batter evenly among pans and smooth tops. Slide onto middle oven shelf, arranging so pans do not touch one another or oven walls, and bake 25 to 30 minutes until springy to touch and cake tester inserted in middle of layers comes out clean.

4. Cool layers in upright pans on wire racks 15 minutes. Carefully loosen around edges with small, thin-blade spatula, invert layers on racks, and cool to room temperature.

5. *For Frosting:* Beat cream cheese and butter in large electric mixer bowl at high speed 1 to 2 minutes until smooth. At low speed, add confectioner's sugar, then vanilla, almond extract, and salt. Beat at high speed until fluffy. Frosting will thin somewhat as you add sugar, but continue beating hard until it thickens a bit.

6. Sandwich layers together with frosting, then cover sides and top of cake, swirling frosting into hills and valleys. Sprinkle with toasted pecans.

7. Cut into slim wedges and serve. Refrigerate any leftover cake.

It's said that when the Marquis de Lafayette returned to America in 1784 after the Revolutionary War to visit his old friend George Washington at Mount Vernon, he traveled on to Fredericksburg to pay his respects to Washington's mother Mary. He found her in her garden raking leaves. Mrs. Washington invited her distinguished visitor inside and served him a mint julep and a piece of her favorite gingerbread. Soon named in Lafayette's honor, Mary Washington's dark and spicy gingerbread recipe remains popular to this day.

Lafayette Gingerbread

Makes One 9-Inch Square Loaf Cake

3 cups sifted all-purpose flour

¾ cup dark seedless raisins (optional)

1 tablespoon ground ginger

1 teaspoon ground cinnamon

½ teaspoon freshly grated nutmeg

½ teaspoon ground mace

¼ teaspoon salt

½ cup (1 stick) unsalted butter (no substitute)

½ cup firmly packed light brown sugar

2 teaspoons finely grated orange zest

3 large eggs

1 cup light molasses

⅓ cup milk

⅓ cup ruby Port, sweet Madeira (Malmsey), or cream sherry

⅓ cup fresh orange juice

1 teaspoon baking soda

1 tablespoon warm water

1. Preheat oven to 350°F. Spritz a 9 × 9 × 2-inch baking pan with nonstick cooking spray and set aside. **Note:** If you want to add raisins to the gingerbread, toss with ¼ cup of the flour and set aside. They'll be folded into the batter at the end.

2. Combine flour (or remaining flour if some tossed with raisins), ginger, cinnamon, nutmeg, mace, and salt in large bowl and set aside.

3. Cream butter, brown sugar, and orange zest in large electric mixer bowl 3 minutes at moderately high speed until light. Beat eggs in one by one and continue beating 2 minutes until light, then beat in molasses.

4. At low mixer speed, add first milk, then Port, then orange juice alternately with combined dry ingredients, beginning and ending with dry. Quickly dissolve baking soda in warm water and thoroughly mix into batter. Fold in dredged raisins, if using, along with all dredging flour—easy does it. Overmixing at this point will toughen the gingerbread. Scoop batter into pan and spread to corners.

5. Slide gingerbread onto middle oven shelf and bake about 35 minutes until it begins to pull from sides of pan, feels springy to touch, and cake tester inserted in middle comes out clean.

6. Transfer gingerbread at once to wire rack and cool in upright pan to room temperature.

7. To serve, cut into squares and top, if you like, with softly whipped cream.

Before 20th-century brownies and chocolate chip cookies, tea cakes were the South's cookie of choice. Recipes vary from state to state and cook to cook. My favorite: this old Virginia receipt.

Old Dominion Tea Cakes

Makes About 3 Dozen

½ cup (1 stick) unsalted butter (no substitute)

1 cup sugar

1 teaspoon vanilla extract

½ teaspoon ground mace or freshly grated nutmeg

2 large eggs

½ teaspoon baking soda

¼ teaspoon salt

3¼ cups sifted all-purpose flour (about; not a soft Southern flour)

1. Preheat oven to 375°F.

2. Cream butter, sugar, vanilla, and mace at high electric mixer speed 2 to 3 minutes until light. With motor at medium speed, beat eggs in one by one, then add baking soda and salt and beat well. By hand, mix flour in 1 cup at a time, adding only enough to make dough about as thick as biscuit dough.

3. Working with half of dough at a time, roll as thin as pie crust on lightly floured surface. Cut into rounds with floured 2½-inch cutter and space about 1½ inches apart on ungreased baking sheets.

4. Bake on middle oven shelf 10 to 12 minutes until cookies smell irresistible and are the color of pale parchment. Transfer at once to wire racks to cool, then store in airtight canisters.

A lot of people consider this a Southern cake—created here and beloved here. Well, they're half right. The cake's a Southern favorite—no question—but the recipe originated at New York's Waldorf-Astoria nearly 100 years ago. So why do so many Southerners claim Red Velvet Cake as their own? Probably because it generated no end of buzz after starring as the groom's cake in the Julia Roberts movie *Steel Magnolias.* Good Southern cooks scrambled to find the recipe and soon thousands of them were baking Red Velvet Cake and raving about its unique flavor and delicate texture. My own memories of Red Velvet Cake date to the early '50s when WWII sugar rationing had ended and we could once again splurge on sweets. "Imagine dumping an entire bottle of red food coloring into a cake!" women would exclaim in the Raleigh of my youth. What few home cooks then knew (and perhaps still don't) was that to boost sales of its red food coloring, one of this country's big food companies simply created a new spin on the old Waldorf recipe. And in no time, bottles of red food coloring were flying off supermarket shelves. If memory serves, the first Red Velvet Cake was a layered affair with fluffy white icing. Today, it's often baked as a loaf cake, even as cupcakes. I prefer loaf cake and top it with a quick buttercream frosting.

Red Velvet Cake

Makes One 13 × 9 × 2-Inch Loaf Cake

2¼ cups sifted cake flour

¼ cup sifted all-purpose flour

⅓ cup sifted Dutch-process cocoa powder

1 teaspoon baking powder

½ teaspoon baking soda

¼ teaspoon salt

1 cup (2 sticks) unsalted butter, at room temperature (no substitute)

1½ teaspoons vanilla extract

2 cups granulated sugar

4 large eggs

¾ cup sour milk or buttermilk

1 bottle (1 ounce) red food coloring (2 tablespoons)

FROSTING

1 box (1 pound) confectioner's (10X) sugar

2 tablespoons unsalted butter, at room temperature (no substitute)

½ cup firmly packed sour cream (use "light," if desired) or well-drained plain yogurt (I prefer thick Greek yogurt)

1½ teaspoons vanilla extract

Milk, if needed for spreading consistency

1. Preheat oven to 350°F. Lightly coat 13 × 9 × 2-inch baking pan with nonstick oil-and-flour baking spray and set aside.

2. Sift both flours with cocoa, baking powder, baking soda, and salt onto piece of wax paper and set aside.

continued on page 252

continued from page 250

3. Cream butter and vanilla at high electric mixer speed 3 to 5 minutes until fluffy, scraping bowl often. With mixer at low speed, add sugar in a slow stream, then beat at high speed 3 to 5 minutes until fluffy-light, scraping bowl and beaters often. Beat eggs in one by one.

4. Combine sour milk and food coloring, then at lowest mixer speed, add alternately with flour mixture, beginning and ending with dry ingredients. After each addition, beat batter only enough to combine—no longer or you'll toughen the cake. Scrape bowl and beaters as needed while adding flour mixture.

5. Pour batter into pan, spread to corners, and smooth top. Bake on middle oven shelf 45 to 50 minutes until cake is springy to the touch and cake tester inserted in middle of loaf comes out clean.

6. Transfer cake to wire rack and cool to room temperature in upright pan.

7. *For Frosting:* Beat all but final ingredient (milk) at low mixer speed, then at high until smooth and fluffy. If frosting seems too stiff to spread, add a little milk, then swirl over top of cake and allow to firm up for several hours.

8. Cut into squares and serve.

My niece Kim, who lives in Fuquay-Varina about an hour southeast of Chapel Hill, discovered a wild persimmon tree at the foot of her street one day while walking her dog. She gathers the windfalls every autumn, purées them, then freezes the pulp to use in future breads and sweets. Don't substitute the big Asian persimmons for the small wild native ones. Their flavor is bland. *Note:* Choose a dry day for making these bars. They will absorb atmospheric moisture in rainy or humid weather.

Wild Persimmon Bars with Lime Glaze

Makes About 3½ Dozen

1½ cups coarsely chopped, lightly toasted pecans (8 to 10 minutes in a 350°F oven)

1¾ cups sifted all-purpose flour

1 teaspoon baking powder

½ teaspoon baking soda

1 teaspoon ground cinnamon

½ teaspoon freshly grated nutmeg

¼ teaspoon salt

½ cup (1 stick) unsalted butter, slightly softened (no substitute)

½ cup granulated sugar

½ cup raw sugar

1 teaspoon vanilla extract

1 large egg

1½ cups firmly packed wild persimmon purée (see Persimmons, page 22)

1 tablespoon finely grated fresh ginger

1 cup unsifted confectioner's (10X) sugar mixed with 2 tablespoons fresh lime or lemon juice (Glaze)

1. Preheat oven to 350°F. Spritz 15½ × 10½ × 1-inch jelly-roll pan with nonstick oil-and-flour baking spray and set aside.

2. Dredge pecans in ½ cup flour in small bowl and set aside. Whisk remaining flour in second small bowl with baking powder, baking soda, cinnamon, nutmeg, and salt and set aside also.

3. Cream butter in large electric mixer bowl at high speed 1½ to 2 minutes until fluffy. Scrape bowl down, add both sugars and vanilla and beat 1½ to 2 minutes at high speed until light, pausing once or twice to scrape bowl and beaters. Beat in egg.

4. Remove bowl from mixer stand. Combine persimmon purée with fresh ginger, then beginning and ending with combined dry ingredients, add alternately to sugar mixture, stirring and folding after each addition only enough to combine. Fold in dredged pecans and all dredging flour, making sure no floury streaks remain.

5. Scoop batter into jelly-roll pan, spreading to edges. Using offset spatula dipped in cold water, smooth top of batter as much as possible—it's very thick.

6. Slide onto middle oven shelf and bake 20 minutes until loaf begins to pull from sides of pan and toothpick inserted in center comes out clean.

7. Cool loaf in upright pan on wire rack 20 minutes. Pour on Glaze, then smooth and spread to edges with offset spatula. Cool 35 to 40 minutes until Glaze hardens—it will have a mottled or marbled look.

8. Cut loaf into bars about 2¼ inches long and 1¾ inches wide and serve. **Tip:** It's easier if you lay an 18-inch metal edge ruler across the rim of the pan to guide each cut.

This early Virginia recipe has been popular forever it seems, especially along the James River Road (Route 5) that meanders east from Richmond toward Williamsburg and Jamestown. Founded in 1607, Jamestown was England's first successful New World colony and the re-created village here with guides in period dress is both appealing and authentic. In olden days, these roll-and-cut cookies (called "cakes" back then) were baked by the hundreds at Christmastime. I think you'll find them better than today's commercial slice-and-bakes because their ingredients are simple and pure. *Note:* This recipe calls for rose water, a flavoring popular in Colonial days and once again gaining favor. Look for it in specialty groceries or online. See Sources (page 264).

Tidewater Cinnamon Cakes

Makes About 3 Dozen

4 to 4⅓ cups sifted all-purpose flour

1 teaspoon baking powder

½ teaspoon salt

1 cup (2 sticks) unsalted butter (no substitute)

1 cup sugar

1½ teaspoons rose water (see Note above)

2 large eggs

1 large egg yolk beaten with 1 tablespoon cold water (Egg Wash)

2 tablespoons sugar mixed with ¼ teaspoon ground cinnamon (Cinnamon-Sugar)

¼ cup finely chopped blanched almonds

1. Sift 4 cups flour, baking powder, and salt onto piece of wax paper and set aside along with extra ⅓ cup flour.

2. Cream butter, sugar, and rose water about 2 minutes in large electric mixer bowl—first at low speed, then at high until fluffy-light. Add eggs one by one, beating well after each addition.

3. With mixer at low speed, add sifted dry ingredients, 1 cup at a time, beating after each addition only enough to incorporate. If dough seems sticky, beat in enough of extra ⅓ cup flour to make stiff but manageable dough. Do not overbeat—your cookies will be tough if you do.

4. Divide dough into four more or less equal parts, shape each into ball, flatten, and wrap in wax paper. Refrigerate at least 30 minutes or as long as overnight.

5. When ready to proceed, preheat oven to 375°F. Spritz several baking sheets with nonstick cooking spray and set aside.

6. Roll dough, one chilled package at a time, about as thick as pie crust between lightly floured sheets of wax paper. Using floured 3-inch round cutter, cut into rounds. Gather scraps, gently reroll, and cut. **Note:** Keep remaining dough refrigerated until ready to roll.

7. Space cookies 1 inch apart on baking sheets, and brush each with Egg Wash, taking care not to dribble it on baking sheets. Sprinkle cookies lightly with Cinnamon-Sugar, then chopped almonds, and gently pat nuts into dough.

8. Bake cookies, one sheet at a time, on middle oven shelf 12 to 14 minutes until lightly browned around edges.

9. Transfer cookies at once to wire racks and cool to room temperature. Store in airtight canisters between sheets of wax paper.

"I remember always having these cookies fresh out of the oven whenever I visited my Aunt Rhoda," my late friend Florence Gray Soltys once told me. Rhoda Gray lived about five miles from the East Tennessee dairy farm where Florence grew up, so visits with Aunt Rhoda were frequent. "You can place this cookie dough in a covered container in the refrigerator," explained Florence, who did just that when her own two girls, Jackie and Rebecca, were little. It will last for several days "so you can bake it as desired." Better yet, you can freeze the dough–a frozen asset that will keep for several months. Baked as is, these cookies resemble the brown-edged crisps we adored as children only these are uniformly brown. To please Jackie and Rebecca, Florence sometimes added chocolate chips and/or nuts—1½ cups of each per batch is about right. *Note:* The nut and chocolate chip cookies may require a minute or so longer in the oven. You'll also get more of them—about 13¼ dozen in all.

Aunt Rhoda Gray's Refrigerator Cookies

Makes About 10 Dozen

4¼ cups sifted all-purpose flour

1¾ teaspoons baking soda

¾ teaspoon salt

1½ cups (3 sticks) unsalted butter (no substitute)

1¾ cups firmly packed light or dark brown sugar

1 cup granulated sugar

2 teaspoons vanilla extract

4 large eggs

1. Preheat oven to 350°F. Spritz two or three large baking sheets with nonstick cooking spray and set aside.

2. Sift flour, baking soda, and salt onto a large piece of wax paper and set aside also.

3. Cream butter, both sugars, and vanilla in electric mixer briefly at low speed, then at high speed for about 2 minutes or until fluffy. Beat eggs in one by one.

4. With mixer at low speed, add sifted dry ingredients and beat only enough to combine.

5. Drop cookies from rounded teaspoons onto baking sheets, spacing 2 inches apart. Bake in lower third of oven about 8 minutes until lightly browned.

6. Cool cookies on baking sheets 2 minutes, then transfer to wire racks. Serve warm or at room temperature.

Whenever I drive over to Winston-Salem, it's almost always to tour New York friends through Old Salem, the restored 18th-19th-century Moravian Village on the south side of town. Our last stop is invariably at the 200-plus-year-old Winkler Bakery right on Main Street to buy those thin, thin, thin Moravian Ginger Cookies (page 258) as well as these buttery sugar cookies. At Christmastime, they may be cut into stars, wreathes, and such, but the rest of the year they're just simple rounds. *Note:* Because these cookies are unusually short, you must refrigerate the dough overnight so it's firm enough to roll. You must also roll a small amount of dough at a time, keeping the rest well chilled. Finally, choose a dry, sunny day for baking these cookies—humid weather makes them doubly difficult to roll. Tip: Do please use freshly grated nutmeg for these cookies. It's faintly spicy, faintly lemony, and far more delicate than commercially ground nutmeg. A few back-and-forths on a Microplane is all it takes for half a teaspoon of freshly grated nutmeg.

Melt-in-Your-Mouth Sugar Cookies

Makes About 7 Dozen

2½ cups unsifted all-purpose flour
½ teaspoon cream of tartar
½ teaspoon salt
½ teaspoon freshly grated nutmeg (see Tip above)
¼ teaspoon baking soda
¾ cup (1½ sticks) unsalted butter (no substitute)
2¼ cups sugar
1 teaspoon vanilla extract
½ teaspoon lemon extract
2 large eggs

1. Sift flour, cream of tartar, salt, nutmeg, and baking soda onto wax paper and set aside.

2. Cream butter, sugar, and vanilla and lemon extracts at high speed in large electric mixer bowl 2½ to 3 minutes until fluffy and almost white.

3. At low speed, beat eggs in one by one, then with machine still at low speed, add sifted dry ingredients gradually. Raise mixer speed to moderate and beat about 2 minutes until soft dough forms.

4. Shape dough into disk on plastic wrap, fold ends of wrap in, enclosing dough, and refrigerate overnight.

5. When ready to proceed, preheat oven to 350°F and spritz several baking sheets with nonstick cooking spray.

6. Quarter dough disk, then roll, one piece at a time (keeping others refrigerated), on well-floured board or marble slab until as thin as pie crust.

7. Cut into rounds with floured 3-inch cutter and space cookies about 1½ inches apart on baking sheets. Gather scraps, reroll, and cut into rounds—but make a note, rerolls won't be as tender as first-rolled cookies.

8. Bake cookies one sheet at a time on middle oven shelf about 12 minutes until color of parchment—pale golden-tan.

9. Transfer at once to wire racks to cool, then store in airtight canisters layered between sheets of wax paper.

Thumbing through my Southern cookbooks—most of them the community fund-raisers I buy wherever I go—I find surprisingly few cookie recipes. At least few that predate the 20th century. My theory is that ovens were then so unreliable that small tea cakes (sugar cookies, etc.) were likely to burn. Cakes and cobblers were bigger, safer. Running tea cakes a close second for popularity in our great-grandmothers' day? Molasses cookies, not chocolate, which was an ingredient so precious few could afford it.

Molasses Chews

Makes About 3 Dozen

2½ cups sifted all-purpose flour

1 teaspoon baking soda

½ teaspoon salt

1 teaspoon ground cinnamon

½ teaspoon ground ginger

¼ teaspoon ground cloves

¼ teaspoon freshly grated nutmeg

1 cup sugar plus ¼ cup for coating cookies

¾ cup (1½ sticks) melted unsalted butter (no substitute)

¼ cup molasses (not too dark)

1 large egg

1. Sift flour, baking soda, salt, and spices into large bowl and set aside.

2. Combine 1 cup sugar, butter, molasses, and egg in second large bowl, then mix in sifted dry ingredients about 1 cup at a time to make a stiff dough. Cover and refrigerate overnight.

3. When ready to proceed, preheat oven to 375°F. Also spritz several baking sheets with nonstick cooking spray and set aside.

4. Working with small amount of chilled dough at a time, shape into 1-inch balls. Roll each in remaining ¼ cup sugar to coat, then space about 2 inches apart on baking sheets.

5. Slide onto middle oven shelf and bake 10 minutes until crinkly on top and irresistible smelling. **Note:** For crisper cookies, bake about 2 minutes more.

6. Remove from oven and cool 2 minutes on baking sheets before transferring to wire racks.

7. Cool to room temperature, then store in airtight canisters.

As thin as paper, these intensely gingery cookies are "sleeved" in cardboard tubes and sold in gift stores across much of the U.S. But in North Carolina—especially in Moravian communities in and around Winston-Salem—they are still baked at home. Experienced cooks know how to roll dough extra-thin and I pass along a few of their tricks here. First, your dough must be refrigerator-cold before you roll it. Second, you must roll only small amounts at a time, preferably on a cold marble slab. I've even seen bakers dip their hands in ice water and dry them zip-quick so the heat of their hands won't soften the dough. I, myself, have tried to roll and cut these ginger cookies right on a baking sheet, then peel away the scraps. Not a good idea. My best advice? Don't fret if your Moravian ginger cookies are as thick as pie crust. Your children and grandchildren will be happy there's more to munch.

Moravian Ginger Cookies

Makes 3 to 3½ Dozen

4 cups sifted all-purpose flour (about)

2¼ teaspoons ground ginger

2¼ teaspoons ground cinnamon

1½ teaspoons ground cloves

¼ teaspoon salt

½ cup firmly packed light brown sugar

6 tablespoons unsalted butter or 3 tablespoons each unsalted butter (no substitute) and lard (not vegetable shortening)

1 cup molasses

2 teaspoons baking soda

2 tablespoons boiling water

1. Sift dry ingredients (flour through salt) onto piece of wax paper and set aside. Place brown sugar in large electric mixer bowl and set aside also.

2. Melt butter in small saucepan over moderate heat, add to brown sugar along with molasses, and beat a few seconds at low speed to combine. Dissolve baking soda in boiling water (it will fizz like mad) and beat into molasses mixture.

3. With mixer at low speed, add sifted ingredients gradually and beat at moderate speed about 1 minute until stiff dough forms. **Note:** If dough seems sticky, beat in another 1 to 2 tablespoons flour.

4. Cover bowl with clean dry cloth and let dough "season" overnight at room temperature.

5. Next day, shape dough into disk on plastic wrap, fold ends of wrap in enclosing dough, and refrigerate 1 to 2 hours until firm enough to roll.

6. When ready to proceed, preheat oven to 275°F and spritz several baking sheets with nonstick cooking spray.

7. Halve disk of dough, then roll, one piece at a time (keeping rest refrigerated), on well-floured board or marble slab until as thin as pie crust—even thinner, if possible.

8. Cut into rounds with floured 2½-inch cutter and space cookies about 1½ inches apart on baking sheets. Gather scraps, reroll, and cut into rounds—but make a note, rerolls won't be as tender as first-rolled cookies.

9. Bake cookies one sheet at a time on middle oven shelf 15 to 18 minutes until lightly browned around edge and soft-firm when touched.

10. Cool cookies, still on baking sheets, on wire racks, then carefully loosen and remove from pans. Store in airtight canisters layered between sheets of wax paper.

Some Southern farmers' markets sell wild persimmon purée or pulp in season (late October through December) and that's good news for those who cherish anything made with our native wild persimmons. With developers bulldozing forests to make room for new housing developments, however, wild persimmon trees are toppling and more's the pity. *Note:* If wild persimmon purée is unavailable in your area, fret not. You can order it online; see Sources (page 264). The purée you use for these cookies should not be sweetened, only sieved, thawed, if frozen, and about the consistency of pancake batter. *Tip:* I used quick-cooking steel-cut Irish oatmeal for this recipe but America's coarser rolled oats work equally well as long as they are quick-cooking.

Spicy Wild Persimmon–Oatmeal Chews

Makes About 3½ Dozen

1¾	cups sifted all-purpose flour
1	teaspoon baking soda
1	teaspoon ground cinnamon
½	teaspoon ground ginger
½	teaspoon freshly grated nutmeg
½	teaspoon salt
½	cup (1 stick) plus 2 tablespoons unsalted butter, slightly softened (no substitute)
½	cup granulated sugar
½	cup firmly packed light brown sugar
1½	teaspoons vanilla extract
1	large egg
1	cup firmly packed wild persimmon purée (see Note above, also Persimmons, page 22)
1	cup dark seedless raisins
1	cup quick-cooking steel-cut oats (see Tip above)

1. Preheat oven to 375°F. Line several baking sheets with aluminum foil, placing dull side up, then spritz foil with nonstick cooking spray. Set baking sheets aside.

2. Whisk flour with baking soda, cinnamon, ginger, nutmeg, and salt together in medium-size bowl; set aside.

3. Cream butter in large electric mixer bowl at high speed about 1 minute until fluffy. Scrape bowl down, add both sugars and vanilla and beat 1½ to 2 minutes more at high speed until light, pausing once or twice to scrape bowl and beaters. Beat in egg, then add persimmon purée and beat at moderate speed a few seconds. Scrape bowl and beaters once again, and beat about 10 seconds at moderate speed to combine. Mixture will have a slightly curdled look but will smooth out as soon as dry ingredients are added.

4. Remove bowl from mixer stand and, by hand, add combined dry ingredients in two batches, stirring and folding gently until no streaks of white show. Fold in raisins and oats.

5. Drop dough by heaping teaspoons onto baking sheets, spacing cookies about 2 inches apart.

6. Bake, one sheet at a time, in lower third of oven 12 to 14 minutes until cookies feel firm and smell irresistibly spicy.

7. Transfer at once to wire racks and cool to room temperature. Store cookies between sheets of wax paper in airtight canisters—they'll keep fresh for several weeks.

Always a tea table favorite, these thumbprint cookies are as pretty as they are easy to make. You can vary the jams that go into the thumbprint but I prefer a crimson one made from the South's finest strawberries. Or maybe a darker one made from homegrown blueberries or blackberries. There are enough cookies here to try some of each. And I'll tell you what I think would also be good—though I haven't tried it: lemon curd, another Southern favorite. Jars of it are sold at many fancy food shops.

Pecan Thumbprints

Makes 3 to 3½ Dozen

14 tablespoons (1¾ sticks) unsalted butter, at room temperature (no substitute)

½ cup granulated sugar

2 teaspoons vanilla extract

¼ teaspoon salt

2 extra-large egg yolks

1 cup finely ground pecans

2¾ cups sifted all-purpose flour (about)

⅓ cup (about) sieved strawberry, blueberry, or blackberry jam

½ cup (about) unsifted confectioner's (10X) sugar (for dusting cookies)

1. Preheat oven to 375°F. Spritz several baking sheets with nonstick cooking spray and set aside.

2. Cream butter, granulated sugar, vanilla, and salt in large electric mixer bowl at high speed 2 to 3 minutes until fluffy. At low speed, beat in egg yolks, then pecans, then flour. Dough should be firm enough to shape. If not, mix in a little additional flour.

3. Pinch off bits of dough and shape into 1-inch balls. Space about 1 inch apart on baking sheets, press thumb deep into center of each ball, and fill depression with ¼ teaspoon jam.

4. Bake cookies on middle oven shelf 12 to 15 minutes until pale tan. Transfer at once to wire racks set over wax paper, and cool to room temperature.

5. Sift confectioner's sugar over cookies one by one, holding ½ teaspoon (from a measuring set) over jam centers so they remain bright and clear.

6. To store, layer cookies between sheets of wax paper in airtight canister. **Note:** If cookies lose their "snowy" look in storage, sift a little more confectioner's sugar over them before serving, once again shielding the jam centers with a small measuring spoon.

The recipe for these unusual cookies comes from my friend Maria Harrison Reuge, who grew up in Tidewater, VA, along the James River. I remember her telling me about "Moldy Mice" years ago when she was an editor at *Gourmet* and e-mailed her recently to ask if she'd send me the recipe to include in this book. "My daughter 'stole' my mother's cookbook," Maria wrote, "and took it with her to college (University of Vermont) where she does a lot of cooking, especially for a local food pantry. I asked her to send me the recipe for Moldy Mice and here it is. I believe my mother used Sauer's sesame seeds—they were a local Richmond spice company but any sesame seeds will do as long as they're fresh." A friend of mine to whom I'd sent the recipe tried it, and pronounced Moldy Mice "yummy!" I think so, too. *Note:* One 2.2-ounce jar of sesame seeds = ½ cup packed.

Grandmommy's Recipe for Moldy Mice

Makes About 2½ Dozen

½ cup (1 stick) unsalted butter, slightly softened (no substitute)

1 tablespoon granulated sugar

1½ teaspoons vanilla extract

1 cup unsifted all-purpose flour

½ cup sesame seeds (see Note above)

¾ cup unsifted confectioner's (10X) sugar

1. Preheat oven to 425°F. Lightly grease large baking sheet and set aside.

2. Cream butter, granulated sugar, and vanilla in medium-size bowl with hand electric mixer at high speed about 3 minutes until light and fluffy. Add flour and sesame seeds and beat at moderate speed only enough to combine.

3. Roll dough, about ½ tablespoon at a time, into logs the size of your thumb, and space 1 inch apart on baking sheet.

4. Slide onto middle oven shelf and bake about 15 minutes until firm and golden brown around edges.

5. Place confectioner's sugar in small paper bag and as soon as cookies come from oven, drop into bag, several at a time, and gently roll in sugar in open bag until nicely coated. Don't burn yourself!

6. Carefully transfer sugared cookies to wire rack set over wax paper and cool to room temperature. Store between sheets of wax paper in airtight container and if necessary, dust with more confectioner's sugar just before serving.

Whenever one of the South's rich desserts leaves me with orphaned egg whites, I like to make these airy cookies along with one of their easy variations. Layered between sheets of foil or wax paper in airtight canisters, they keep for weeks—one good reason why they're a Christmas favorite below the Mason-Dixon. *Note:* In the frenzy of holiday baking, many good Southern cooks use sweetened flaked coconut in this recipe instead of wrestling with a fresh coconut. To be honest, I do, too, to save precious time and energy. *Tip:* Pick a dry, sunny day for making these cookies. In humid or rainy weather, they will absorb atmospheric moisture and never crisp up properly.

Coconut Kisses

Makes About 3½ Dozen

4	extra-large or jumbo egg whites
¼	teaspoon cream of tartar
¼	teaspoon salt
¾	cup granulated sugar
⅓	cup unsifted confectioner's (10X) sugar
1	teaspoon vanilla extract
1½	cups sweetened flaked coconut (see Note above)

1. Preheat oven to 250°F. Line several baking sheets with foil, placing dull side up, and set aside.

2. Beat egg whites in large electric mixer bowl at moderate speed until foamy, add cream of tartar and salt, then switch machine on and off to combine. With mixer again at moderate speed, add granulated sugar, then confectioner's sugar, 1 tablespoon at a time. Add vanilla, raise mixer to highest speed, and beat 2 to 3 minutes until meringue is glossy and stiff enough to peak when beater is withdrawn. By hand, fold in coconut.

3. Drop meringue by rounded teaspoons onto foil-lined baking sheets, spacing about 2 inches apart and rounding tops with back of spoon.

4. Bake, one sheet at a time, on middle oven shelf 35 to 45 minutes until the palest of ivories. For chewy cookies, remove from oven, lift cookies—foil and all—to wire racks, and cool to room temperature. For crisp cookies, turn oven off when cookies are done, and leave in oven—no peeking!—for 2 to 3 hours.

5. Peel cookies from foil and layer in airtight canisters between sheets of foil or wax paper.

VARIATIONS

Pecan Kisses: Prepare as directed but substitute 1 cup finely chopped pecans for 1½ cups coconut. Makes About 3½ Dozen.

Angel Kisses: Prepare as directed, adding no nuts or coconut. When cookies have baked, leave in turned-off oven 2 to 3 hours until shattery-crisp. Makes About 3 Dozen.

Sources

Note: For more information about some of the items listed here, see Ingredients (page 14).

All Things Southern

boiledpeanuts.com: Everything from sorghum molasses to stone-ground grits.

southernconnoisseur.com: The foods that made the South famous: boiled peanuts, Carolina Gold Rice, Duke's mayonnaise, Key lime juice, etc.

virginiatraditions.com: Field-fresh peanuts, Virginia hams and ham slices, smoked bacon (sliced or slab), sausage links and patties plus such ready-to-eat Southern classics as barbecue, Brunswick stew, she-crab soup, and rum cake.

Bakeware & Tableware

bakerscatalogue.com: Pan shapes and sizes not often available in retail stores.

benowenpottery.com: Like his grandfather Ben Owen, Sr., Ben Owen III is a master potter working in North Carolina's "red clay country." Though Owen's pieces are largely decorative, he also makes a few functional items of rare beauty.

cadyclayworks.com: Lidded stoneware casseroles—many colors, many sizes—made by potters Beth Gore and John Mellage at their pottery near Seagrove, NC.

cooksdream.com: Hard-to-find 7- and 8-inch tube (angel food cake) pans plus a variety of decorative pans both large and small.

discoverseagrove.com/nc-potters.asp: A who's who of Seagrove, NC, potters, many of whom produce elegant but earthy bakeware that you can buy online; most of them welcome visitors. I name particular favorites separately.

jugtownware.com: The form-follows-function clay casseroles, pour bowls, and pie plates long favored by local country folk. Hand-thrown by members of the Owens family, all pieces—wood-fired—are glazed in blues, grays, bronzy greens ("frogskins"), mustardy yellows, or browns ("tobacco spits"). There's a small pottery museum here.

kitchenworksinc.com: Headquarters for baking pans of all shapes and sizes as well as kitchen gadgets galore.

siglindascarpa.com: Unglazed terracotta-colored stoneware roasters, casseroles, and bean pots made by a gifted Italian clay artist now living near Chapel Hill, NC. Featured in *Gourmet* magazine, Scarpa says her designs are reminiscent of those of Tuscany.

southernseason.com: Excellent selection of casseroles and Dutch ovens. Also headquarters for Vietri hand-crafted Italian dinnerware, glassware, and table linens.

surlatable.com: Huge inventory of baking pans (all major brands) including Le Creuset's lidded square and rectangular bakers in nonporous enameled stoneware.

westmoorepottery.com: Reproductions of 17th-, 18th-, and 19th-century redware including Moravian pieces of stunning detail. All are made by Mary and David Farrell, Seagrove, NC, potters "inspired by the past." Redware, the first pottery made by Europeans settling in North Carolina, is superb for baking because heat penetrates it evenly.

williams-sonoma.com: Everything the home baker needs.

Cheeses

bellechevre.com: Alabama goat cheeses and goat cheese spreads in a variety of flavors.

gethsemanifarms.org: Mild, aged, and hickory-smoked cheeses made by Trappist monks in Kentucky.

Condiments, Jellies, Sauces & Seasonings

freshfromne.com: Wild plum jelly in 4-, 5-, 8-, and 10-ounce jars.

mexgrocer.com: Headquarters for authentic Mexican sauces (salsas red and green, mild and incendiary, chipotles, moles), masa harina (tortilla flour), tortillas, and much more.

penzeys.com: Every extract, herb, and spice you can imagine.

simplycajun.com: Mayhaw jelly and tabasco pepper jelly.

southernsupreme.com: Blackberry jelly, peach marmalade, and hot red pepper jelly plus mustards sweet and hot and an outstanding tomato relish.

thencstore.com: Bone Suckin' barbecue sauces hot and mild (voted "America's best" by *Food & Wine* magazine) plus mustard, salsa, rib rub, and hot pepper sauce.

tonychachere.com: Gumbo filé, Cajun and Creole seasoning blends, and more.

Cornmeal, Flour, Grits & Grains

ansonmills.com: Not only the place for organic stone-ground cornmeal and grits but also for the precious Carolina Gold Rice.

loganturnpikemill.com: "Best in the nation," *Atlanta Cuisine* calls Logan's stone-ground speckled yellow and white grits. Logan also grinds cornmeal and a variety of flours, even produces pancake, biscuit, and corn bread mixes.

louisianapridegristmill.com: Stone-ground cornmeal and grits plus peppery Cajun seasonings.

old-mill.com: An ancient gristmill in Pigeon Forge, TN (Dolly Parton's hometown), is kept busy grinding cornmeal, grits, and flour. There are Old Mill mixes, too.

oldmillofguilford.com: Stone-ground yellow or white cornmeal and grits, unbleached plain or self-rising flour, high-gluten flour, rye flour, buckwheat flour, and more.

southernconnoisseur.com: Carolina Gold Rice in 2-pound bags.

southernfood.com: Nora Mill White speckled grits ("Georgia ice cream") in 16- and 32-ounce bags plus many more strictly Southern specialties.

southernseason.com: By the bag: the grits used at Chapel Hill's beloved Crook's Corner. The James Beard Foundation recently named this restaurant an American Classic.

Note: There are, in addition, many fine regional mills selling stone-ground cornmeal and grits, among them Pollard Milling of Hartford, AL (said to have been Edna Lewis's favorite).

Fruits & Vegetables

byronplantation.com: Both spring and fall Vidalia onions; baby Vidalias, too.

gapeaches.com: Dickey Farms of Musella, GA, founded in 1897, grows more than 20 varieties of peaches and will pack and ship to your door. Freestone peaches, ripening in mid-June, launch the summer peach season.

keylimejuice.com: Nellie & Joe's Famous Key Lime Juice in 12- and 16-ounce bottles.

http://www.localharvest.org/persimmon-pulp-C14148: Frozen wild persimmon purée from the Red Rosa farm near Spencer, IN. To quote Cathy Crosson of Red Rosa Farm: "Wild persimmon purée is generally available from sometime in September through January, sometimes later. It is frozen in 2-cup (1-pint) quantities, and ships with ice packs. And it is 100 percent pure persimmon pulp—the persimmons are as sweet as dates, so they certainly need no sweetener! You might tell your readers they can go easy on the refined sugar in any recipe using mostly persimmon pulp!"

http://www.ncfreshlink.com/shipperdirectory/peach-gsl.htm: A list of North Carolina peach orchards that pack and ship.

peachstand.com: Sun-blushed South Carolina peaches from Springs Farm.

sciway.net/shop/peaches.html: South Carolina peach orchards that pack and ship.

vidaliasfinest.com: The L. G. Herndon, Jr. Farms of Lyons, GA, ship jumbo Vidalias May through September.

vidaliavalley.com: Stanley/Manning Farms grows, packs, and ships Vidalia onions in season as well as myriad Vidalia onion products year-round.

Hams, Bacons, Sausages & More

bentonscountryhams2.com: Hams sugar-cured, hickory-smoked or unsmoked plus hickory-smoked bacon from Benton's Smoky Mountain Country Hams in Madisonville, TN.

http://www.biteofthebest.com/surry-farms-surryano-sliced-dry-cured-ham: Domestic serrano ham that's an excellent substitute for country ham. It's presliced and packaged.

cajunspecialtymeats.com: Cajun tasso, andouille, boudin, and more.

comeaux.com: Featured on *Emeril Live* as a source for andouille, some dozen different boudins and sausages (from alligator to crawfish to rice to pork), and not least, a splendid hickory-smoked pork tasso recommended by Slow Food USA.

heritagepork.com: Supremely succulent fresh pork—everything but the squeal, you might say—plus bacons, hams, and sausages.

newsomscountryham.com: Fine Kentucky hams aged and cured according to a 200-year old process. Also available: smoked bacon and sausages as well as aged prosciutto.

nueskes.com: Applewood-smoked bacon, ham, and sausage.

nimanranch.com: Top-quality meats from small family farms. Carried by high-end grocers but some cuts are also available online, among them beef steaks and pork roasts and chops.

smithfieldmarketplace.com: Famous Smithfield hams, country hams, bacon, and sausage.

virginiatraditions.com: The beloved hickory-smoked Edwards Virginia hams (cooked or uncooked, bone-in or out, whole, halves, or slices); bacons (sugar-cured, hickory-smoked, or nitrite-free), and sausages (smoked or fresh, links or patties).

Honeys, Molasses & Syrups

blueridgehoneycompany.com: Order sourwood honey ("Appalachian gold") by the 16-ounce jar, order it by the case. Also available: 16-ounce jars of sourwood comb honey.

byronplantation.com: Blackberry, blueberry, peach, and other fruit syrups in 12-ounce bottles.

dutchgoldhoney.com: 1- and 5-pound jars of tupelo honey from Southern Georgia and the Florida Panhandle.

floridatupelohoney.com: Unfiltered, never-heated tupelo honey "with all of the natural ingredients nature intended"—both comb and liquid honey—from the Smiley Apiaries. Available by the jar, jug, or squeeze bottle.

lltupelohoney.com: Jars and jugs from 12 ounces to 2½ gallons from L. L. Lanier & Sons Tupelo Honey, founded in 1898. Ben Lanier and his wife Glynnis were consultants for the Peter Fonda movie *Ulee's Gold* and several family members appeared as extras.

markethallfoods.com: Bottled tupelo honey and sometimes honey-in-the-comb from the Savannah Bee Company.

mtnhoney.com: Sourwood and tupelo honey in 1- and 2-pound jars. In 2005, this Georgia sourwood was named "Best Honey in the World" at the World Honey Show in Dublin beating more than 400 entries from 21 countries.

peachstand.com: 8-ounce bottles of peach syrup and rare black walnut syrup.

http://ruralroot-store.stores.yahoo.net/pantry.html: Several brands of "sweet sorghum" (a.k.a. sorghum molasses).

slowfoodusa.org: Once on this website, search "sourwood" or "tupelo honey" and you'll not only find descriptions of them but also reliable sources.

smokiesstore.org: Sorghum molasses made the age-old way and sold in 1-pint jars.

steensyrup.com: Golden pure sugar cane syrup; good for baking and glazing hams and meatloaves.

stsimonsoutfitters.com: Savannah Bee Company raw comb tupelo honey as well as liquid honey.

Nuts

ab-nc.com: Home-style southern peanuts: blister-roasted, raw redskins, raw blanched peanuts.

auntrubyspeanuts.com: North Carolina peanuts in the shell, blanched or unblanched raw peanuts, and country-style peanuts roasted in corn oil.

black-walnuts.com: Hammons, a family company in Stockton, MO, sells shelled black walnuts not only in major markets across much of the country but also online through Hammons Nut Emporium. It even sells bottles of wild black walnut oil.

byronplantation.com: Extra-large Georgia pecans in the shell or out.

pearsonfarm.com: Fresh from Georgia, U.S. Grade No. 1 fancy pecans—pieces or halves, plain, roasted and salted, or spiced.

pinenut.com: Unshelled wild hickory nuts as well as a limited supply of the shelled.

priesters.com: Fresh-crop Georgia pecans in the shell or out, roasted or raw.

rayshickorynuts.com: Shelled wild hickory nuts by the pound.

sunnylandfarms.com: Georgia pecans, plus peanuts, plus hard-to-find black walnuts.

vapeanuts.com: Ready-to-fry-or-roast "super extra-large" blanched Virginia peanuts.

werenuts.com: Louisiana pecans large and small, plain and fancy, plus black walnuts.

wildcrops.com/wild_nuts.html: Wild hickory nuts both shelled and unshelled. Also wild butternuts and pine (pignoli) nuts.

wildpantry.com/wildnuts.htm: Unshelled wild hickory nuts. **Note:** It takes about 4 hours to extract the meat from 1 pound of hickory nuts.

Seafood

alwaysfreshfish.com: Skinned farm-raised catfish fillets, fresh jumbo lump crab meat, and many sizes of shrimp—raw unshelled or cooked, shelled, and deveined.

cajuncrawfish.com: Live farm-raised Louisiana crawfish and fresh-caught Gulf shrimp.

cbcrabcakes.com: Jumbo lump crab meat plus a variety of prepared chowders, crab cakes, casseroles, and pot pies.

ilovecrabs.com: Pasteurized Maryland lump and backfin crab meat, also jumbo Gulf Coast shrimp, and live littleneck clams.

lacrawfish.com: This family-owned Louisiana firm guarantees that the crawfish shipped to your door will arrive live and kicking. They also pack and ship jumbo Gulf shrimp as well as a variety of Cajun meats.

lintonsseafood.com: Chesapeake Bay lump crab meat. A good source, too, for oysters, clams, and sea scallops, even Gulf Coast shrimp and Louisiana crawfish. Also available: flounder, salmon, and tuna fillets.

Index